CONFUSED

A True Story of Flawed Love, Control and Abuse

Susan K. Green

Publisher Susan K. Green

Book Cover Tanja Prokop BookDesign Templates

Layout, Print and Distribution BookBaby
7905 Crescent Blvd
Pennsauken, NJ 08110

Confused A True Story of Flawed Love, Control and Abuse/ Susan K. Green. — 1st ed.

Print ISBN: 978-1-54395-895-9
eBook ISBN: 978-1-54395-896-6

Sweet Expectations

DESSERTS

CUMBERLAND FESTIVAL   ATLANTA, GEORGIA

TABLE OF CONTENTS

TO THE READER

This story occurred forty years ago. Plenty of time for wounds to heal and emotions to wane. Wary of waking long-sleeping beasts, however, I've assigned pseudonyms to all characters, a move you'll come to understand. Protagonist Rosie Browning first appears as she is today: seventy, seated in her backyard glider, perusing journals, letters, and other records dating from late-1976 to mid-1983. Prompted by these verbatim accounts or by the most accurate recollections her memory can dredge up, Rosie drifts backwards, reliving the darkest period of her life.

PROLOGUE

A short burst of breath parts my pursed lips. The slightly jarring, slightly flatulent sound used to crack up my students whenever I became exasperated. Today, disgust more accurately describes what I'm feeling. My attention returns to the journal in my lap:

Thursday, November 4, 1976... I am excited but also wary.

Rereading the forty-year-old entry only deepens the smirk on my face. Right there. Even at the very get-go, like an earnest crossing guard who herds the wayward student, my gut was trying its best to point me in a safer direction.

Why didn't I pay attention? How did I allow a man toting such unacceptable baggage to continually pass through the checkpoint? What fueled my Great Self-Escape?

I settle into the green and white striped cushions of my back-yard glider. Sollie, the latest in a long and storied line of fabulous felines, has claimed her spot beside me, unconcerned that I had to chuck to the ground the many journals and papers I've lugged out here.

My gaze rises to a multi-layered web of leaves, thrown across the November sky like tattered scarves of scarlet and gold. They alternately reveal and conceal patches of clear, cobalt blue. I'm relying on my canopied cloister to perform its usual magical smoothing of my brow, furrowed now by the questions just posed. My emotions will no doubt run the gamut today, the entirety of which I've devoted to My Quest.

Which would be...what? To find contentment? Nah! But for a hole, my contentment is whole. I giggle at my silly self. That hole, of course, is the lifelong lack of lasting love, if you will kindly allow the alliteration. My quest is to understand why, after all this time, that hole remains. Understand the hole and you understand the whole. I have to giggle again. Surely within these old writings some key resides, some crystal nugget that will shrink that hole once and for all.

Dread and hope fill me as I ruffle the pages filled with memories forgotten, repressed, or misunderstood. With one hand marking the page and the other resting on Sollie's flank, I lean my head back again. Yes, it was autumn...oh, right, Halloween. Another rude blurt escapes my lips. How apropos is that? The feast of fools that celebrates mistaken identity...

CHAPTER 1

OFF TO THE MONSTER MASK MASH

Braking carefully on the rain-smeared street, I brought my car to a gentle stop, right next to Bozo.

God, I love Halloween! The one night when perfectly sane adults revert to unhinged adolescence without apology or embarrassment. Seeing straight-laced executives and provincial housewives morph into monsters, witches, rock stars—or, as in the neighboring vehicle, a clown—never failed to amuse me. How could a party *not* be a hoot if it had Godzilla and Snow White engaging in a serious tête-à-tête, or Beauty jitterbugging away with her Beast? *Good for them.*

I engaged Bozo's attention and placed my hands on my cheeks, my mouth forming a big, round *O* of surprise and delight. He rewarded me with a wacky grin, yellow-toothed against red and white face paint. The instant the light changed, he accelerated, inducing a slight fish-tail. Direction corrected, car and clown sped out of sight towards an evening promising crazy costumes and much merriment.

Such enticements were only secondary motivators for my venturing out on this dreary night. The primary draw was the likelihood of—what else—*meeting a guy*. For several weeks, good friend Lucy had been trying to set me up with a new manager at the hotel where she worked in Convention and Hospitality.

"I'm telling you, this man's hilarious!" Lucy had reiterated when she'd called earlier to confirm my attendance tonight. "I think you'll like him, but you'll just have to see."

Yep, I'll just have to see. I squinted through the blurred windshield, not altogether sure of this par-tay's location. *Maybe this time,* like Liza Minnelli belted out in "Cabaret," *maybe this time he'll...* My tongue thrust through puckered lips, expelling a quick raspberry. *He'll what? Stay?* Hells bells, I can't even get him to ask me out. Or if he does, most times I don't even want him to stay.

I clucked wryly. Man, it's not like I'm a dog. At twenty-eight, I'm no beauty, but I do occasionally get second glances, particularly from the legs and ass men (the boobs men, not so much). Whatever I've got going for me apparently hasn't been enough to attract anyone to whom I'm attracted right back.

My mind filled with the oft-repeated, well-intentioned suggestions as to why I was without a guy: 'Well, you're too independent; men like to feel needed, you know.' Or, 'You've got such a strong personality; a lot of men probably feel a bit overwhelmed.' Or, my personal favorite, 'You're too picky.'

Damn right I am. True, I have perhaps failed to delve beyond less-than-stellar first impressions. I bristled. I'm a pretty good package on the inside and out; why can't I have that in a guy?

I slowed to turn into a large apartment complex. Would tonight hold a meeting with the proverbial knight? I shook my head. *Alors, ce type-là n'existe pas.* No such animal. But I conceded keeping an open mind was wise strategy.

I spotted the building number, parked and turned off the motor. Even if I didn't like the guy, I ought to get some laughs from watching silly adults act like idiots. I yanked down the visor for a last-minute check of my hair (the recent streak job had improved my Farrah Fawcett locks) and makeup (what there was of it). Satisfied nothing was horribly wrong, I snapped the visor back into place.

I exited the car and mumbled, "OK, here goes nothing."

If only I'd been right.

A quick glance around the room told me this Halloween party would not be making the social column. There was not a single decoration. How hard could it be to throw up some fake spider webs, orange mini-lights, a witch's hat, a pumpkin or two? A no-brainer, to be sure. Besides lacking the Martha Stewart gene, the host had apparently missed the class on basic social etiquette, since no one was coming forth with a welcoming smile or handshake.

I scanned the twenty or so unfamiliar faces, beginning to wonder if I'd crashed the wrong party, when I finally spotted Lucy. Relieved, I sidled up to her.

"So, is he here?"

"Not yet, but I'm sure he's coming," Lucy said.

"Who are these people?" I whispered.

"Mainly friends of friends of somebody from work. I only know about two or three people myself."

At that very moment a voice yelled, "Hey Luce, c'mere!"

I rolled my eyes as Lucy, who could endear herself to a telephone pole, made for the voice.

"Back in a sec!" she giggled, slightly sheepish.

A second sweep of the roomful of strangers detected no humorous or impressive costume. Had I repeated last year's creation—a piece of flesh-colored material sewn to a rear pants pocket, resulting in my half-assed Halloween costume—I might've won the prize for Best or, in this case, Only Costume. Decked out in unfestive street clothes myself, I wandered into the kitchen and mixed a drink. After chatting with a few folks about absolutely nothing of interest, I found a seat on a beige couch. Beige couch for a beige party. Haha.

I'd been anticipating meeting this guy far more than I cared to admit. With odds of his being a no-show increasing by the minute, I felt a bit deflated. Rather than pout on the couch, though, I forced myself to rise and mingle. I approached a couple clusters, segueing artfully into germane jokes drawn from my ample supply. But thirty minutes of vanilla encounters fueled my decision to split this soirée. I edged back towards the kitchen to retrieve my jacket and make my getaway.

As I tipped my half-empty Solo cup over the sink, the front door opened. I chuckled. *Probably someone else slipping away.* But then, much like the air that greens and crackles before a huge thunderstorm, the atmosphere turned electric. I felt a slight prickling at the nape of my neck.

Within moments, a roar of laughter thundered throughout, followed by another. Curious, I leaned on the counter and peered through the arched pass-through above the sink. From across the room, Lucy shot me a news-bulletin look. *This was the guy.*

Delighted to have lucked upon my own private observation post, I watched as he and another guy named Kevin launched into Comedy Club mode, regaling the crowd with one hilarious quip after another. I began my assessment.

In the 'tall, dark, handsome' category, I gauged he was good for two out of three, maybe two point five. At about six feet, he was plenty tall for my five feet and change. His deeply tanned skin was irregularly shaded; I decided to call it exotic. Prominent cheekbones and square chin formed a strong profile. His eyes, black as a witch's cat, were arresting, almost spooky! From my proximate position, I also noticed a few brownish spots tarnishing the whites of his eyes. *What the hell is that?*

Suddenly, those eyes, as though sighting an intended target, settled upon me.

Embarrassed to have been caught almost gawking, I cast my eyes down, demurely I hoped. I slowly lifted my gaze, determined to match his. My eyes met the back of his head—hmmm...needs a haircut. The man's entire attention had reverted to the show at hand. I felt like a piece of merchandise that had held momentary interest only to be returned to the shelf.

Shrugging off this mini-rejection, I resumed my appraisal. Now I heard him laugh. I'd never heard such a sound: a wheezing jeer, followed by a deep-throated giggle, ending in a gut-bursting explosion of laughter with head thrown back. Utterly engaging and infectious! I noticed his teeth, exposed during a wide-mouthed laugh. Oh dear! That must be a gap between a couple of the side teeth..or was a whole tooth missing? Jeez, can't this guy see a dentist? *Oop, there you go again, Miss Picky. C'mon now, nobody's perfect.*

Still studying him, I took in his wardrobe choices, finding nothing perfect about that leisure suit, with its hideous swirl of Irish Spring Soap green imprinted onto one hundred percent pure polyester...Lord! I sniffed and tossed my head. Hey, if this man's interest in me could only last one fleeting moment, just watch how I could deflect any humiliation by listing his numerous unacceptable traits! And topping the list, I was appalled to realize, was that his right hand, previously hidden from me, held a freaking cigarette. Lucy hadn't mentioned that he was a smoker. *Omigod, I haaate smoking!* Forget this dude.

For an entire nanosecond, I did. Flaws be damned! I could not peel my eyes off this entertaining spectacle. Not that it mattered one whit; he had not turned back in my direction.

I returned to departure prep, telling myself I was likely avoiding another train wreck of a relationship. I poured out the rest of my drink, grabbed my jacket and muttered, "I'm outta here."

I spun around and plowed right into someone's shirt. From above the shirt came a voice, *his* voice, which moments ago had addressed no one in particular but which now was zeroing in on me. Soft, husky, kind, the voice said, "Whoa there! Where're you headed, lady?"

Dumbfounded, I pulled my face away from buttons and strange material, hoping to God I hadn't smeared lipstick or drool. I looked up into those eyes, devoid of spookiness now and instead filled with amusement, warmth, and—was I imagining it?—interest. For the second time this evening, this man's powerful, magnetic, steadfast gaze enveloped me and me alone.

I managed to snap, "Nowhere, thanks to you, but at least I got there fast."

Watching his face fill with gleeful approval, I felt as though I'd passed his pop quiz on wittiness.

"I'm Carl," he said, hefting his sizable supply of booze—a veritable bar—onto the kitchen counter. His hands flicked at the wrist, relieved of the load. "Can I fix you a drink? Or...were you about to leave?"

"No, no, I wasn't leaving," I said, casually dropping my jacket on the chair behind me. "And, sure, a gin tonic would be nice."

He expertly mixed our drinks. As he handed me mine, I could barely say "thank you" before someone approached and engaged him in high-energy conversation. As I observed Carl one-up the man's wisecracks with rejoinders of Robin Williams/Billy Crystal ilk, an oddly uncomfortable sensation overtook me, as though my own easy wit and charm was packing up to go AWOL.

How could I hold my own with this dynamo who'd commanded everyone's attention, this magnum force who'd caused this party to go from bust to boom? I felt like the clumsy kid who wanted to be chosen for the A-team, but secretly knew she was out of their league. *Oh, for silly's sake, Rosie-Rose, at least show up for tryouts.* I determined to learn more about this...this...what was he?

"Food and Beverage Director, for about a month now," Carl responded to my inquiry about his position at the hotel. "And no, not exactly Lucy's boss." Noticing Lucy had come within earshot, a playful, wicked glint flashed in his eye. With increased volume Carl added, "Although she'd be damned foolish to think of me otherwise."

Lucy rolled her eyes, grinning. As she exited, she shot me an inquisitive look, wondering how things were going. I shot back a look that said, "Who the hell knows?"

I'd not entirely cast aside those earlier, somewhat off-putting external imperfections of this nearly knock-down gorgeous man. But that was surface stuff, easily fixable with the help of a barber, a dentist, possibly an ophthalmologist, and most definitely a tailor. Taking pride in my newfound open-mindedness, I once again reminded myself nobody's perfect. As for his smoking...well, no need to worry about that right now.

I was more interested in what lay beneath. There was something about his manner, the way he'd turn back to me after conversing with someone who'd interrupted us, as though my company was highly preferable. Such singular attention was pulse-quickening indeed.

"And so," Carl asked me, seemingly intent to know, "how does one go about teaching? What's your favorite thing about it?"

Latching on to an opportunity to be amusing, I scrunched up my brow as if weighing the many attributes of a teaching profession, and then deadpanned, "Holidays." Puffing up with pleasure at Carl's amusement, I added, "Like tomorrow, for instance; it's Veteran's Day." I praised my cleverness at sneaking in that tidbit.

Eyebrows raised, eyes twinkling, tone a tad huskier, Carl whispered conspiratorially, "Well, then, I guess we better take advantage of that, shouldn't we?"

"Guess we better," I murmured, trying my best to contain all that was jumping around inside of me. I felt like the old Jello ad which touted that, on the outside, you're saying, "Oh, okay, Jello," while on the inside, you're screaming, "Yeah-USSS! JELL-OOOO!!"

For the next couple hours, Carl's company transformed the party's beige to technicolor. Around midnight, as Carl helped me on with my jacket, I surveyed the remaining Halloween party-goers, still nary a costume nor mask among them. It had taken no small effort on my part to mask a hippety-hopping interior beneath an oh-so-cool exterior. I turned back to Carl to say goodnight, acknowledging another quickening of pulse.

What I didn't acknowledge was I was actually staring straight into a mask, one that took no effort at all.

.

CHAPTER 2

REALLY BIG

I couldn't remember a morning when I'd awoken bathed in such excited anticipation and satisfied affirmation. How many times had I shown interest in some guy who managed to make me feel invisible? Or, almost worse, the flip side, when I would reciprocate a man's fawning with a brief smile that never traveled to my eyes. But here! Here was a guy who, for some reason, set something off deep inside me and, lo and behold, he'd immediately made plans to see me again.

I thought about my original game plan for today. Besides grading the never-ending pile of French quizzes and English compositions, I'd anticipated further progress in making my house—moved into a mere three months earlier—a home. *Scrap that plan!*

I took extra care with my hair and make-up, which meant ten minutes instead of five, as I had never been one to go bonkers with beauty products. (I preferred the 'uncluttered look,' a description offered by a department-store beautician. Only upon hindsight had my ears caught her tongue-in-cheek tone.) Over tight jeans I slipped on my favorite bateau-neck, turquoise tee, guaranteed to make my blue eyes pop. Laughing at all my fuss, I mimicked Ed Sullivan and intoned, *"After all, this could be the beginning of something rrre-ally big!"*

Having made sure all cats—all *three* cats, for heaven's sake—were inside and fed, I took the steep front steps two at a time and hopped in my trusty '72 Camaro, aka The Merry. (How could anyone *not* name their car?) That I was driving over to see Carl, as opposed to his picking me up was hardly any skin off my back: he didn't have the entire day off work as I did.

Off to see my Prince! I grinned, made a speedy three-point turn, and headed to Camelot. Prince Carl awaited me in the hotel lobby.

"I was wondering," he asked solicitously, "would you mind helping me pick out some rental furniture? It's for an apartment, close by, until I have a chance to look around for something permanent. Kevin, the General Manager—remember from last night?—and I will switch out nights we have to be on the hotel property, but it'll be good to have someplace approaching a normal home. In the mean-time, I have no clue when it comes to decorating. Whaddaya say?"

Inwardly thrilled he was inviting me on a playing-house errand, I simply said, "Sure, why not?"

Carl placed his hand lightly on the small of my back and guided me through the parking lot to his spanking new car.

Wow, fancy wheels. Not that I gave a rip about makes and mod-els—except for my beloved Merry—I recognized an expensive car when I saw one. A Lincoln Mark V, navy blue with caramel accents and interior, with genuine leather and a wood-grain dash. Carl opened the door and I eased down onto the smooth, soft surface. He slid behind the wheel, familiar with and well suited to such a plush ride. He nimbly backed the car out of its space while glancing over at me with a comical 'Here-we-go!'

And off we sped on our first date: a trip to the rental furniture store.

I'd have been pleased no matter where we went—laundromat, post office, license registration—but our unusual destination proved highly entertaining. This, thanks to Carl's non-stop commentary of the wildly differing furniture suites, bundled up for on-the-spot carry-out. One set featured a couch with extremely overstuffed cushions, "fashioned for our hemorrhoidal customers," Carl exclaimed like some late-night-TV car salesman. For a set featuring no couch but a couple rigid straight-back chairs, Carl explained it was "for those customers so uptight you couldn't drive a needle through their ass with a sledge-hammer." A bedroom suite with a huge mirror made Carl cut his eyes wickedly at me, hissing, "Kinnnky!" While the store clerk was unimpressed with Carl's humor, I was constantly cracking up. (I was, however, slightly unnerved that laughter—not witty rejoinders—was all I could manage. I attributed this to simple, sheer excitement I was with someone who'd finally piqued my interest.)

Our jolly affair continued through lunch back at the hotel restaurant and bar. I was pleased to note Carl's interest in my animated account of my recent home-purchase.

"I'd sure like to see it sometime, hon" Carl said, "but I can't say when..."

Thinking he was hinting at an invitation, I said, "Well, how about—" but Carl interrupted, lightly placing his hand on mine.

"What I want to do," he said, "is treat you to dinner in a fine restaurant." His eyebrows squeezed together in frustration and regret. "But right now, with all the work needed to get things running smoothly, and me only a few weeks on the job, I just can't."

I nodded, tsk-tsking his apology; besides, the only word I heard was *hon*.

"I hope you don't mind coming over to spend some time with me in here—" Carl's glance encompassed the bar, "—whenever I can slip in for a few minutes. And when I'm not with you, at least the band'll keep you entertained. They're pretty good." Carl gently squeezed my hand. "I'd really, really appreciate it."

"I don't mind at all," I cooed.

A slight restlessness in Carl's shoulders intimated he needed to return to work. I made motions to leave. "Great fun, *really*," I said, putting on my jacket, "but I've got tons of stuff to do at home and, anyway, I know you're busy, so..." Afraid of sounding too forward or, worse, needy, I didn't add, 'see you again soon?'

"See you again soon?" Carl asked, hope written all over his face.

"Well, why not?" I chirped, hoping he'd not detected my rush of relief. Carl leaned in for a brief brush of lips, nothing more, but I felt sure I was reading a stronger message in his eyes, those magnetic eyes.

As soon as I was out of sight of the parking lot, I allowed a grin to plaster itself across my face. Never had I experienced this level of excitement that tingled, shook, and burned within me! Carl was so different from *anyone* I'd dated. I referred to my pathetically small number of past love affairs. So different from, say...Tristan. Hmmm... Tristan. Now, there was a character!

As The Merry continued wheeling me homeward, my memory rolled backwards about four years.

Tristan was twelve years beyond my twenty-four when we met, and that alone had attracted me. Somebody who knew a lot, not so silly. Behind his rather unkempt appearance resided a sharply intelligent mind and a wickedly insightful sense of humor. Deep, interesting conversation comprised much of our time together, as did sex. Not a virgin, but still unversed at the time, I often felt like a student to a sometimes wise, sometimes overbearing teacher. Over the next three years, sex became more of a power struggle while those wonderful conversations became depressing, cynical harangues, fueled by Tristan's constant drinking.

Initially, I had tried to fix all that with encouragement, patience and, well, love. Surely, Tristan would see the light and cross over to my positive lifestyle. But there would be no leading this horse to healthier waters. I began to move on. This did not set well with Tristan. Days before I was to sign papers for my house, Tristan's opposition to my independence finally exploded in the form of his sizable fist pounding into my right eye.

My back tensed against the car seat, remembering this debacle. I shuddered. Never in my life had I encountered any sort of physical altercation. It hurt like hell! My neighbors, thank heavens, had come to my aid, and Tristan was sent home, tail tucked under. I had refused to see him afterwards, no longer able to trust him. I feared Tristan, but mostly I pitied him, because I knew, somewhere beneath his inner turmoil, lay kindness. However, his genuine remorse could not persuade me to resume any sort of relationship with him. No way was I going to be one of those women who kept running back to their brutal boyfriends or husbands, '*cuz I know he really loves me!*'

From behind me, a car's horn blasted me back to the present. I'd sat through an entire green light.

I chuckled. Yeah, you could say Carl was *slightly different* from Tristan. While Tristan's humor was dark and cynical, Carl's was light and silly. Tristan was introverted, lazy and sorta sloppy. Carl was comfortable as the center-of-attention, a workaholic, and oh, so impressive in a three-piece suit. These two were so different it was silly to compare them further. Even from what little I knew of Carl so far, I was certain he was my kind of guy.

My earlier grin re-plastered itself from ear to ear. I made no effort to contain it the rest of the way home.

CHAPTER 3

_____

DIFFERENT DIMENSIONS

"Boring!" whined a student. "Nothing's more boring than verb conjugations!"

I smiled, acknowledging his point but reminding him untantalizing conjugations were part of the package if he wanted to correctly *parler français.* With grudging acceptance, the student rattled off a verb in the passé composé ending with a sly smile. I was in my element with these high school kids. They were old enough to enjoy and produce sarcasm and wit, and I was certain they enjoyed and respected mine.

I felt anything but bored, returning to my teaching job the next day. I delivered lessons with added zest, brilliant clarity, and humorous asides. No doubt about it, the notable Halloween encounter had imbued even the most mundane task with a whole new dimension.

Hold on now, let's not get too carried away. Noting this warning-to-self with an insouciant shake of my head, I quickly fell back into the sheer enjoyment of having someone exciting to think about. I indulged all scenarios running rampant through my head.

"Sorry, no can do," I said to Vivien, my best friend, who taught across the hall, and who'd suggested we go shopping that afternoon. "Don't faint, but I have a date."

Vivien's eyebrows raised in near disbelief but excitement as well.

"I know, I know, I can't believe you know nada about this, but you and Frank"—I was referring to Vivien's recent romantic interest—"were at the Biltmore this weekend, and I was with Carl Sunday evening, all day Monday, and now tonight." I absolutely tittered, giving the full update.

A teeth-shattering bell rudely interrupted us and sent us trotting back to our classrooms. Now that Vivien and I were *both* in budding love affairs, it would be *such fun* to relate and compare *actual* experiences—rather than references to books or movies. I could feel my life getting fuller by the moment.

As soon as the three-o'clock bell rang, I zipped home, fed the cats, showered and primped. Twenty minutes of negotiating rush-hour traffic brought me to the hotel. I wandered into the bar which was dark and smelled dimly of cigarettes and stale beer. Carl was nowhere to be seen. I perched on a barstool, crossed my legs from under my short skirt, trying my best to look cool and unconcerned. *Where was he?*

Twenty minutes passed and I began to wonder if he'd stated a time for 'cocktails.' What if Carl had forgotten? I would wait five more minutes, then disappear; I didn't need him thinking I was one who'd breathlessly come at his beck and call.

"Omigod," Carl panted as he hurried into the bar, "I'm so sorry! It's been crazy: food delivery truck delayed with a flat tire; we're short a waitress *and* a cook; and there was a small fire in the kitchen. Shit, I need a drink!" A single slap of his hand on the counter and a pointed look produced the swift appearance of Carl's scotch on the rocks and a Chardonnay for me. As Chip, the bartender, turned to serve a waiting customer, his eyes rolled slightly. The teacher in me smelled a bad attitude.

Carl plopped on the barstool and whooshed a long sigh. Apparently regarding my presence as a welcome balm to the day's crazies, he raised his glass toward me. "I'm so glad you're here," he said, eyes enveloping me.

I felt sympathy for him, taking time out from his stress-ridden job for me. I wondered if he'd sensed I needed a little reassurance of his interest. I sipped my wine, enjoying its warm wake.

"So..." Carl swiveled his stool, positioning his knees so they surrounded but barely touched my crossed legs, like a pliant prison. He leaned into me, as though to block out everything else in the room, "...so, lady, how was your day?"

My earlier anxiety now history, I gaily launched into a tale about one of my wittier French students who'd suggested discovering the gender of the word *bureau* was as simple as looking underneath the desk. "And so," I laughed, "I said—"

"Damn!" Carl nearly spat out the word upon hearing his name called. The chef stood at the kitchen door at the far end of the bar, waving a towel. Carl rose to his feet. "Sorry, hon,"—I loved this term of address—"apparently there's another crisis in the kitchen. I'll be back as soon as I can!" He placed a quick but gentle kiss on my cheek and was gone.

"I'm home!" I grinned at my Siamese feline trio—Mona Bone Jakon, Frau Eva and Sinclair—intricately entwined together like a furry octopus with limbs askew. From this entanglement rose three heads and six sleepy eyes, telegraphing varying degrees of disinterest in their mistress's return.

"What? Not thrilled to see me, pusseroos?" I gently jostled the pile. The heads—two tan and black, one cream and gray—snuggled back to their former positions, deeming further interaction unnecessary. I giggled, fully appreciative of a cat's penchant for aloofness and near arrogance in deciding when and to what extent they'd display true affection. Nothing doormat-y about a cat!

Nothing doormat-y about me either!

I had remained in the bar after Carl's sudden rush to the kitchen. Occasional small talk with bartender Chip revealed a much more pleasant attitude than I'd originally pegged him for. Still, I couldn't quite read the guy. I'd noticed his sideways glances, sometimes quizzical, sometimes—I couldn't put my finger on it—scornful? Pitying, even? Surely not. Probably he was simply keeping his distance around his boss's girlfriend, not saying anything that might be misinterpreted and come back to haunt him.

Determined not to appear stood up, I had gathered my purse with airy nonchalance, said a simple good-bye and left. I hoped Carl would return to the bar to find I was no longer waiting patiently for him. *It'll be good to teach that boy a lesson early on that he best not be showing any disrespect to me!* My chin jutted out, punctuating my self-worth.

Humming a favorite Joni Mitchell tune, "A Woman of Heart and Mind," I took on a hefty pile of English compositions, energetically adding detailed comments. Before I knew it, I was done! *Amazing how having a man in my life brings out the best in me.*

Now I could turn to journaling. Whenever plagued with dilemmas or, better, delighted by titillating events, I sought out my journal, my best friend actually. I'd kept journals since I was a little girl in third or fourth grade. Back then they were *diaries,* sporting cats or horses on the cover, and a small golden clasp lockable by a ribboned key. I'd saved them until high school, when Mama found and read a few. I'd been so furious I threw them all out, a move I deeply regretted later, even if they did contain ninety-nine percent silliness.

But I resumed journaling and seldom neglected my secret confidant. Sketchy entries of late were due to the time-gobbling rigmarole of buying this house. Plus, I'd actually had dealings with other men, but—I felt a ripple of giddiness—none of whom had gotten my attention like Carl.

One of those men was not entirely a closed chapter, even though I'd lost interest in reading further. Hailing from California, Warner had come into my life not by his, but by his mother's, volition.

A few days after Tristan's blow-up last spring, my laying low was cut short by Mama's insistence I pay a visit while her dear friend Scout (Warner's mom) was in town. The moment I entered Mama's kitchen, I heard both of them inhale in horror when I pulled off my sunglasses, revealing the sizable shiner surrounding my bloodied right eyeball.

"My God!" was all either could say.

Unbeknownst to me, Scout had at that very moment anointed herself my rescuer, deeming her son Warner the perfect choice for me. A few weeks later, I found myself enjoying a two-week visit on the west coast. My mid-summer visit would be reciprocated with Warner's visit here. Not a bad plan, except I felt no attraction to Warner other than friendship. (This due in part, perhaps, to my resounding aversion that anyone plan my life and to the slow dawning that Scout was attempting exactly that.) I'd hardly given Warner a thought the past few months. Now, I jolted upright on the bed realizing his Thanksgiving visit was a mere three weeks away! What to do? If ever there was a time to journal, it was now.

As I reached for the journal, though, the telephone jangled, startling me so much I knocked the phone, journal, and glass of water off the table. I fumbled the receiver to my ear and, much to my delight, heard Carl's voice:

"Damn, woman!" Chuckling at my *oofs* and *ouches* as I resettled, he said, "I didn't realize you left here drunk as a coot!"

"Not drunk then or now. Just klutzo."

"Well, Miss Klutzo, I feel bad about leaving you stranded at the bar this evening, and I was wondering if I might pop over tomorrow for a quick visit to see what all the fuss is about with this new house of yours."

So it wasn't mere lip service when he'd said he wanted to see it! I swelled with delight. "What a great idea! How's about I fix us a really simple dinner?" *Yeah, it'd be simple all right*; my forte did not reside in the kitchen. "Sound OK?"

"Sounds perfect. See you tomorrow."

I cradled the phone and folded my arms around my chest in a warm self-embrace. I put the journal aside and pulled back from the cats, who'd immediately jumped on the bed when the journal appeared.

"Sorry, puddy-tats, no time for journaling right now. It's time for James!"

I jumped off the bed and, for the rest of the evening, James Taylor crooned away as I straightened up for Carl's first visit to my digs. Wired, I zipped from one household task to another. Buying my own home at age twenty-eight had filled me with pride and a wonderful sense of stability. Of course, Mama and Daddy had helped with the down payment, which I was already repaying in small monthly amounts, as much as I could manage on my paltry teacher's salary.

Three years into teaching, I tried not to get depressed about the gap between my income and that of many of my non-teaching friends. Luckily, I loved my crazy, funny high-school kids. I would repeatedly milk that contentment to mitigate frustration with my financial strappings. Not that I was in debt; no, no, nothing like that.

"Lord, Rosie, you can stretch a dollar like a bungee cord! CPA's would kill for your monetary wizardry," both Lucy and Vivien commented time and again. True, I'd been confident I could handle a reasonable mortgage payment, which, so far, was the case.

Wonder what he'll think of my place? Wonder if it's anything as nice as places he's lived? Which, by the way, is where? Gosh, I've got so much schtuff to ask him! Oh, this is *fun!*

Everything ship-shape, at least by my standards, I made out a list so I could zip by the grocery store after school and get home to cook. That thought brought on its usual smirk. Whatever, I was bound and determined to give my best effort for our first meal together, away from hotel diners or interruptions.

Journaling would have to wait. No matter, I didn't want to *write* about my feelings now; I wanted to *feel* them. I sighed in contentment as I crawled into bed and nudged between the cats. It occurred to me Carl had better like cats, too. But I figured, between my powers of persuasion and the irresistible charm of my three charges, this would be a non-issue.

Grocery list in hand, I was hurrying out the front door of the school when an office aide flagged me down.

"Hey, Miss Browning! Some guy called and asked you to call before you left."

I felt a vague uneasiness. I found an empty office, dialed the hotel, and was transferred to Carl. He could not have sounded more apologetic.

"Oh, thank heavens you called before you went to the grocery store! I'm sorry hon, but they called a staff meeting and there's no way I can miss it." Not one to reject a sincere apology, I made to respond, but Carl continued. "But I wanted to make sure we're still on for this weekend. I want to see you again." Carl's voice lowered. "Like, soon."

I hoped Carl hadn't heard my sudden intake of breath. "Just how soon is soon?"

"Well, I'd say tomorrow afternoon, but didn't you say you had some kind of meeting?"

I did in fact have to chair a ballet support group meeting. *Wow, even this registered with him?*

Carl continued, "So, maybe as soon as you can, afterwards?" Carl's voice sounded hopeful.

My entire being was warming from head to toe. This man, so busy with his new job, was making a special effort to keep our little flame going. Thinking of how he made a point to reach me before I spent money on groceries, to apologize, and then to ensure our next get together...all made me feel so...*desirable.* Allowing my voice to reflect a trace of my growing desire, I replied, "I think that kind of 'soon' will do nicely."

I hung up the phone, smiling. With no small relief, I crumpled the grocery list and tossed it. Any residual disappointment dissolved upon opening the front door to my now spotless home. I'd have no problem enjoying it all by myself, knowing I would see Carl in a little over twenty-four hours. The evening passed quickly and pleasantly after which I rounded up the cats and headed to the bedroom, determined to resume journaling. After a few pages of gushing about what was looking to be a significant upturn in my life, I felt oddly compelled to add the following closure:

I am excited but also wary.

CHAPTER 4

LEVELING THE PLAYING FIELD

"So, have you slept with him yet?"

Lucy's wickedly pointed question elicited cackles from The Inner Circle, namely me, Vivien, and fellow teacher Louise. Banded together three years now, we had no idea our friendship would stretch over forty years. Tonight, we were gathered at a restaurant to celebrate Louise's birthday and to hear the latest about Carl, beginning with an answer begged by the question just posed.

I took a sip of wine and assumed a mockingly drunken slur. "Well, hey-ull yeh-ussh! At leasht, I thing zo."

"What the hell does that mean?" Lucy, the funniest of the foursome, flicked her eyebrows in Groucho Marx fashion as she did when delivering perfectly timed punch lines. "What we want to know is, how the hell was it?"

Laughing at three mildly confused, highly expectant expressions, I began to recount The First Time.

"Right before I trucked over to the hotel for the fifth time in that first week after Halloween, Carl called and asked 'Why don't you pack a toothbrush?' which I took as his very cool, subtle way of asking me to spend the night."

"Either that or he thinks you have a really bad case of goat breath," Lucy said.

I cupped my hand over my mouth, exhaled quickly, fell sideways and gasped, "Aw, it's not so bad!" Righting myself, I continued. "So there I am in the bar doing my thing—nope, *not* pole dancing, but playing the waiting game for one of Carl's three-minute swing-bys."

Louise, in her straightforward manner, spoke up. "Bit of a pattern, that?"

My face soured briefly. "You could say so. I'd mind this if I didn't enjoy the band so much, but I do wind up drinking more than I should. You know, I can't handle liquor like I could in my lush college days."

"Is there a point anywhere in here?" Vivien asked serenely.

"OK, OK. Carl whizzes by, slips me the key, and says he'll follow shortly. Off I go...and promptly...get *lost*...because, you know, all those hallways look alike."

Everyone tsk-tsked, picturing a half-wasted woman, toothbrush in hand, listing from one wall to the other.

"Somehow—do not ask how—I find the room and Carl arrives right after me. I'm thinking we're about to engage in passionate, romantic lovemaking—trust me, I'd had multiple scenarios of our first time—but I also wished I'd been more sober to fully experience the whole performance. We're undressing each other and I need to sit on the bed to unlace my boots, and, oh God, I missed the whole bed and landed on my ass on the floor!"

Tsk-tsks became guffaws of disbelief.

Lucy pressed on. "So then what?"

"Well, whaddayathink? We *did it*."

"And?" said everyone.

I paused. "I wish I could say I was, um, 'sassafied,' but that just didn't happen." I toyed with my food. "It doesn't make sense: Carl can simply look at me, or lay a hand on my shoulder, squeeze my thigh... and I go weak in the knees. But in bed with him, at least that night, I went stiff as a board. We're talking, nun-like! I felt like an actor who'd memorized her lines perfectly only to lapse into morbid stage fright. True, we were both pretty lit. But I gotta give the boy credit, he kept at it for my sake, until finally—" I grimaced, remembering, "—he said 'to hell with it.' Then he passed out."

Nobody said a word.

I spread my hands in 'tah-dah!' fashion. "How's that for an anticlimax?"

"Maybe your body knows something you don't," Vivien said, her tone earnest, thoughtful.

Most anything Vivien said, I took as sound wisdom, but this didn't strike a chord with me. "I think my body felt like it was with someone of much greater sexual prowess and was embarrassed it wasn't as, ah, *schooled*." I sipped some wine. "But to have been so turned on by this guy and then fall pitifully short in performance... it was strange."

"No big deal," Louise said. "The first time usually stinks for everybody..." She ignored our inquisitive looks. "...according to *Glamour* magazine. Once you know him a little better, you'll feel less uncomfortable, although for the life of me I don't know how you can think you're a Dull Girl." Lucy and Vivien nodded in agreement.

"Remember the comedian Marcia Warfield?" Lucy asked. "She said she's not into sex whenever she's mad at her man. Well, the way she put it was, 'When I be mad, my pussy be mad, too!'" Our shrieks of laughter caused some diners to look our way. Lucy continued, "So in your case, it's 'when I be uncomfy, my pu...blah blah blah!'"

My laughter changed to a short harrumph. "For sure, I'd feel more comfy if he'd quit breaking dates. *Three times* in the last three weeks he reneged on coming to my house for dinner."

"Uh-oh," came the chorused response.

"But he's sincerely apologetic; it's always *hotel obligations*." I made no effort to hide my sarcasm. "And it's always me over to the hotel, not vice versa. It feels, I don't know...cheap." I held my finger over the straw of my water glass, raised it, released my finger, and watched the water dribble out. "Especially when he doesn't always call me the next day after we, you know, *do it*." I sighed. "But he eventually calls and, I swear, my heart sings when I hear his voice."

"So...who is this dude?" Louise asked. "Really, what do you know about him?"

My lips puckered. "Not a helluva lot, but that's because he usually keeps conversations focused on me." A prideful smile. "He studied hospitality and culinary management at some northern college. He's worked all over, 'getting experience,' he says. He's from New Jersey—right, I know: of all places... As for his family, he calls his dad 'Cap'n'—kinda cute, huh?—but doesn't seem to be as close to his mom or younger brother." I reflected a moment. "Not that my family's what you'd call close. Whatever, I'm not dating his family." Expressions had turned skeptical now.

"Look, all I know is this man makes me laugh more than *anyone* I've been around; to me, that in itself is sexy as hell." I sensed my audience wanted more. I tried to downplay my next reason: "He respects my aversion to smoking by always cupping his cigarette in his han—"

"Whaaa?" Louise jerked forward in her chair. "*You're* dating a *smoker?*"

Shrugging sheepishly, I hurried on. "And he *listens* to me! He's always making references to stuff I've said. Hell, I remember dating one guy who, when I was talking about a friend whose house had been destroyed by a tornado, this guy's response was he thought his calves were getting bigger. Carl would never be so gauche." Going for a strong close, I said, "Standing next to him, my whole being feels electrified! That's got to be a good thing, right?"

My friends' smiles of hope and encouragement relayed their happiness for me.

Lucy brought us back to the bottom line. "Speaking of sexy... you only told us about y'all's first time. Any improvement since then?"

I resumed my drunken slur, "Well, hay-ull yeh-ussh." I grinned. "After all, he is IIII-tal-yun!"

At that moment, several waiters approached our table, bearing birthday cake and candles. We sang Happy Birthday as quickly as possible so we could dive into dessert and watch Louise open her presents.

Licking icing off my fingers, I pointed one at Louise and said, "OK, birthday girl, that's enough about you. Let's steer this thing back to *moi* 'cuz I've got a question."

Now everyone regarded me in mock exasperation as if to say, "What now?"

"Remember Warner from California, with the matchmaker-from-hell mom, and whose visit is *next week*?" I asked. "What if this messes up whatever's happening with Carl and me?"

Lucy spoke first. "Seems to me it could be a timely test of Carl's sincere interest. You gotta admit he's been sending mixed messages."

"Can't argue that," I said. "But I think it's *rude of me* to allow Warner to go to all the effort and expense—and expectation—of coming out here only to realize I'm not nearly into him as he is into me. I think that's almost cruel."

"Could you call him and explain that things have changed?" Vivien asked.

"I discussed this very thing with Darrah, my sister. She said it wasn't all about me—" I shot a sour look around the table, "—and I should consider others. She's right: Mama would have a duck fit, Scout would be downright pissed, and Warner would be hurt... though not as much as he's probably going to be."

"Shit's gonna hit the fan pretty much any way you throw it," Louise stated. "Still, since it's a done deal, I say let the chips fall where they may. Maybe Carl will un-mix his messages."

"What if Carl thinks I'm some kind of player, a tricky woman who likes to—" my voice lost force, "—keep men on a string?" I looked around. "OK, OK, that dog don't hunt. Hell, at college, I'd get nervous if I accepted two dates in the same weekend."

We began gathering purses and coats to leave. Vivien summed up everyone's thoughts: "You're probably making a mountain out of a molehill. You know, you do tend to be a bit on the anal side." Energetic nods all around.

Lucy joined in. "This thing with Carl is barely a month old. Just give it some time."

Driving home, I decided to put full stock in my friends' advice and lose some of my angst. Upon entering my house, the phone was ringing.

"So...ya been thinking about me?" Carl's husky voice rippled down my spine.

"Who is this?"

A wheezing, gurgling giggle pronounced firm approval of my quip. Apparently my new go-with-the-flow mindset had ushered my wit all the way back to its regular seat. I curled up with Mona Bone, who took his regular seat in my lap, and settled in for some easy conversation.

"I've got a great idea," Carl said, enthusiastic. "How's about let's rent a cabin at Mount Cheaha—it's only twenty miles from here—for a couple days next week? Just you and me, hon! Scenery will be beautiful, and I'm not talking outside."

So much for easy conversation. Time to bite the bullet. "I'm afraid I have plans."

Carl went silent, much as I had done the last time he'd broken a date with me. That he was obviously taken aback by my unavailability was strangely exhilarating. Making sure my voice contained no smugness, I continued. "I've been meaning to tell you this was coming up; it's something that's been planned for months and it's too late to change things now."

"So, what's going on?"

Did I hear the slightest tone of disbelief or, even anxiety? I let out a soft laugh. "A set-up, I fear." I explained the circumstances and ended with, "Warner's simply a good friend and I need to play gracious host. I hope you understand."

Carl grunted a few times, formulating what to say. "Damn, girl! Kicking me to the curb for a week!" His voice contained no anger, just disappointment.

For the next forty-five minutes, we spoke of our days, with my having to wake a student who'd drooled all over his blank test, and with Carl's tale of a rookie waiter's screw-up with a Bananas Foster dessert, igniting the tablecloth and the waiter's pants.

My laughter was loose and hearty. It felt good. I felt like our playing field was more level.

"So..." Carl said, "are you going to have time for me after next week?"

"You bet."

CHAPTER 5

WANTED: WANTED COMPANY

Because I felt more settled about Carl, the following week proved surprisingly enjoyable...for the most part. Initially, Warner and I assumed a bemused attitude towards being pawns in our mothers' matchmaking game. I had no problem *liking* Warner...*so long as he kept his distance.* The first few days were jam-packed with activity: city tour, hikes, nightlife, even a party (touted as a house-warming but—to the matchmakers—serving as an introduction of *Rosie's new beau*...). Our conversations flowed with mutual interests of creative endeavors or with Warner's sincere compliments of and suggestions about my house.

But Warner's easy-going persona belied his sincere interest in me, and things became strained as I repeatedly brushed off his more romantic advances. The most awkward of these was the night he walked down the hall from the guest room and appeared at my bedroom door, his expression a mixture of hurt, questioning, and desire.

Trying hard to keep pity out of my voice, I fumbled, "I—um, oh dear, this is awkward. I really do *like* you, Warner, but, um..." I lowered my head to silently curse, *damn Scout and Mama! This is exactly what I knew would happen!* I continued, "God, I'm so sorry my mother and Scout have made things uncomfortable for us."

"It's not them," Warner said softly. "It's you."

Deep inside, I knew Warner had spoken an absolute truth. "Right. I know I've done a terrible job of handling the pressure of what's supposed to be happening here and not...not being able to deliver the goods, so to speak." Warner waited, expecting me to continue, but I remained silent.

With a long sigh, as though to finally get things off his chest, Warner said, "You know, what's really made me uncomfortable this week is seeing how affectionate you are with everyone—your friends and students at the party, people we've run into all week long—with everyone but me. You've hardly held my hand. I'd actually kinda been thinking these past few months I'm in love with you, but now I'm seeing I'd never be able to handle your coldness."

Stung, I took a moment to gather myself, digging deep to be sure I was telling the truth, since that was what Warner deserved.

"I do withhold affection—false affection—*especially* if I think that person cares more for me than I do for him..." I looked at Warner. "...which seems to be the case with you and me, even though I wish it weren't." My gaze lowered. "That doesn't mean I'm cold." Anger seethed within me, but I kept it below surface. "I should've canceled this whole thing but opted to go ahead with it. Bad decision."

Warner, the consummate gentleman, rose above his hurt to show understanding and acceptance that we remain friends. On departure day at the airport, we gave each other a platonic hug and managed to laugh ruefully at how disappointed our mothers would be.

I watched Warner board the plane, feeling a strange wave of regret or, possibly, fear that my independent streak—close cousin to hard-headedness—was letting the good one get away.

I turned, hurried to my car and damn near clicked my heels. On the drive home, I felt the shackles of control falling away. As I hurried into the house, the phone rang. I knew who it was.

For five minutes, we stood and hugged each other. Some four hours after Carl had called, I was back at the airport. He'd gone to a one-day conference in Washington, D.C., and had asked if I minded picking him up. *Well, duh.* My scenario of our returning to my house so Carl could finally see where I lived wasn't realized, as he was anxious to get back to the hotel property. Whatever irritation I felt about this quickly evaporated as Carl showered me with attention, reiterating how glad he was to see me. Our mutual delight in reuniting was evidenced further by an immediate, heated romp between the sheets (proving to myself I could show plenty of affection when I felt like it. Damn it.).

Even though it was a hassle for me to stay overnight at the hotel, what with the increasingly familiar routine of packing up my clothes and school stuff and dealing with food and litter for the cats, I did so not only Sunday night but Monday night as well. Since our lovemaking was becoming more satisfying with each round, since our TV watching, eating dinner, or having drinks at the bar (the sum total of our activities thus far) were filled with warm snuggles, laughter, and more of those sweet-nothings that sent thrills through me, I decided a little inconvenience on my part was worth getting the stuff I craved.

CHAPTER 6

TÊTE-À-TÊTE

"Well, where in the hell have you been?" Over the phone, Mama's voice was more worried than demanding.

"Busy, busy as usual," I answered. Keeping my voice neutral was difficult, in light of some disturbing tidbits passed along to me by my good friend, Cindi, who'd attended the previous week's 'house-warming' party. There had definitely been more behind-the-scenes activities afoot than I'd been aware of. I needed to vent. "OK, Mama, you and I have to talk about that fiasco of Warner's visit."

"Why? I haven't done anything!" Mama's immediate reversion to defiance told me perhaps she knew she'd crossed the line. Or maybe she feared whatever closeness we had built up over the past few years was about to go up in smoke. I was beginning to understand my mother really was a mixed bag. Gushing with pride and admiration for me one minute, resorting to sarcasm and judgment the next. I knew this whole drama with Warner had been ninety-percent orchestrated by Scout because Mama really wasn't much of a schemer. Even if she'd deemed Scout's recent machinations as over-the-top, though, she lacked the mettle to stand up to her friend's more flamboyant, A-plus personality. I didn't want to discuss anything further over the phone.

"I'm going to drop by after school tomorrow, OK?"

"Sure, honey, come on. I'll fix dinner."

Driving to my parents' home the next afternoon, I implored myself to keep calm, stay focused, and, for heaven's sake, not to dissolve into tears, an instant argument weakener, and one of my less admirable habits. Rather than prove a point, I came across as a weepy whiner. I felt confident I could stay on track, probably buoyed by Carl's unquestioned interest in me of late. I wouldn't call it *love* yet, but if he continued this way, I couldn't envision any other outcome.

Mama and I chose to sit on the deck since the early December day had not ushered in enough chill to keep us from enjoying the forty-mile view. I was glad to have the calming backdrop.

"So. Number one, do *not* try to arrange my life." All wide-eyed innocence from Mama. "I mean, this whole Warner enterprise, with you and Daddy telling him to '*move to Birmingham,*' to '*give me some time...*'" Mama fussed with her drink. "Cindi told me everything. I mean, Jesus H. Christ!"

Somewhat taken aback, Mama countered, "Now, Rosie, Warner is a fine, fine man, and—"

"Who said he wasn't?"

"—and if you give this a little time—"

"Time is not the problem here. The problem is I'm not in love with Warner!"

"—and...but this Carl, this Carl seems kind of—"

"And that's another thing: Do *not* pry into my life!" My insides seethed as I delivered the most unnerving item Cindi had relayed.

"I cannot believe you and Daddy hired, or, at least, got somebody to investigate Carl's—"

"We only did it because we were concerned! You've not even introduced him to us, which makes us think maybe he's not—"

"Not what? As good a catch as Warner? Well, it just so happens this guy interests me way more than Warner does. And I'm more interested in how *I* feel about somebody, not in how somebody else thinks I *ought* to feel!"

Mama shot right back. "You know, that's exactly what Scout said—"

"*Enough* of Scout! Damn, what is she, your master? She—"

"She *said*," Mama elongated *said*, determined to make a point, "and I quote, 'Rosie needs one kind of man and wants another.'"

Infuriated anyone could label me as having poor judgment skills, I said, "Well, she is wrong, dead wrong!" My voice began to quiver.

"I think you're being a tad over-dramatic, don't you?" Mama asked, her voice perfectly calm now.

"Absolutely not!" I hated to sound shrill. Controlling myself, I said, "Look, if I make a mistake, at least it's *my* mistake! Hell, I'm twenty-eight years old. You and Daddy can't change me now."

The sliding door opened and Daddy stuck his head out, not venturing any further. "What the hell's going on out here?" he asked cautiously.

"Your daughter's telling us to mind our own business," Mama's answer was laden with sarcasm.

Having no desire to enter the fray, Daddy muttered a vague "Ah..." and headed for the bar. I knew he'd fix his usual pitcher of martinis, his number one method of dealing with conflict.

Mama and I remained silent for several moments, processing. Even though I had voiced my most pressing points, turmoil remained within. My whole argument had been presented in anything but graceful fashion. My initial attack-like mode had disallowed any civil discussion towards a mutual understanding. Why am I always so danged untactful, so clumsy?

And yet, Mama's moves regarding Warner had been clumsy, too, underhanded without malice but, importantly, without communication either. I sighed, realizing I'd touched on the root of the problem with my parents. Our relationship was fine and dandy so long as nothing worthy of or demanding real discussion came into play. I regained control of my voice.

"Look, you and Daddy are going to have to accept what I do—and whom I choose—and not be so quick to judgment. I'm not stupid, and I'm not on any path of self-destruction, as y'all seem to fear."

More subdued herself, Mama said, "No, honey, your Daddy and I know you're not stupid; you're anything but! We're worried, that's all."

"Well, all I can say is I truly don't think you have anything to worry about. So please, try not to, OK?" I paused. "And I promise, y'all will meet Carl soon."

"OK." Relieved the argument was not going to escalate, Mama asked, "So, are you staying for dinner?"

"Nah, gotta get home; you know, cats, papers to grade, the usual." We walked back inside.

Daddy sat in front of the TV, drink in one hand, a kernel of popcorn in the other. In front of Daddy and at full attention sat Jimbo, the world's best dog. I had to smile at this nightly ritual which was in full swing.

"So, Daddy, how was your day?" I ventured, trying to return to normalcy.

"Oh, fine." His hand was poised for the next toss to Jimbo, whose eyes were fixed on the prize. Seeing the current game was for two participants only, I turned to go. "See ya."

Admiring Jimbo's quick catch and readying for the next throw, Daddy managed an offhand "Yeah, see you next time."

Yeah, next time, I thought ruefully. I maneuvered Merry out of the impossible driveway, necessary with a house perched on the side of a mountain to ensure a dynamite view. A familiar emptiness filled me as it usually did after visits with my parents. Our frequent encounters seemed to serve no purpose other than keeping up appearances of a good solid relationship. Ours was rarely hostile—today's brief outburst being the exception—but I could never describe it as close. (Years later, a therapist would find this lack of closeness 'remarkable.') The likelihood of sharing my current thoughts about Carl, whether full of anticipation or uncertainty, was nil. This, because previous ventures into such dialogues were usually met with judgment or disinterest. Nope, Norman Rockwell would not be painting a portrait of this family.

I turned the volume up on the cassette player, hoping my loud accompaniment to Elton John's "Philadelphia Freedom" would dispel my vague uneasiness. But it wouldn't go away. I tried to pinpoint what in our discussion was continuing to needle me. Not anything Mama said, really. No, it was that quote of Scout, the one that implied I was too stupid to make a wise choice about men. Sorry, not true. Scout said that because she was mad I didn't choose her son. And I had a handle on this thing with Carl; no problem there. I joined in with Elton again, sounding as though I had not a care in the world. My reflection in the rear-view mirror indicated otherwise.

A light shower of leaves ripples downward as my foot seesaws against the ground, keeping the glider in motion. So many thoughts have crowded my mind I hardly know which one to address first.

A man who made me laugh and whose very presence turned me to a puddle of flesh and bone... A bittersweet smile creeps across my face. I gotta admit, it *did* look good. In tandem with my own giddy anticipation, though, had been the weightier, often unspoken expectation that I'd sooner or later be joining the ranks of *married*. At almost thirty, it was getting to be later. I was *ready* to be *normal*.

I slide into my habitual self-talk mode. I'm still on board with you, Rosie-Rose, for not choosing Warner, albeit a great catch...for someone else. That unsolicited campaign certainly got your independent shackles bristling, but it was Scout's aggravating 'need/want' comment that went deep and stayed a while. It wasn't like you renounced Warner and chose Carl in some conscious, rebellious attempt to prove Scout wrong; it was more a matter of locked-down determination to prove yourself right. Too bad you didn't sit back to take full stock of your feelings; a small helping of crow wouldn't have killed you.

This is not to say Scout's comment was indisputable. *Needing* someone for your own fulfillment and happiness is a big old heavy cloak woven of melodrama, guilt and insecurity, whereas *wanting* someone is a lightweight garment, a fun frock laced with threads of joy, freedom and confidence. The trick is to recognize whether what you're wearing makes you dance or trudge. If you struggle to even try it on, it's probably never going to fit. Of course, Rosie-Rose, being the seamstress that you are had you hell-bent on making alterations.

CHAPTER 7

HIGH TIME

With Christmas holidays fast approaching, I was inundated with the usual flurry of activities. School was insane, as semester exams meant preparing, copying, giving, grading, and recording. This, along with making merry with the kids who brought every snack and soft drink known to Winn Dixie for partying it up on the last day of school. I looked forward to telling Carl about all the craziness, this evening, *at my house.*

On a Friday evening in December, some six weeks after we'd met, Carl's seemingly set-in-stone pattern of Always There, Never Here was finally broken. As I opened the front door, I saw no need to begin with some sarcastic in-the-nick-of-time greeting. His slightly sheepish expression disclosed he knew full well his visit was long overdue.

I had wanted so long for Carl to see my own little nest and had flitted about the house all afternoon to make sure everything looked warm and welcoming. As I watched his square-shouldered, six-foot frame cross the threshold, I could hardly contain my excitement and pride.

"So. This is it? This is all you got?" Carl said as he took in the surroundings, his expression reflecting an entirely different opinion.

"Well, you know, my decorator's been in Europe."

"Which means, *you* really *did* do all this yourself?" Carl wasn't patronizing; he seemed truly impressed.

"Aw...gawlee, shucks amighty, I guess I did," I said, pointing one toe to the floor at an angle and twisting my forefinger on my cheek.

"So, where are those famous cats?"

I was doubly delighted Carl had started the evening asking about the most important things in my life. A quick 'Pusserroos!' summoned all three, who entered the living room with varying degrees of curiosity, nonchalance or caution. Watching Carl kneel down to scratch behind Sinclair's ears, to rub Frau Eva's tummy, to coax Mona Bone forward—while saying their names, no less!—filled me with a lovely sense of satisfaction and, well, home, as if this was the way it should—or could—be with Carl.

"Here." He handed me a bottle of wine and another of scotch along with a couple Styrofoam boxes of tasty hors d'oeuvres. "Compliments of the hotel."

"Goodness! It's the least the hotel could do for keeping you away from here so long." I cast mocking eyes at Carl and then said, "And now, if you have an hour—or maybe two minutes—allow me to give you a tour of my estate." I took Carl's hand and led him through what could have been an ordinary three-bedroom-one-bath house. A Dutch-door and brick grill added charm to the kitchen, huge double-hung windows brightened the bedrooms, and a small, bay-windowed front parlor lay in wait for its unique furnishing. "That would be a baby grand piano," I pronounced, grinning. "Well...one of these days!"

In short order, we sat on the couch and grazed on cheeses, crab and shrimp while sipping our drinks. Conversation was free-flowing as we enjoyed the lights from the tree and the glow from the fire. The only reference to Warner's recent visit was as a rude interloper to our unspoken goal of tightening our relationship. We paid scant attention to the program on television, other than by Carl's occasional commentary which never failed to send me into giggle fits.

Laughter was an integral part of our foreplay. Carl would usually punctuate many of his hysterical remarks with some sort of move, be it nestling into my neck, a gentle placement of his hand at the top of my inner thigh, or a lingering kiss. Every move he made ignited me throughout. This, I was convinced, was the way two people should feel when they were on course to a deeper union. Our embraces became more and more heated until, having shed half our clothes on the couch, we moved to the bedroom. Sated with good food, wine, and tantalizing foreplay, I glided onto the bed, Carl never breaking contact with me.

I yielded to his firm grasp as he pulled me towards him, our eyes steadfastly acknowledging the pleasure we'd been anticipating for the entire evening. Whereas our last time together was marked by heat and passion, this time was decidedly more intimate, gentle and, well, I could think of no other way to describe it, loving. Carl appeared intent on convincing me I was someone he very much wanted to treasure. To see his dark eyes deepen into softness and adoration as he entered me, I exulted not only in the sheer physical pleasure of the moment but also in deep pride knowing I was with the man I'd chosen.

As I lay in exquisite afterglow, I heard Carl clumsily fumbling his way out of the tangled sheets, going into one of his mock-grumbling routines, "What the hell? I'm trapped! This sheet's alive!" Thrashing about madly, "Leggo, leggo! I can't breathe!" he clutched his chest, mimicking Redd Foxx of "Samford and Son," "Hold on, Elizabeth, I'm coming! It's the big one!..."

And so on. It wasn't that his lines were so funny; it was Carl's delivery of them, with eyes rolling wackily, mouth pouting or grimacing. My stomach heaved with laughter.

Carl crashed to the floor and plopped his head on the edge of the bed with eyes crossed. "Sorry, hon. Gotta go. You know that hotel's only gonna let you have a little piece of me at a time."

I scrunched my lips in good-natured disgust. My resentment of the hotel had dissipated considerably in light of the pleasant evening. I lay in bed, watching him dress, recalling how our bodies were becoming more and more in sync. Carl leaned over, kissed my brow softly, and turned to leave. In my most syrupy Scarlett voice, I murmured, "Come back anytime now, ya heah?"

I heard him chuckle. I was further delighted to hear, as he opened the front door, "See ya next time, cats."

CHAPTER 8

THE WINTER OF SLIGHT DISCONTENT

Many 'next times' would occur over the ensuing six wintry weeks, as would many 'no times,' always justified by Carl's go-to excuse. *I'm about up to here with your frigging maybes and your it's-the-hotels*, I would itch to say, but I did *not* want to get all weepy and needy. Or bitchy. 'OK' would remain my go-to response.

But the 'no times' infuriated me. Why was he treating me this way? Couldn't he step up and be a gentleman, for chrissakes? Yes, furious is what I was, but at myself. Why did I repeatedly say 'OK' when it was decidedly not? What the hell was wrong with me?

To answer these questions, I'd pace around the house, muttering to myself while my cats gazed on, mildly curious as to what all the fuss was about. Eventually, I'd plop on the bed and plow into my journal. What if rebelling against Carl's poor behavior sent him packing? Nothing could be further from my wishes. Trying to imagine how I might express my grievances only caused my shoulders to scrunch tightly rather than level squarely. Thoughts of taking a stand dredged up an image of Tristan's balled fist heading straight for my eyeball.

Confrontation—no matter what the degree—had become anathema to me. Acquiescence, equally unappealing, would be my option until I could get a grip on my emotions, an ongoing duel between hurt and desire which turned my brain into mashed potatoes.

As duels go, Desire held the mightier sword. If I wanted great sex and fabulous wit—and I did—Carl was gratifying me in fine fashion. Our first ridiculously clumsy liaison had sputtered into oblivion; now, whether in bed, the hallway, the car, wherever...Carl and I fell into rhythm effortlessly, breathlessly, beautifully. I loved it.

My sense of humor had fully returned from its early perceived Lazarus-like state. Our conversations were much more animated, no longer one-sided, and punctuated more often than not by Carl's hoot at something I said. I considered such high-energy banter a hallmark of a solid relationship. I loved it.

Around others, Carl and I exuded a strong connection, what with sideways glances of mutual enjoyment, sharing a private joke, or a quick show of affection. An entertaining, dynamic duo we were; I was sure that was the impression we made. I loved it.

Carl and I must have been adequately impressive at a holiday dinner at my parents' house.

"I promise, they're really nice people," I assured Carl as we exited the car. I'd made no mention of the *investigator*.

"What? Do I look nervous?" Carl had asked. "Trust me, I'll be fine."

My parents, always gracious hosts, greeted us at the door. Whether Carl detected their slight reserve, I couldn't tell. When Carl offered Mama a tasteful seasonal floral arrangement, her surprise and delight was genuine. Daddy could find no fault with his gift bottle of gin. "I hear you're a martini man," Carl said. Daddy grinned in spite of himself.

Dinner began with a flurry of questions—job, family, interests—which Carl fielded easily, always enhancing with humorous tidbits: "Oh yeah, Italian dad, Irish mom...well, we're talking fireworks!" or, "Right, the gift of gab is helpful in my job...as it is (looking at Daddy, a consulting engineer), I imagine, Edward, in yours," or "Josephine, do I taste nutmeg in these mashed potatoes? Brilliant!"

Perhaps my parents heard the excitement in my laughter, or sensed my hope they'd approve of Carl; by evening's end, the invitation for a repeat was sincere. From what I could tell, my parents had moved their concerns about Carl to the back burner.

I was disappointed Carl and I wouldn't be able to shine as a couple on New Year's Eve. Spending Christmas Eve together was pleasurable, but I'd especially looked forward to the holiday so full of symbolism for new beginnings.

"I'm so sorry, hon," Carl had informed me two days beforehand. "We now have four functions scheduled and, trust me, if you came, you'd hardly lay eyes on me at all. I'm going to be slammed." This time, Carl's 'excuse' was valid. I'd been his date at another hotel event and he'd been on high alert the entire night, intent that operations ran smoothly. So, another New Year's Eve found me home in bed with no company other than cats and journal. I couldn't believe snow was forecast the following day and I wouldn't be able to experience its magic with Carl. A perfect opportunity missed.

Carl's missed opportunities to solidify our fledgling romance rendered me in a position to seize, albeit halfheartedly, other chances. Since the New Year's Day winter wonderland would not be a cloistered, before-a-fireplace romantic interlude with Carl, I grudgingly accepted an invitation from a former boyfriend to spend the day outdoors with several other friends. Within short order, I was an enthusiastic participant in sled races and snowball fights followed by pizza and hot chocolate at my house. I couldn't help but regard the pleasant day as a weapon of sorts. A few other dates cropped up, but not frequently enough to knock Carl out of the picture. That Carl made scant mention of these infrequent intrusions upon our sketchy routine made me wonder if he regarded them as permission to do likewise.

But insecure thoughts or alternate diversions would dissolve into nothingness the moment Carl painted himself prominent in the picture. I absolutely preened like one of my cats whenever he paid the least bit of attention to me. A simple telephone ring would send a thrill through me, not only in anticipation of his voice but in contemplation of his thought processes leading him to dial my number. As for encounters not separated by a telephone line, his all-consuming attention left me wanting little else.

If only his attention were consistent!

"A mixed bag, you say?" Cindi, one of my favorite friends, elbowed me as we sat on her piano bench, her face contorted into one of the rubbery masks only Cindi could make. We were about to do an initial run-through of Beethoven's Fifth for four hands but, for the moment, a Carl-update took precedence. "Well, he looks like he ought to carry one of those skinny black suitcases, after seeing that pimp mobile he drives. You sure he's not Mafia?"

"Nah, hell no!" I laughed even though, if pressed, I couldn't say for sure. I still had learned next to nothing about Carl's past.

"What I want to know is..." Cindi said, "...did your parents' private investigator come up with any juicy stuff?"

With mock drama my right hand played the opening ominous four notes of Beethoven. "Not much, best as I could gather from Mama. The guy—who, by the way was *not* a professional, he just knew somebody who knew somebody—reported something about an unpaid bill or some such, but I don't think it was a certainty...I don't know, it didn't seem terribly important."

Cindi gave me a quizzical look.

"I mean, I don't think this guy came up with anything that should raise eyebrows. What raises *my* eyebrows is that this Dick Tracy crap went on in the first place!"

"But wouldn't you want to know if there were something really bad going on?"

"Well, sure, but I kinda think I could figure that out myself." I straightened my back and placed both hands on the keyboard. "C'mon, let's give this a whirl."

Cindi folded her arms. Tall, blonde, gorgeous, hysterically funny, seemingly ditzy but far from it, Cindi had an uncanny ability to cut straight to the chase of any conundrum...especially when the subject was men. "So, did you figure out whether he's seeing anyone else? Lucy suspects so, doesn't she?"

Lucy had indeed voiced suspicions about Carl at work: unexplained disappearances or long phone conversations with some woman named Sherry from Huntsville. "Only sorta. Lucy conceded he could've been running errands or the call was business-related. Nothing she could put her finger on." With some defiance I added, "So, see? Just like with the *investigator:* No proof positive."

Cindi waited, sensing I had more to divulge.

"Um, about two weeks ago, I slept at his apartment—you know, the one he and Kevin, the manager, share; they don't both need to be at the hotel overnight." My fingers brushed back and forth over a few keys. "After lights-out lovemaking, Carl fell asleep and I got up to pee. There was a hot-roller pin on the bathroom sink counter and one long black hair in the bathtub." I looked down, knowing Cindi was looking at my streaked brown hair that hadn't seen hot rollers since college. "Of course, one of Kevin's dates could've used Carl's bathroom..."

"Hmm," was Cindi's only comment. She changed the subject. "So tell me about these dates you've had recently. I think it's great you're not sitting at home waiting on Carl."

"Yeah, I just wish these guys could excite me as much as Carl does," I said with a touch of dejection. "Take Robert, for instance: Fit. Well-mannered. Plays tennis. We have—well, had—plans for dinner and the symphony." I regarded Cindi's widening eyes. "But I'm not sure he even has a personality. And..." I repeated Beethoven's familiar four-note intro, "...he is undoubtedly the worst kisser in the world!"

Cindi's eyebrows scrunched downward in disgust. "Oh dear! And we know what they say about a guy who can't kiss..."

I nodded with a quick eye roll. "Well, Robert won't be confirming that one way or another because he called things off." Cindi blinked rapidly. "Yep, he asked if he should pursue me any further, meaning, was there anybody else. I told him there was, but only sorta, because things were very up and down. So he said—and jeez, Cindi, he was so forthright and reasonable—he said he really didn't want to play second fiddle to anyone, even though our relationship was in the very beginning stage. Of course I told him I understood."

"Wow," Cindi said, "a man who doesn't play games. How refreshing."

"Tell me about it. I really admire the heck out of him for doing that, and there's a part of me saying maybe I better not let such an admirable man get away. Only thing, I wasn't torn up at all about his putting a stop to us. The man simply does not turn me on in the least. And, like with Warner, that's not entirely because of Carl."

"Come on, now," Cindi chided.

"No, really. I've sorta liked going out with different guys. Shoot, I even think if somebody turned up who really, really got my attention, ol' Carleroonie would fade out of the picture."

"I find that a tad hard to believe, given all the emotional energy you've spent on him so far," Cindi countered.

"Right. Howevah..." I paused to add emphasis, "something's gotta give with Carl. That second-fiddle comment got me to thinking, what in the hell am I playing with Carl? Fifth fiddle?"

Cindi nodded in rueful agreement. "Oh yeah, it's time to put that journal down and quit analyzing."

I balked. "What? Are you saying six pages of bitching, moaning, longing, wondering, worrying is being over-analytical?"

"Ya think?" Cindi's expression rubberized into something worthy of the front cover of *Mad Magazine*. "Not to be blunt, Rosie, but it's time to shit or get off the pot!"

On the way home, I stopped by the drugstore to stock up on some household items and wandered into the greeting card aisle. Sending cards was one of my favorite things to do. I enjoying both the search for the perfectly toned message and the anticipation of the recipient's reaction. I skipped the cards under the Love category, finding them too presumptuous or way too gooey. Moving to the Just For Fun selection, I came upon a card showing a heavenly scene on the front with the message, "*I had a long talk with God today.*" Eschewing anything remotely religious, I almost replaced it but, slightly curious, looked inside: "*He says for you to either shape up or ship out.*"

Sure that others in the drugstore heard my abrupt snort, I put the card in my shopping basket, as though placing an arrow in my quiver of weapons. I could easily imagine Carl's gleeful giggle at the sarcastic message. I only wished the card wasn't quite so spot-on. At home, I signed it, "*Just kidding!? Your Hon...*" and placed it in my purse, supposing an opportune moment to give it would crop up soon.

CHAPTER 9

CARDS ON TABLE

The next day, goaded by Cindi's ultimatum, I strode through the hotel lobby, turned left, and entered the administrative offices. Before seeing Carl, I needed to check with Lucy about her mysterious message I'd received earlier at school. Lucy sat behind her desk; Carl, my lover-apparent-but-maybe-not-for-long, perched nonchalantly on its front edge. As I approached, I saw twin expressions of gleeful expectation.

I stopped dead in my tracks. Both gazes shifted to a small box on the desk.

"Happy Early Birthday to You, Happy Early Birthday..."

My birthday was in June, not January. I remained where I was, totally confused.

"What are you waiting on? Bus Number Seven?" Carl's laugh was full of mirth and kindness. "Get over here and open your damn birthday present!"

Lightly muttering, "OK, what the hell is going on?" I pulled the ribbon, lifted the box top, pulled back the tissue paper, and found a string of seven tickets, one for each day of the upcoming Birmingham International Invitational Tennis Tournament. I stared at the tickets, dumbfounded. I'd long known about the tournament and had figured my rigidly-allocated-teacher-salary budget might swing a ticket for one, maybe two days. I'd now be able to see the likes of Connors, Gerulaitis, even nasty ol' Nastase for an entire week. I'd never received a more perfect gift and I looked at Carl and Lucy with utter, tearful appreciation. "Holy yowza yowza! Talk about the best present ever! Whose idea was this?!"

Carl sheepishly tilted his head Lucy's way, but she quickly splayed her hands wide in innocence. "Nope," Lucy said, "I merely suggested to him if he was even remotely thinking of getting you a cool present, this was a ringer." Carl beamed. "And this bad boy," Lucy laughed, "jumped right on it!"

I spread my arms wide and brought my hands to rest on Carl's cheeks, pulling him forward to plant a loud smacking kiss on his puckered lips. Spreading my arms wide again, I airplaned around the desk and planted another smackeroo on Lucy's cheek. I was close to bursting with love and appreciation. "Omigod! Thank you, thank you, thank you!"

"You gals go ahead to the bar; I'll be there in a minute and we can all celebrate..." Carl cast a goofy look my way, "...your birthday."

"So, did he really 'jump' at this amazing gift opportunity?" My elated expression turned slightly quizzical as Lucy and I awaited Carl at the bar.

"Like, in a New York minute, was how fast he said 'OK!' Really, all I did was mention it in an off-handed way, after Carl had said he felt kinda bad about not having done more for you over the holidays."

"Omigod, really?" A thrill traveled down my spine, but at the same time I felt a tiny bit of deflation. "Hmm...this is going to make it harder for me to, you know, show my hand." I quickly summarized my talk with Cindi.

"Cindi's right, it's time to let Carl know you're, ah, less than enchanted. Who knows, maybe he's gotten an inkling of that and he's trying to cut you off at the pass with these tickets."

I considered this and then scoffed half-heartedly at Lucy's suggestion. "Maybe. But man, I don't want to appear unappreciative." Lucy looked at me. "Then again, tennis tournament tickets hardly qualify as bedrock foundation for a relationship, huh?"

We clinked glasses as Carl entered the bar. He'd barely reached us before Chip, with Pavlovian efficiency, slid a vodka tonic with a twist towards Carl.

Taking a deep swallow, Carl stood close to me and allowed his free hand to trace across my shoulders and rest lightly on the nape of my neck. I wondered if he had any idea how deeply his touch affected me. "So, what are you two talking about now?"

"What, do you think we're still on those tickets?" I sputtered. "I mean, big deal! Really, passé."

"Well, maybe you oughta give them back and I'll give them to someone else."

"The hell you say! Here, Lucy, put these someplace safe." I handed the tickets to Lucy who promptly thrust them into the lengthy cleavage of her sizable breasts. Carl made a lunge towards her.

"Don't even think about it, Buster!" Lucy crooned, eyebrows arching wickedly. I laughed at Carl's enjoyment of my good friend, who never missed a beat when it came to their dueling repartees, most times infused with off-color, lewd remarks. Carl finished off his drink and ordered another round.

"Not for me," said Lucy, "The office calls; gotta follow up on a couple things." She dug into her chest and retrieved the tickets.

"Here." She handed them to me. "Don't let that son-of-a-bitch get hold of these, or I may have to do something to him...something rough!" Like Tina Turner, Lucy growled the last word with a string of *r*'s.

Carl grabbed his chest as though in full cardiac arrest. "Lawzy, hep me, 'Lizbeth, it is the big one this time!"

"Yeah, don't you just wish," Lucy smirked, and waltzed out of the bar.

"So, is my lady happy?" Carl asked, his voice soft and content. We'd moved to a small table. Carl placed his ashtray on a neighboring table, making sure the cigarette smoke wasn't drifting my way.

"You did believe me when I said I've never received a better present, didn't you?" Carl puffed up with pride that he'd hit such a home run. "Plus, it was a total surprise, which makes presents even more perfect." His homer was out of the park.

Hating to spoil the moment, I lowered my head, trying to summon the resolve I'd been building en route to the hotel. "But.."

Carl's head jerked ever so slightly.

"...but my surprise wasn't just about the gift."

I had Carl's full attention now; he gazed at me with a mixture of curiosity and guardedness.

I summoned all my strength to keep my voice steady, telling myself to keep going. "I was surprised you even did that, based on how you've practically...ignored me recently." A flash of comprehension on Carl's face was replaced with utter astonishment. I faltered briefly, wondering if I was being melodramatic, making this up. "I mean, you know, not going out on New Year's Eve and then—"

Carl extinguished his cigarette and nudged his drink to the side of the table so he could lean in closer. "But, hon, surely you know I care for you! Surely you read that the last time we were together." I knew exactly what he was referring to: probably the best lovemaking we'd had to date.

"Yeah, but that was, what, ten days ago?" Carl met my questioning eyes but said nothing. "I mean, have you even missed me?"

Carl leaned further forward, his hand traveling up my arm to the back of my neck to cradle my head.

"Have I missed you? Well, hell yes, I've missed you! I really hate it there's always stuff here at the—"

"The hotel, I know. Maybe you should've looked more closely at that twenty-four-seven clause in the contract." I pictured Cindi in the wings, applauding.

Carl deflected this mini-zinger and regarded me as if I didn't quite understand the gravity of his responsibilities.

"Look," I continued, "I know this is a different sort of job, and because of that, I try not to ask too much of you, which I don't believe I do..." Carl smiled, appreciative. I felt more emboldened. "...and...and I think—well, I know—you see other women from time to time..." Slight surprise from Carl, as though he'd been caught at the cookie jar.

I exhaled evenly, "...as I see other men." I was careful to gauge Carl's reaction; he only looked slightly taken aback.

Having no interest in playing games, I wanted Carl to understand. "But these guys don't mean anything—*anything*—as much to me as you do." I looked straight at Carl, his face a mixture of pleasure and gravity. "Look, I know three months is sorta early on in our... whatever this is, so I don't want to pry, but I really need to ask if any of these other women you're seeing is especially...special..." Carl's head moved from side to side, his eyes adamantly signaling 'No.' I stopped, feeling it was time for him to say something.

"Look, if you're referring to Sherry in Washington—"

"You went to Washington for a conference." I hoped Carl couldn't hear the thumping in my chest after laying this thinly veiled accusation on him. I plunged ahead. "I thought Sherry was in Huntsville."

Though Carl's expression didn't change, I bet he must be wondering how much information I actually had.

"First," Carl's voice was firm while sounding ever-so-slightly insulted, "there *was* a conference in Washington. And, second..." now as if acquiescing to address something totally irrelevant, "...Sherry and I...we used to sorta have a thing but now we're just friends and—"

Noticing he'd ignored the Huntsville factor, I stayed on task.

"So, why did you go to Huntsville last weekend?" I pictured Lucy applauding next to Cindi.

"I told you," Carl said patiently, "sometimes it gets to be too much here and I have to get completely away. From everything." As though the thought just struck him, he continued, "And I knew you were busy with that Pointe Society thing—or I would've asked you— so I figured it'd be a good time to go somewhere and chill."

Sounding not at all convinced, I asked, "So...what did you do up there?"

As though trying to hold impatience at bay while keeping his voice level and kind, Carl said, "Like I said, nothing. I watched some TV, ate in a restaurant instead of a hotel for a change." (I refrained from saying, *Yeah, that'd be a nice thing for us to do.* If this discussion became an exchange of sarcastic remarks, I knew I'd lose. I was quick, but still no match for Carl's rapid-fire, sometimes cruel, comebacks.)

Carl continued, "I slept late, I—" At this point he stopped short. He sat back in his chair, his gaze of affection towards me taking on a tinge of condescension and defiance. But his voice remained kind and patient. "Actually, not only is all this totally unimportant, it's sorta like none of your business."

I jerked back in my chair, shocked. Carl continued, his tone becoming worldly and persuasive. "Look, we're not in high school; we've both got some living under our belts and we both have some experiences we'd just as soon not revisit." I considered the validity of this statement. I decided it was a wise remark, coming from Carl's thirty-five years as opposed to my mere twenty-eight. Carl took my hands and looked earnestly into my eyes.

"What I know is I would never, ever hurt you." His voice, swelling with sincerity, became a caress. "You've got to know you are my *very* special lady." I searched Carl's face for the slightest sign of deception and found absolutely none.

I drew a deep breath, drawing upon my dwindling supply of determination. "It's not that I'm so scared of getting hurt. I'm just scared of getting hurt when I know it could've been avoided."

Carl's look relayed this was an utter impossibility.

"Just be honest with me," I implored quietly, "and I'll be honest with you."

Leaning forward again, he laid his hands gently on my shoulders, brushed his lips against my cheek until they touched my ear. "Count on it," he whispered with absolute conviction.

Tension melted from my body, soothed as I was by Carl's protective hands and voice. I pictured Cindi and Lucy, no longer applauding, apparently underwhelmed with my decision to remain on the pot.

"What's this?" The bright pink corner of the envelope in my purse caught Carl's attention.

I smiled, realizing he'd spotted the '*shape-up-ship-out*' card. "Funny, when I bought this card for you last night, I didn't know

I could use it so soon." Handing it to Carl, I added, "What do you think? Is now a good time?"

I watched Carl as he read the card. Crinkled eyes, scrunched lips and nodding head conceded he'd been cleverly one-upped. "Pretty timely," he chuckled, standing behind me as he helped me on with my coat. He pulled me close and whispered playfully in my ear. "But, trust me, I have no plans to ship out."

I felt giddy. "Good thing, because I have no plans to give those tickets back."

CHAPTER 10

OF FITS, STARTS AND STOPS

Early in February, after several weeks of intense attention (possibly fueled by that silly greeting card), Carl surprised me with news that he was looking for another job in Baton Rouge because he 'couldn't work for that asshole of a new general manager' who'd replaced Kevin, Carl's fun sidekick. He surprised me further by adding that, should he be hired, there were 'plenty of teaching jobs there as well.' I took Carl's suggestion as a bold uptake in his professed desire to have me with him.

Lucy informed me the hotel employees were not nearly so desirous of keeping Carl with them. Tales of harassment of kitchen staff and a decidedly unfair incident involving Lucy herself made my heart sink. It was unsettling to learn others weren't as impressed with Carl as I was. Carl's interview came to nothing, as 'they hired some turkey from who knows where.'

A mere three days later, Carl was fired from the hotel.

Now, Carl's remaining in town was a crap shoot. I'd hardly had time to entertain Carl's 'plenty of teaching jobs' remark, now moot.

But the thought of my breaking bonds in Birmingham to follow him elsewhere, while romantic, was as alarming as it was unlikely. Recent euphoria notwithstanding, I couldn't deny a sense of relief that I may no longer have to deal with the angst of the past few months if Carl just got the hell out of town.

Of course I was sympathetic with him for having been dealt such a blow and hoped he would confide in me, his girlfriend-apparent, as he grappled with this unexpected life event. But Carl became uncommunicative to the point my nearly evaporated grievances voiced a few weeks earlier resurfaced with a vengeance. Scant, brusque phone calls and infrequent visits fueled my irritation to the breaking point.

Carl broke our Valentine's date for a supposed last-minute, strong job opportunity at a hotel in...Huntsville. When Carl begged my understanding, I chose to forgo lengthy reiterations of his mistreatment. Much to my amazement, I discovered a simple '*No*' did the trick for putting a stop to any and all of Carl's shenanigans.

It only took me a week to back down from my stance. To Carl's fevered apologies and groveling for one more chance, I finally conceded with a simple '*OK. One chance.*'

I had recently chanced upon new armor in the wealth of words found in a book: Ayn Rand's humongous *Atlas Shrugged*. As Carl and I tiptoed into the week following our make-up, I was agog with Rand's all-but-irrefutable philosophies which both reinvigorated and compelled me to take another strong look at our relationship.

Within a week, Carl used up his one chance. Discomfited that *No* had failed me so swiftly, I vented my frustration this time from a much stronger tack.

"Look, Carl, the reason we've even stayed together this long is because we...I've been operating under a breach of morality."

"A what?" asked Carl, nonplussed.

"A breach of morality. Ayn Rand says, and I quote, 'a breach of morality is when you make a conscious choice of an action you know to be evil, or when you willfully evade knowledge'..." Carl regarded me as if I were speaking Hebrew. "It's a suspension of sight and thought."

"What the ever-loving fuck are you talking about? What, are you saying what's been going on between us is *evil*?" The last word dripped with incredulity and derision.

"No, no, that's not it. I hardly think we're *evil*. But, like, for example, back when I told you I didn't mind if you saw other women...I actually did mind—"

"Who says I'm seeing other women?" Carl acted insulted. Then he added, "Now, I mean."

I halted, feeling as though the conversation was going adrift somehow. "Nobody says that!" Trying to explain my newfound philosophy I felt sure would ultimately benefit us both, I continued, "Listen, when I said I didn't mind, but I really did, well, that was a flaw, see? Because it was a lie. I was lying to myself and to you."

"So...we need to break up because *you* lied to *me*..."

"No! I mean, yes, but not on purpose. I had suspended sight and thought, which causes a breach in morality."

Carl snorted. "'Suspended'? What, like 'levitated'? Who the hell is this Rand woman, some kind of wacko voo-doo witch doctor?" He shook his head, his expression moving into unmasked ridicule.

"No! Damn it!" I was frustrated I couldn't make my point. "There's nothing voo-doo about her saying you can't fake reality."

Carl, beginning to get irritated, said, "Who's faking anything? Well, other than you, who just admitted to lying. What, are you saying what we have isn't real?"

"That's exactly what I'm saying! I'm—"

"You mean, when we make love, when we share our little private jokes, when we—"

"OK, yes, that's real, but—" My shoulders squared. "—it's not... it's not real *enough*. But here's something real: Ayn Rand says A is not non-A."

Carl wheezed with laughter as he would at a drunk whose words, instead of being intelligible and profound, were complete gibberish. "Lord, woman, what are you saying?"

I was exasperated now. "I'm saying," I said pointedly, "our relationship that we think is so wonderful, so *real*, is *not* so damn wonderful." I looked at Carl, his expression now one of surprise and hurt. "Look, you don't treat me the way I think I should be treated. Your bad treatment is *not* good treatment."

Finally, I had made a point. Carl simply looked at me and then started up again.

"Look, hon, I'm sorry I broke those plans last—"

"No, Carl. I gave you one more chance, and you blew it in less than a week. I really am so tired of all this." Carl made to speak, but I held up my hand. "I'm sorry, Carl. Let's just call it a pretty damn good ride and let it go at that."

"I can't let it go."

"I'm betting you can." I opened the door and Carl, disbelieving but resigned, made his exit.

"Can I just kiss you goodbye?"

I tilted my head and turned my cheek. Carl balked momentarily but then bent and gave me a tender kiss on my cheek. "Not exactly what I had in mind," he chided lightly.

With a small smile and gentle voice, I said, "No sense trying to make something what it isn't."

Carl rolled his eyes, turned, and, with hands slightly flicking at the wrist, he descended the steps into the dark.

"Wow!" said Vivien. "I mean, you're so energized, you seem so sure of yourself!" Still in her own on-again-off-again roller coaster ride with Frank, himself a charismatic and witty force, Vivien listened with something akin to envy as I recounted my *Atlas-Shrugged-*armatured split with Carl, some three weeks past.

"Yep, ol' Ayn, she tells it like it is." I was pumped by Vivien's enthusiasm. "Rand's book made me realize that, despite our great humor and sex—" I quickly glanced around, making sure the students entering the classroom hadn't overheard, "—our emotional bond was not nearly strong enough. Trying to convince myself Carl and I had enough for a strong relationship...*that* was the breach in morality...you know, telling myself I had A when I had non-A."

My smile at the simple explanation was slowly edged out by a puzzled look. "Actually, I do have a slight problem with the woman's insistence one stick to one's moral code in striving for perfection. This is all fine and good except for the troublesome shortcoming that, until I find the man who's perfect for me, I ain't gettin' laid!" I paused to give that statement the gravity it deserved. "And if that's the case," I flashed a wicked grin, "I might be having myself a few of them breaches every now and then..."

I exhaled in mock exasperation. "For sure, keeping in lockstep with my two new allies—'No' and Ayn Rand—ain't easy!"

"I hear ya, I hear ya," Vivien laughed. Then she looked at me with some seriousness. "But, it is over with Carl, isn't it? I mean, y'all are broken up for real, right?"

"Oh, yeah. Yes!" I nodded my head enthusiastically but checked it. "Well, pretty much." I smirked. "It's just that, over the last three weeks, he's called about every two or three days, merely saying he wants to check in. No heavy-duty conversations or anything; just funny stuff. One time he said he didn't need to speak with me, just Sinclair. God, the man is witty." I stifled my laugh when Vivien cast me a vaguely suspicious look. "Really, no big deal."

Later that evening, still flush with pride in having gotten—and stayed—on track, I spent a long time with my journal.

February 24, 1977 - I know that my hanging in there was partly due to my "hope," my "faith" that Carl would come around. Patience such as this is foolishness, I'm afraid, since everyday Carl didn't come around and I remained was another day that I sanctioned his flaws. And that was my own flaw, one I could wipe out simply by telling Carl no. Which I did...yeah! ... The next man...will have to be one with whom I believe our relationship could be—no, not could be—is real. Not perfect. But consciously working towards perfection. There! Yeah!

CHAPTER 11

BUT FOR THE CATS

After Carl kissed me and Ayn Rand good night and goodbye nearly a month earlier, he rarely allowed three days to pass without giving me one of his quick check-ins, most of which stayed light-hearted, waxing platonic. Faced with the seemingly interminable dearth of diversions of the male flavor, I became less and less inclined to brush off Carl's low-key attention. Along with lending a casual ear in Carl's direction came my vague distress that my recently embraced armor was already developing tiny cracks.

My flagging determination to turn away from Carl was waylaid further with the approach of spring holidays. An invitation from my sister Darrah to spend the break at her home in St. Simon's Island seemed the perfect opportunity to lengthen and strengthen the distance between Carl and me.

Of course, for me, taking a trip wasn't a matter of packing a few bags. There were the cats to deal with. I'd need two cat-sitters, since Mama and Daddy remained steadfastly disenchanted with Sinclair, who definitely had a High Maintenance gene. Enter Carl, whose phone call came a few days before my trip. I'd still found no solution for Sinclair's care and was beginning to feel desperate.

"Look, hon," he coaxed. His insistence to keep calling me 'hon' did not go unnoticed, but I chose to ignore it. "Rather than cart them off to different places, why don't I stay there with all three while you're gone?" Before I could accept or refuse, he hurried on, "Hey, they know me already, they can stay home, and it'll be one less thing you have to take care of before leaving...or worry about why you're gone."

I hesitated. Let Carl stay at my house for an entire week? Hell, the most he'd ever spent there was two nights. Plus, this would hardly stretch the distance between us. "Oh, I don't know if that's such a good idea—"

"Aw, c'mon hon, this is simply an easy solution to your problem. Nothing more." Carl, sensing I was weighing the issue, remained quiet a moment. Then he added, "Besides, you know Sinclair has a thing for me. Hell, maybe even more than for you." His laugh was as full of hopeful expectation as it was of glee.

It was true. Sinclair, by far and away the most idiosyncratic of the three cats, had inexplicably bonded with Carl.

"No way!" I shouted. "No way does that cat prefer you to me!" But then my laughter blended with Carl's. Whatever misgiving I had in letting him stay in my home for a week was trumped by relief my cats would be happy and well cared for. "Oh, OK, I guess."

Carl stopped by the evening before my early morning departure so I could give him explicit instructions and the key to my house. Much to my relief, all was businesslike except for Carl's occasional suggestion that he add a small glass of Kahlua to the cat's meals, perhaps some ice cream for dessert, or, should he take them for walks around the neighborhood? Key in hand, Carl made no suggestion of staying the night, simply promising he'd be there by noon the following day.

I thoroughly enjoyed my time with Darrah. Five years separating us, my older sister and I had operated in separate spheres during childhood. We weren't enemies, more like irritating intrusions into each other's universe. Occasional shared moments of mirth proved too infrequent to fortify a foundation of closeness such that I now shared with Vivien and Lucy. Adults now, Darrah and I seemed on the threshold of the slow discovery we quite enjoyed each other. During my visit, we shopped, ate out, went to the beach, and attended a tennis tournament featuring Chrissie Evert. I even had had a date, another nice-company-end-of-story type.

Throughout the entire visit, Carl kept popping into my mind, to the point I rather liked the idea of having him in the house while I was gone. The arrangement resembled something dependable, solid, permanent...the trappings of a bona fide couple.

Upon my return, I entered my house to find Carl asleep on the couch with Sinclair—The Slink, as he called him—stretched from Carl's chin to his kneecaps. I had to smile.

Carl woke as I approached the couch, stretching one hand toward me while he gently removed The Slink with the other. He sat up and patted the space next to him. "I'm glad to see you."

Such simple words, but so welcome. They elicited my only possible response: "I'm glad to see you, too."

My kind tone prompted Carl to ask with something approaching humility, "Hey, since it's kinda late, would you mind terribly if I stayed over tonight—" He acknowledged my frown. "And I mean stay in the guest room. Hey, I'll fix a really good breakfast in the morning."

Bleary-eyed and exhausted from my nine-hour drive, I didn't want to do anything but take a hot bath and go to bed. To wake up to a breakfast prepared by someone other than myself was tempting indeed. With a meaningful look of guarded assent, I said, "There are fresh linens and a blanket in the top drawer of the dresser." Fifteen minutes later, soothed by a hot bath, I collapsed into bed.

Had I remained awake to worry whether Carl would keep his word, I would have found he did indeed. When I walked into the kitchen the next morning, I was stupefied at the gorgeous breakfast Carl had prepared. Omelettes, hash browns, French toast, bacon... I was touched. And ravenous!

Settling back in our chairs after the feast, we sipped our coffee. Carl gazed at me as I watched his expression turn from sated pleasure to one more serious.

"What?" I asked, dead neutral.

"Can I please say something?"

I knew I should have bristled, but I was feeling so content and rested this morning; besides, I was curious as to what he could possibly have to say. I said nothing, shrugged to give him the go-ahead.

"Rosie," Carl's voice was low, steady, insistent, "that talk we had the other day—"

"When?" I tried to think of a recent phone conversation.

"—a few weeks back, I guess, when we...when you...when things between us were pretty much called off."

My lowered chin and raised eyebrows asked, *"pretty much?"*

Carl remained on task. "A lot of what you said really got me to thinking."

Remembering the valid arguments I'd presented to him, I was bound to not be swayed from them today. Also remembering how unimpressed with them Carl had been, I doubted there was anything he could say to sway me from my position, even if it did seem somewhat weakened of late. Still curious, I said, "Really? And what were you thinking?"

"It's beginning to get through this thick head of mine that if I don't make some changes, I'm going to lose you."

Bingo, I thought but said, "I'd have to say that's a bit more than a distinct possibility. I'd say it's pretty much the case as it stands now."

Undeterred, Carl continued. "And, you see, that doesn't set well with me at all, because, I've also figured out that..." a pause, with fingers of one hand tapping his forehead, those of the other, his heart, "I'm in love with you."

Dang. Those magical words. There they were, delivered to me for all the world in total sincerity. I couldn't ignore the melting sensation inside of me. My fledgling idealistic philosophy went up in smoke as soon as Carl imposed himself into my current state of mind. It wasn't that I'd *never* heard this catchy little phrase before, but never, never from anyone who had enthralled me as much as Carl had. He was simply so much more exciting than anyone—the few!—I'd ever been with, dang it! And, when Carl was good, oh, he was very, very good.

Was I really going to swat this away like some bothersome fly buzzing around my head? Would this not be something to fight for? And didn't people tell me all the time I was too picky? And, for all that great philosophy in *Atlas Shrugged*, wasn't it really a bit too idealistic?

Still, I had to ask Carl, "What makes you say that?"

Carl, encouraged I hadn't slapped him, spouted, "Because you're the best thing that's ever happened to me. Because you're kind, and good, smart and funny, and, well, I have a huge amount of respect for everything that you are and do."

I lowered my head, trying to hide my pleasure at hearing this affirmation. This sounded like *treasuring*. The warmth inside me was increasing and it could only be from finally hearing these words from someone whom I had actually sought out. This was a man who'd caught my attention at the very get-go, and now, apparently, he was appreciating me for who I was. Goodness, if the two of us could get on—and *stay* on—the same wave length, there was no telling how fantastic our relationship could be.

I cocked my head slightly, coquettishly, "What else?"

Carl exhaled in relief. "And...let's face it, you've got just about the cutest tush I've ever seen."

I certainly didn't mind hearing these words either, but it was those others that had me tossing away those simply impractical ones of Ayn Rand.

To add fuel to the fire, Carl pulled me to him and let his kiss speak volumes more than what he'd already said. Clasping my hand, he headed to the bedroom. Waxing delirious with newfound joy and hope, I followed, a willing participant.

It was a short walk from the kitchen to the bedroom, but it was a very, very long fall I was setting into motion. All the while Carl spoke his lovely words, I was deciding this was what I wanted and I would—and could, by God—do anything to make it work.

Without any real discussion of what was happening, the clothes and belongings Carl had brought for the week remained. As did Carl.

The glider's squeaks and creaks are drowned out by my sputterings, mutterings and moanings. Well, girl, what you *thought* you heard was a man treasuring you. What you *really* heard was a man without a job needing a place to stay!

Despite my disgust, I allow myself an iota of pride at my short-lived deliverance. I chuckle at one of my 'franglais' remarks that Carl and I had '*fini'd for sure.*' Ah yes, that was a good moment. While it lasted...

In the lengthy February entry, I notice several more Ayn-Rand-fueled comments relating to perfection. My head cocks slightly as though listening to a child's emphatic declaration that Santa Claus exists because she *saw* him. Ah, Rosie-Rose, being a tad idealistic there, weren't you? Hey, telling Carl it was over? Excellent move! Reverting to striving for perfection? You were setting yourself up for a fall...

A wistful smile tugs at my lips as I reread the ultimately powerless proclamation of fervent naïveté. Less than a month later, I had allowed myself to be pulled back into the muck. Looking back now, Carl's move-in appears to be The Single Incident, The Aha! Moment that so changed my life's trajectory. I flip the journal's page in search of my thoughts during this period.

The next entry eradicates my smile:

September 18, 1977 - Well, the last time I wrote was Feb. 24. To say that things are back on with Carl and me is to make the big understatement since Carl and I are getting married. Oh yes, I am dealing with those points of philosophy above and I really question what I'm doing

*and yet I can't convince myself that Carl and I can't work.
I'm too tired to write now but intend to before Nov. 19.*

The glider jerks to a halt. *Whoa!* I check the dates of the two entries; nearly seven months separating them. One, an exultant recount of a grand exit à là *Atlas Shrugged*; the other, an irresolute, infelicitous, inexplicable announcement of impending marriage.

My journal temporarily useless, I turn to one of several small pocket calendars by Hallmark, once a handy method of tracking my day-to-day doings. I scour it for any notation that Carl had moved in. Nothing. Failure to mention such a momentous event is jarring indication I had begun my slow-motion hurtle towards disaster.

"What we've got here," I take on the nasalized sneer of the captain in *Cool Hand Luke,* "is a failure to communicate."

Sollie, disturbed by the unfamiliar voice, communicates her irritation with a single tail twitch.

"What we've *really* got here," my voice softens with pity, "is undeniable proof I had left a smooth, solid track and taken a rough and treacherous escape route. An escape not from Carl, but from myself."

It is difficult now to imagine how I became so lost. But noting the numerous *fini*'s and *commencé*'s, denoting our breakups and makeups, I realize that each time I'd capitulated to Carl's persuasions and pleas, I'd lost another degree of self-respect and confidence. No wonder I hadn't turned to my journal. It had become far too humiliating, far too difficult.

Laying the calendar to the side, I decide I've had enough for the moment. How draining to elicit and struggle through these memories! I bend over to whisper in Sollie's ear: "Food! Want food?" Sollie perks up straight away, recognizing the words that are somehow magically followed by good eats. I definitely am going to need some fuel to get through the rest of this. Cat and cat owner (or is it human and human owner...?) head inside for some lunch.

Forty-five minutes later, I return to my seat outside, refueled from a light lunch of a shrimp-stuffed avocado. Sollie, full of Fancy Feast, curls into an O snugly encircled by her tail.

My eyes squint to decipher my scribbles on the tiny calendar squares encompassing the mysteriously unjournaled period. Between the brief, inconsistent notations and random memories, a foggy account of that unfathomable interim emerges...

CHAPTER 12

BACK IN THE FOLD

Spring of 1977 began with its magical transformation of Birmingham into a panoply of color and ended with Carl's landing a promising managerial position at a nightclub called "The Caboose." One glitch: The Caboose was in Orlando, Florida. Whatever unhappiness or skepticism I felt was assuaged by Carl's infectious enthusiasm. Such drive could only lead to success; I wanted to be a part of Carl's forward motion. I abandoned Birmingham several times over the summer to help out however I could.

Cocktail waitressing would be my contribution. Initially gung-ho for a job totally unrelated to teaching, I soon realized that rushing around in high heels, balancing heavy drink-laden trays, and maintaining a smile while actually wanting to spit on the occasional obnoxious customer, was basically grunt work in a scanty costume. But if it meant I could be with Carl, I felt little need to complain.

Even though I was with Carl, it was rarely without the presence of someone else associated with work. So when Carl suggested in mid-June we take a three-night break to the Bahamas, I jumped on it. Just think, *the Bahamas*! Merely saying it forced one to pronounce a breathy, smooth 'aaahhh!'

The first twenty-four hours of our exotic getaway were *aahh*-worthy indeed. The jaw-dropping beauty of aquamarine waters, luxurious hotel, and fascinating casinos were all trumped by Carl's obvious delight in having me all to himself. Lusty afternoon sex ended with spooning and drifting off to sleep. Sometime later Carl woke me, gripping me tightly, licking my ear, and making all sorts of lascivious noises. Gasping and grunting, he assumed a Jack Nicholson 'Heeere's Johnny!' voice and leered, "I want youuuuuu! I neeeeed you!" I acted like this drove me up a wall, but we both loved it. Silly mutterings continued poolside while we baked to healthy tones of toffee and cinnamon, providing the finishing touch to our evening attire. I practically felt the admiring glances as we strode through the lobby into the casino.

Whatever romance, exoticism, and beauty that had already occurred was to be the sum total for our entire stay. Carl was either in a stupor by the pool or planted at the poker table. Dinner was room service. I got in bed alone the next two nights, Carl stumbling in a few hours later. Except for the occasional pat on the ass or kiss on the neck, Carl appeared to have gone into a completely different world, one which commanded his full attention.

Only because I had witnessed firsthand the multitude of responsibilities Carl juggled at the Caboose, I decided this was his way of blowing off steam. Besides, it wasn't like I had had a terrible time. I gave him a free pass.

Carl and I had been invited to a July Fourth celebration at the home of my college friend, Glenise. She and her husband Bob lived in a high-end community of Orlando. Unbelievably, this would be the first time Carl and I had actually socialized with several other couples. I felt pleasure and pride watching everyone latch onto Carl's humor and strong presence. Sitting on the terrace with Glenise, I gave a condensed version of the past several months.

"And so, after all that crap—I mean, back in February I was all but outta there—heeere we are," I said. "Pretty solid for four months."

"Well then, the two of you must really love each other. Take Bob and me: we had some really trying times—alcohol being a biggie, money-handling another—but we got past all that and, to use your phrase, heeere we are!" We laughed at the men in the pool playing a ridiculously rough game of volleyball. "One thing for sure," Glenise continued, "Carl is gaga for you. I don't know if you notice his expression but it's saying he wants to be all over you!"

I tittered with delight. "Really?" I gushed. "Well, and me him, that's for sure!"

Back at the apartment, I lay in bed filled with sweet anticipation of accumulating memories similar to this evening's fare. Tonight had a richer, more robust flavor to it, and I not only hungered for more like it, I was certain they were within my grasp.

I felt Carl slide into bed. He drew me close. We both had showered and our naked bodies produced a sweet, enticing scent.

"Know what I want?" Carl whispered into my damp hair.

I felt Carl's heart rate take a decided uptick. My own pulse quickened in response. I whispered back, "Uh-uh. What?"

Several short breaths passed through Carl's lips after which I heard nothing at all for thirty seconds. Then, very quietly, Carl said, "I want to marry you."

Now it was my breath that stopped. Every moment—the good and the bad—of our relationship completely disappeared from my mind. All I was aware of was this beautiful, naked, and increasingly aroused man next to me. My head was a riot of sounds: water whooshing, bells ringing, choirs singing, beasts bellowing. But above it all I heard Carl's racing heart, saw his adoring, imploring eyes, and felt his love—yes! Love!—completely enveloping me.

"OK," I said.

We lay in bed the next morning, silently contemplating the momentous step we'd taken. Sighs of satisfaction indicated our rec-ollections weren't just of conversation. Finally, Carl broke the silence.

"Know what I want?" He sounded almost confessional. I turned on my pillow to see him staring at the ceiling, almost in a trance. I hoped to hell he hadn't forgotten what he'd asked me a few hours earlier.

"What now?" I murmured sleepily, adding a touch of feigned irritation.

"I want to get you a house at least as nice as Glenise and Bob's, a car, clothes...just anything you could possibly want. And I'm telling you that I've never wanted that for any woman I've ever been with. I am so in love with you, Rosie. It just makes me want to do whatever is in my power to make you happy."

"I must be lying next to a blind man, then, or else he'd see my happy-quotient is off the charts." Carl smiled and drew me close as I added, "I'm especially happy you didn't say 'what you wanted' was kids."

On one of my back-home stints, with cats close by and Joni's "Fire and Ice" on the stereo, I was happily occupied at the sewing machine creating a bathrobe. Knowing that Carl—my fiancé!—would soon call, I was feeling pretty good in my skin. Soon enough, the phone's ring was followed by Carl's still completely endearing

"Hey, hon." I listened attentively as he related the happenings of the last week.

"...so those damned owner-investors are saying they're not seeing the profit they should be seeing, given that the place is full every night. But, they're idiots and just don't understand how expensive it is to keep this gig going."

I recalled a scene from the wee-hours one morning at the Orlando apartment, when I'd woken and gone to the kitchen for a glass of water. I had surprised Carl and Kevin (who'd hooked up with Carl as co-manager), seated on the couch in front of the huge coffee table, the glass top of which was smothered in bills—singles, fives, twenties.

"Cover charge take," Carl had mumbled. This recollection flashed through my head and quickly receded as Carl's diatribe of the owners' stupidity continued.

Eventually, he turned the conversation to me to ask how I was doing. I rattled on about my day of invigorating tennis, a funny cat story, and now my determination to finish this sewing project.

Carl was silent a moment. "Gosh, you didn't say anything about missing me."

I was taken aback. "Well, of course I miss you. That kinda goes without saying. What, did you think I was going to go fetal when you're not up here or I'm not down there?"

"Well, you don't have to get bitchy about it." Carl managed to sound defensive and offensive at the same time.

"I'm not being bitchy. I'm just...I'm just content knowing, I guess, that we're both doing our part, even though we're not always together, working towards *eventually* making it that way. You know, together."

Somewhat abashed, Carl harrumphed. "Well, yeah, when you put it that way. You're just so smaaarrt, hon, one of the things I love about you."

I took his sarcasm as all in fun. "Well, it shows how smaarrrt you are to have the good sense to luuvvv me."

"Yep, you got me there. G'nite hon, we got a busy night ahead of us, expecting a busload of folks from Kissimmee. I love you and I miss you."

"Me too, you," I hung up and, with a smile on my face, returned to my work.

On my next and final visit for the summer, I noticed that Carl didn't seem as enthralled—'gaga' as Glenise had put it—with my presence. This I attributed to his heightened attempts to appease the owners and assure them they had no reason to worry. His total immersion in his work reminded me of myself at the beginning of the school year; it was imperative that I set a firm foundation early on for smooth sailing later.

I'd treated my role as cocktail waitress with similar earnestness, seeking help and advice from Sharon the bartender. While some waitresses regarded her as a domineering bitch, she became my favorite. Not only was she kind to me, I considered Sharon the most accomplished, level-headed, and trustworthy employee.

One afternoon, I arrived at the Caboose to see if I could help Carl with anything so we could take off for a quick dinner before returning to work. As I entered the bar, I heard a terrible tirade of curse-laden shouts which, I realized after a moment, were directed at Sharon and coming from Carl. I was shocked by his snide, belittling, unfair remarks. He finished his harangue with a pounding of his fist on the bar and a huff and puff off to his office in back, never noticing me. I carefully approached a bar stool and sat quietly while Sharon gathered herself.

After a while, I whispered, "So what the hell was that all about?"

Sharon just looked at me, her expression a mixture of hurt, indignation, and wonder. She seemed to grapple with what she was about to say. "I don't know why in the hell someone as nice as you would stay with—much less marry-someone as...as horrible as him. That guy's a fucking monster."

I hung my head, disappointed that someone I liked so much disliked so much the person I liked so much. Was I totally in the dark about Sharon? What could she have said or done to elicit such harshness, the likes of which Carl had never displayed with me, not even during his stressful search for employment back in the spring. He must have had good reason to explode like he did and I wanted to hear his side. Just not right now; I'd let him calm down.

In the meantime, I would prove myself worthy of being, as Carl had told me ad infinitum, 'the best thing in his life.' I was engaged to a man I really wanted to marry and with whom I wanted to build a life together. I would love him, understand him, be his safe harbor. I could make this man happy.

Ah! To be back home! Summer came to a close, and with it, the few instances of disappointment or ill-omen. These were far out-numbered by the positive aspects of our relationship, the most nota-ble being that we had not had a breakup or even a huge argument since Carl had moved in over five months earlier.

My last waitressing stint done, I was all the more excited about the upcoming school year. Standing before a bright, full-windowed roomful of mostly attentive students was much more appealing than doling out drinks to sometimes-unsavory customers in a dark, loud, dank cave. I didn't know exactly how Carl and I would manage so far apart, but I acknowledged a strong unwillingness to leave my very solid, enjoyable position.

One evening early on in the school year, I sat at the desk tweaking lesson plans when Carl arrived, unannounced. I rushed to meet him, at once thrilled to see him but also confused why he was taking a break just now, especially when I'd emphasized how crucial the first few weeks of school were. "You'll be better off missing me from afar," I'd told him. "I won't be the best of company."

One look at Carl's dark and troubled face, however, told me he hadn't endured the nine-hour drive just because he missed me. My heart sank as Carl relayed the news of his firing, attributing it all to the short-sightedness of those 'idiot investors.'

"Those guys don't know the first thing about the food-and-beverage scene. It's one of the most difficult enterprises to pull off. Operating costs, staff turnover, and on and on. That place was on the brink of tanking when Kevin and I took over. But did they give us a real chance to turn it around? Hell no! Fools!"

Troubled as I was by this bombshell, my heart went out to Carl. In Orlando, I'd watched him head over to the club around noon and rarely leave until closing in the wee hours. When I'd arrive at the club later, I'd see him heading back into his office, where I'd then find him busily going over papers. It surely *looked* like he was packing in twelve-hour days. As for the capriciousness of the whole restaurant/bar scene, I had only to consider the many such businesses in Birmingham that went belly-up after mere months.

"Maybe you might want to consider another line of work?" I said gently. I anticipated a look of incredulity, but instead heard Carl agree with me.

"As a matter of fact, I've interviewed with a guy from La Cuisine. Looks like I'm going to be selling cookware."

"Pots and pans!" I couldn't believe it. I pictured him going door to door like the Fuller Brush Man. "That sounds *awful*!"

Carl looked slightly hurt and immediately became defensive. "This is *high-end cookware*, the commission's great, hours are flexible..." Seeing that I looked less repulsed, Carl continued with mounting enthusiasm, "...and hon, it's temporary, you know, until a decent food and beverage position comes up."

With this, his hands held my head in a gentle but firm grasp, so that my face was inches from his. I recognized that all-encompassing, singularly focused gaze, which meant whatever Carl was about to say was coming from his heart. "Hon, I *know* I can make this work, because I *know* I love you and I want more than anything in the world to make our life together the very best life ever."

Well, OK, that's good enough for me. I could practically feel Carl's words caress me. I absolutely craved the sensation.

CHAPTER 13

INNER CIRCLE'S LAST STAND

"Again?" A unified groan reverberated from the entire Inner Circle. We'd gathered to celebrate my engagement. "You're telling us Carl got fired *again*?"

Looking at the deeply concerned faces of Vivien, Lucy and Louise, I feared this might not be the cheeriest of celebrations. I had summarized Carl's complaints about the investors' cluelessness regarding the many facets of bar/restaurant business. Upon listing troubles with staff turnover, I divulged the yelling incident with Sharon.

"So did you find out what that was all about?" Lucy asked.

"No, I left for Birmingham early the next morning. I was going to let the touchy subject rest a few days. But then he got fired, so I figured discussing it would be like sour grapes."

No one said anything.

I scooted back in my chair and leveled my lowered chin. "Wouldn't it be nice if the hotel/restaurant/bar industry had tenure like education does."

In not unkindly fashion, Louise said, "You gotta teach three *years—not three months—*to get tenure."

Vivien asked, "Aren't you a little worried to marry someone who doesn't have a job?"

"But he does have a job! Well, sorta. It's commission-only the first three months, but he'll probably land another job before that occurs. Carl's very impressed with the quality of the cookware."

Now all eyes looked dubious.

I placed my hands on the table. "Look y'all, you haven't been around him enough to see how *effective* he can be. He's really a hard worker." Louise and Vivien looked slightly encouraged; Lucy not so much. "I know he can have great success once he finds the right position. The Caboose was not rock-solid."

As though unable to remain quiet any longer, Lucy spoke up. "Well, when he was at the hotel, his blowups *effectively* turned off nearly the entire staff..." she paused, then added, "...even me."

Lucy was referring to the time Carl had threatened to fire her if she didn't brave snow and ice to get to work. I was embarrassed I'd not stood up for my friend at the time. I lowered my head, still embarrassed. "I know, that was a major faux pas. But our principal..." I sought confirmation from Louise and Vivien, "...gives us the riot act from time to time. Guess it comes with the territory." Before anyone could rebut, I added what I hoped would be a strong argument. "But I'm telling y'all...Carl *treasures me.*"

Vivien chided gently, "Like he treasured you when he broke dates, what, half a dozen times?"

"Like he treasured you when he'd make it to your place once for every five times you trucked to the hotel?" Now Louise's tone had a slight edge to it.

"Those would be really good points, except that it's old news. Carl wasn't in love with me then. He is now." I smiled broadly. "As I am with him."

My closing remark wasn't nearly as persuasive as I'd hoped. Vivien, Louise and Lucy spoke one after the other: "Rosie, we love you and want you to be happy. But we think you're making a big, bad mistake. What you've told us doesn't look like a few flags...it looks like freaking Arlington Cemetery on Memorial Day."

My smile remained broad. "I love y'all, too, and I appreciate you're looking out for me. But I truly don't think you have anything to worry about. I'm going to be fine—great!—with Carl."

On the way home, I prided myself in having stood my ground against the well-meaning confrontation. I wasn't aware of it, but the Inner Circle clearly saw that the ground I was standing on was above a yawning sink hole.

CHAPTER 14

DAMN THE TORPEDOES, FULL SPEED AHEAD!

A bridesmaid more times than I could count, I—*now the bride!*—had learned a few things, the number one lesson being that weddings were damned expensive. Determined not to incur any unnecessary or ludicrous expense, I snubbed the common practice of hiring a wedding planner. (What? Please.) I set to work on every aspect of my special day: the venue (where else but my parents' home, with its gorgeous view?); bridesmaids (none; the *marriage* was between Carl and me; my closest friends would be in attendance without any bridesmaid hassle or expense); invitations (hand-written, in calligraphy); flowers (hand-picked, a bounty of fall color); music (the adagio movement from Rachmaninoff's second symphony for the ceremony, and anything from Motown to the Allman Brothers for the reception); and my wedding dress (well, of course, I would make it myself). All these preparations I did while continuing to work through the Friday before the Saturday ceremony.

I wanted tons of people to join in the *celebration* of my marriage, but I decided the ceremony itself would be much more meaningful, more intimate, if only family members and the bestest of best friends attended. I assumed the brevity of Carl's guest list was to honor this preference.

"So, just your parents, your bro and his wife, the preacher and... what's this...the Chief of Police?"

Carl chuckled as if he'd heard an inside joke. "Yeah, he's been a friend of the family for years. I don't know if he'll be able to come, but I know he'll be interested to hear I'm finally tying the knot." I shrugged, smiled, and resumed multi-tasking.

One evening in my sewing room, I was admiring my handi-work on my nearly finished, luminous wedding gown (so unlike the puff-sleeved, crinolined, cotton-candied atrocities I'd had to wear as a bridesmaid). As I made a slow twirl to observe the changing tones of the fabric in the light, the phone rang. I smiled, figuring it was Carl, who'd had a late afternoon appointment, to tell me he'd be home soon for supper.

I answered with a honeyed "Hello?" after which I heard nothing. I waited for one of Carl's ridiculously funny lines, but then heard an entirely different male voice.

"Is this Rosie?"

For some reason, a cold chill traveled down my spine. "Who's this?" I demanded.

Another pause, and I was about to hang up, when the caller said, "Is this the Rosie who's engaged to Carl Ballini?" The chill made a second run.

"Who is this?" I tried to keep my voice imperious, allowing no fear to weaken it.

A deep, nervous breath, and then, "I'm sorry I can't tell you. But I must...I feel compelled to tell you that you are making a huge mistake if you marry this man."

Fear was trumped by rage and indignation. "Who in the hell do you think you are? For one thing you're a coward for not identifying yourself. For another you're going to have to explain why you made such an insanely false statement!"

More nervous breathing. "Can't. Can't tell you. But you should take my word for it. You need to get away from this guy."

The next thing I heard was a click and a dial tone.

I shuddered and bristled at the same time. Who *was* that? Some sicko who's pissed at or maybe jealous of Carl for some reason? Has some ex-lover of Carl gotten somebody else to make this call? Is it one of my yukkier students playing a trick on me? I racked my brain for other possibilities. One of my ex-lovers—OK, it's a short list— who doesn't want me to be happily married? The more I thought about it, the more weird the phone call became. What a crazy fluke!

Aggravated I'd been so rudely interrupted, I turned back to the mirror. The dress was absolutely lovely, but my expression, so pleased a few moments earlier, now held a slight frown. Irritated, I forced a wide smile, expecting it to readmit my earlier sense of contentment. When it didn't, I sputtered in exasperation. I refused to be bothered with such nonsense.

"Total nonsense!" Carl had confirmed later when I related the strange incident.

Much to my relief and delight, all my planning and preparations came to polished fruition on what should be the most symbolic day of my life: a celebration of my future with the man I loved. Everything was indeed beautiful. Light from the brilliant autumn afternoon diffused the wide open living-dining-den area with soft colors, playing over the flower arrangements, beautiful clothes, smiling faces, and the simple ceremony. In my mind, there was the perfect mixture of gravity and levity.

Moments prior to the ceremony, Carl and I had jostled for position as we were about to march down the hallway leading to the great room:

"Now, hon, it's only fitting *the man* be first in this marriage," Carl's face, full of mock seriousness, sent me into my usual giggle fits.

"The hell you say! Surely you know by now that behind every successful man there's a woman."

"Make that underneath, which is where you're going to be in a few hours." Carl's eyebrows crunched into a devilish *V* while he thrust his leg in front of mine.

"Remember, I'm a dancer and an athlete and a thousand times more graceful than you'll ever be," I chimed as I nimbly stepped around him yet again.

We burst through the hallway door, like Archie and Meat Head, holding hands and laughing. Could there have been a more perfect picture presented to the guests? We moved to the huge sliding glass doors which framed the glorious expanse of fall color. We positioned ourselves on either side of the preacher, Jack Goodman.

Having long drifted from the church, I had had no qualms with Carl's proposing we use an old friend of his family to conduct the service. Father Jack—in his three-piece suit, topped with a bow tie, a full head of silky white hair, a twinkle in his eyes, a smooth voice full of mirth, wisdom and kindness—immediately endeared himself to me. He was the ideal choice to consecrate our union.

Once I had slipped the ring onto Carl's finger, I completed the ritual with a quiet but decisive pat of my hand on top of his, drawing soft chuckles and murmurs of approval from everyone. According to plan, the last lines of the ceremony coincided with the final exultant chords of Rachmaninoff. *Perfect!*

After a sweet, brief kiss, Carl and I turned beaming faces towards the happy gathering. For the next four hours, everyone enjoyed the whirlwind of guests coming and going, a full-fledged bar, delicious hors d'oeuvres, and cake. (I smiled that my odd choice of carrot wedding cake was nonetheless consumed to the last crumb.) When I found brief occasions to observe the lively scene around me, I delighted in watching Carl move with ease among my friends and those of my parents, all of whom regarded him with enjoyment and admiration. Carl and Lucy drew amused attention as they faked a battle of smushing cake in the other's face.

Any reservations held by Lucy, the rest of the Inner Circle, or my parents were held firmly at bay. After all, this occasion demanded it was time to put one's best face forward.

I was especially pleased to see that the small number of Carl's side of the family was mingling as well with members of mine. There was Carl's brother, Donnie, with his new bride, in lively conversation with my aunt and uncle from New Orleans. And over there on the love seat sat my grandmother with Carl's mom, Penny, whose red hair was piled to an impressive summit.

Taking in the whole scene, I decided the inscription on the wedding cake, 'Toujours Comme Maintenant,' was joyfully apropos: with all the goodwill enveloping Carl and me, how could we *not be* 'always as now'?

When the last of the guests left, Carl and I began opening the pile of presents, but quickly decided we were too tired to do one more thing other than go home and *sleep*. The next morning we'd commence our short honeymoon to a rustic cottage in the forests of Cheaha Mountain. This, of course, was my idea as well, partly remembering Carl's long-ago, never-realized suggestion for a get-away. Mainly, though, I didn't want to spend huge amounts of money—*which wasn't exactly rolling in, given Carl's job situation*—on some exotic vacation. To spend a couple days and nights curled up in front of a fire, barely coming up for air from one passionate love-making session to another, appealed to my sense of practical simplicity. And romance.

Riding from my parents' home to—now—*our* home, I was amazed to hear Carl say he was hungry. Hardly believing we were stopping at the window of a Kentucky Fried Chicken on our wedding night, I giggled upon hearing Carl's order for two of the biggest breasts they had, so he could remember what they were like. Nearing the house, we joined in with Rita Coolidge on the radio as she sang "Your love is lifting me higher..." Carl opened the moon roof of the car, straining to lift his head through and howl like a wolf, causing me to fall back in the seat with laughter, completely exhausted but completely happy. To have this much silly love, this much *fun* in a marriage...this was going to be *good*.

As planned, the next day, another beautiful one, we headed twenty miles up the interstate to our little rental cabin in the woods. Unfortunately, the cabin wasn't nearly as ready for us as we were for it. A dank smell greeted us as we surveyed the sloppily made bed, the fireplace full of leftover ashes with no logs in sight, and a naked light-bulb hanging from the ceiling.

"Oh my," I looked around in wonder and disgust, "this is not what it looked like in the brochure."

Carl walked into the bathroom and immediately came back to stand in front of me. "Well, hon, you gotta admit this place has all the creature comforts..." I tried to assume my good-attitude face. "...and the creatures are in the bathroom!" He grabbed a suitcase. "C'mon, we're outta here." The honeymoon was over.

There was a pleasant post-script, though, as we pulled back to the house. We were surprised to see Cindi—who had a key for cat-care—running down the front steps.

"Jeez! Y'all aren't supposed to be back for two days!" came her distressed cry. "I left a surprise for y'all. Check the fireplace and the fridge!" And she was gone.

Curious, we went inside to see what Cindi was talking about. Stacked neatly on the grate and on the hearth was a large supply of firewood. In the fridge, two steaks, two potatoes, and salad fixings. On the table, wine and flowers.

"Perfect," we said in unison. Then, again in unison, *"but not right now."*

And husband and wife made their way to the bedroom.

My drawn-out, startling raspberry destroys the afternoon stillness. I eject from my seat, the glider sashaying wildly. Sollie bolts towards the woods.

"How?" I'm obliged to produce a few more rude outbursts. "How could we not be 'always as now'?" I'm referring to my syrupy wedding-day prediction. "Omigod, let me count the ways..." I begin pacing.

For starters, that kindly preacher-man of God, Father Jack? Hey, that man, while bestowing his blessing that day, did so with guarded hope at best. A few years down the road, I would be dumbfounded to realize he'd known from the get-go that I was most likely stepping into the depths of hell.

And Carl's brother, Donnie? I search my memory for the exact point in time when I'd learned that Donnie had recently been released from a fifteen-year incarceration. For exactly what charge—involuntary manslaughter resulting from a barroom brawl, maybe?—I never could say. My memory of when and how Carl had divulged this little tidbit is ever so faint; I guess I'd simply clung to Carl's insistence that he and his brother were nothing alike. That was all that mattered.

And just what was that conversation going on between my grandmother and Carl's mother, Penny? It wouldn't be until years later, while visiting my grandmother in Meridian, that this scene would be recalled by both of us.

"Oh, yes," Granny Browning had said, "I remember that quite well, mainly because it was so odd."

"Odd?" I had looked confused by such an unexpected description.

"Yes. I remember Penny and I sat there, watching Carl talk to a group of people who seemed completely enthralled. So I said to his mom, 'You must be very proud of your son.' And what she said was, I thought, very odd."

"Which was...?"

"'No, I'm not at all proud of my son.'"

I had been dumbfounded by this piece of information, so long past its usefulness, but still unnerving. "Holy cow, Grandma, why didn't you tell me?"

"Well, I didn't figure it'd do any good. I mean, you'd already married him."

CHAPTER 15

SO THIS IS THE FAIRYTALE?

Since Carl and I had been cohabiting for nearly seven months, our first week of living as husband and wife, while not exactly ho-hum, was nothing new. There would be no setting up of household, seeing as the household was basically mine and had already been set up. This didn't strike me as anticlimactic, however; I preferred to look upon the somewhat vanilla beginnings as a more realistic, practical step towards building a life together.

I had been nothing short of ecstatic to turn over most cooking duties to Carl, who had a flair for preparing simple but tasty meals. Most evenings, Carl was content to watch TV and I joined him as much as I could, once schoolwork was caught up, or I reached a good stopping point in whatever project was in the works.

My latest, a massive macrame project, hung over one of the front French doors. Carl stared in wonder at the hundred or so bobbins that hung below the finished portion, wondering why anyone would undertake anything so complicated. Sometimes I would walk in the room to find him huddled underneath the threads and bobbins which draped over his head and shoulders, making him look like some weird Medusa. I enjoyed his good-natured ribbing, even when he'd casually walk by with scissors and pretend to stumble, scissors snapping wickedly.

Cuddled up on the couch in front of the fireplace, exchanging silly stories of the day's happenings, appreciative of each other's humor, even more appreciative of each other's sensuality...all these little things, in my mind, were conducive to and important in the making of a wonderful marriage. As the first couple months came to a close, I found myself constantly reliving these many special moments not only as a source of joy but as sustenance for fighting off anything that might threaten such contentment.

One such threat was Carl's continued unemployment, growing more oppressive by the day. Each morning I left for work saying a silent prayer that I'd return to find Carl with some very good news indeed. Our wedding gifts included a nice sum of money—nearly two thousand dollars—so there was no hint of desperation in the air, but I had to control myself to keep my worry hidden from Carl.

"So here I am," I told Vivien, upon returning to work after the Thanksgiving holiday, "a brand new bride and principal—oh, 'scuse me, make that *only*—breadwinner of the household. On a teacher salary, mind you..."

"What happened to the pots and pans?" Vivien asked. We both realized how ridiculous the question sounded and laughed, albeit ruefully.

"The pots and pans ain't happening, best I can tell." I grabbed a pile of freshly run-off papers, arranging them into four smaller stacks. "I can't help but feel sorry for Carl because I know that is *not* what he wants to be doing..." my fingers whisked over the piles, grabbing a sheet from each. "...but still..." I glanced at Vivien's mildly worried expression which matched my own. "I mean, it's not like we're starving or anything, but I *hate* to use that wedding money for the damned power bill, know what I mean? And, more importantly, I sure as hell don't want to start out this marriage by nagging about money. Or nagging about anything, for that matter."

"So, are there any job possibilities for him?"

"For sure, he's got lots of irons in the fire, seems like to me. He's always checking the classifieds, I hear him talking on the phone setting up interviews...I mean, it's not like the man isn't trying." Vivien's face relaxed. "Really, the worst thing right now is my parents. They've not said anything but their silence speaks volumes. I'm sure Carl feels the pressure of convincing them their daughter hasn't married an unemployed no-count." I shrugged lightly while stacking the stapled tests together. "I'm not all that worried, though; this is more like an aggravation. Just one of those little bumps in the road during the first year of marriage."

"Yeah, back in my first marriage, I remember that first year was really hard," Vivien offered.

My shoulders squared. "So, until a good job offer comes along, looks like I'm married to Pots 'n Pans Man." More laughter, and then I added, "And don't you *ever* call him that!"

"Got it!" Vivien saluted. The bell rang and we returned to our classes.

A little less than two months into our one-income marriage, a solid job offer did indeed come along as if to reward Carl's and my efforts at keeping our spirits high. Carl would be general manager of a well-established restaurant-bar. Only thing: this establishment was in Auburn, some ninety miles southeast of Birmingham. I was sorely disappointed that we must contend with another long-distance job, but felt it best to keep that negativity under wraps for the time being.

We needed that money. Plus, I wouldn't think of throwing a pall over Carl's nearly palpable delight in returning to his chosen line of work, his forte. Relief, as well, on both our parts, would serve as a huge impetus to align this marriage's slightly off-kilter inaugural. We would deal with the distance, simple as that.

That both wife and husband were now gainfully employed, the heretofore unspoken tension completely evaporated, allowing our first Christmas together to be one of contentment and contained merriment. My practical gift to Carl, another dress shirt and tie, was meant to be more of a celebratory symbol of his new job. Upon opening my gift from him, a two-hundred-and-fifty-dollar knit pantsuit from one of the most expensive stores in town, I had to call on every ounce of grace to express my gratitude. Yes, he was employed, but we were in no position yet to indulge in such extravagance. I simply wouldn't be able to enjoy this outfit that I could make myself for less than twenty-five dollars, in a better color, nicer material, and which fit.

"Too long? So?" Carl looked puzzled. "Can't you hem them?"

"Not this material. I know it'll bunch up and look homemade."

Perhaps having realized himself that this outfit did absolutely nothing for me, he conceded, "Well, the beige color does kinda drain you out. We'll exchange it for something else."

"Why don't let's just return it for now and wait until something special comes up and then we'll find something else." I didn't add 'that costs about one-fifth as much.' Carl shrugged his agreement. I couldn't resist adding, "Besides, we could use that money for something else right now."

"Aw, c'mon, hon! I just wanted to show my wife how much she means to me!"

I was surprised by Carl's tone, a mixture of hurt, defensiveness, and, what was that other, belligerence, maybe? I turned on my best coquettish attitude, sidling up and then straddling him as he sat on the couch.

"Now, babe, I know how much I mean to you because you *married* me. So don't be worrying yourself about what kind of, or how expensive a present to give me." I lowered my lips to his, planting a warm, wet kiss. "You're the only present I really want."

"Well, OK, if you put it that way," Carl grinned, pulling my hips closer in. "Now what I suggest is that you take that Christmas present off before I rip it off."

I pushed myself back to stand just in front of Carl's knees. In one swift but careful motion, I removed the top and let it puddle on the couch. Placing one palm on Carl's thigh, I slipped one leg, then the other, from the pants which I gently placed to the side. I tugged at my bikini panties as I eyed the growing mound under Carl's robe. "Actually, I prefer gifts we can share..."

Much later, I lay dreamily next to Carl who was snoring softly and steadily. Smiling, I relived the couple hours or so of eroticism in which the two of us had so enthusiastically engaged. The sensuous vision was occasionally interrupted by something...a sudden flicker, like a troublesome gnat...what was it? Oh, yes, that. The thought about Carl's handling of money, so very different from my way. I hoped this rather irresponsible gesture was a mere isolated whim, spurred on by the recent good fortune of a job and the spirit of the holiday.

I would eventually realize that this was no whim but a harbinger. And, unlike daffodils, not a happy one.

CHAPTER 16

SEARS HAS EVERYTHING!

My thoughts became more and more centered on financial matters, which seemed to be cropping up on several fronts the first month of the New Year. For starters, Carl's out-of-town job put daily commuting out of the question. Irked at being a newlywed and home alone, I was further distraught that part of Carl's salary was immediately earmarked for an efficiency apartment.

I fully expected that another chunk would soon be going to an Orlando bank trying to collect on a thirty-five-hundred-dollar loan, taken out by Carl and Kevin, for reasons unknown to me. When I got yet another collections call, I was relieved that with his new job Carl could make payments. I told the collections office Carl's number.

"What the fuck were you thinking?!" Carl's voice was a low hiss over the phone line. "The last thing I need right now is a harassing phone call at work!"

I was speechless. Carl had never used this tone of voice with me. My voice reflected my confusion. "Harassing? That man was very nice, very classy. He just needs to know what terms of repayment y'all can agree to."

Carl said, "Look, I've told you I've been holding off on starting payback because I'm waiting on Kevin to get a job so we can share the payments. And now *you* throw this monkey wrench in the works and add even more stress to what I'm already dealing with!"

"But, Carl, you can at least pay *something* to show good faith."

"Fuck good faith right now!" To my shocked silence, he quickly added, a bit more patient, "Of course I'm going to pay this loan back, but I plain and simply don't have the money right n—"

"But you do! I know you and Kevin got some severance pay from Orlando and now you're making a decent salary—"

"Well, aren't you just Little Miss Financial Wizard," came the sneer. I heard Carl take a huge gulp from whatever he was drinking. "I hate to tell you this, but there's more to this job than meets the eye, so you best stick with your little teaching job with all your little airhead students."

I was stunned. Practically whispering, I said, "That is not fair."

"Fuck fair, too! Can't you see I'm trying my best to make a go of it for us—us!—and thanks to you, it's suddenly become a lot more difficult." I heard a voice in the background. "I can't talk right now," came Carl's hurried voice. And he hung up.

I was shell-shocked for the rest of the afternoon and evening. Not only had he completely ignored the main point that he was shirking responsibility, he'd managed to put the onus on me, making me feel like a stupid, naïve housewife who'd unwittingly put him in an unpleasant position.

As I wrote thoughts such as these in my journal, I kept one eye on the phone, waiting for it to ring so Carl could deliver a much-called-for apology. But the phone remained silent, allowing me to contemplate other troubles.

Besides that bank loan, there was a year-overdue bill to Goodyear, which I had inadvertently discovered when emptying the trash. Carl had assured me he had taken care of it long ago, blaming any additional bills on computer glitches. If my unquiet was somewhat mitigated by this rational explanation, it erupted once again with the annual arrival of one of the two certain things in life: taxes.

Unlike the world of procrastinators who wait until the last minute to do taxes, I was on it the moment I received my W-2. To me, taxes was my most distasteful task, bar none. The sooner done, the sooner unburdened. But (sometimes arguably) nerve-wracking efficiency wasn't the primary motivation this year. My pitiful—but steady—teacher salary had been barely supplemented by the unsteady income produced by my husband. Growing desperation, then, was the primary force driving me to get my return done quickly to get that refund in the bank. In early January, I urged Carl to do likewise.

"Holy shit, woman! That's four months away!"

"More like three, actually, but I'd just as soon have the refunds in one."

"I haven't even received my W-2 yet. I can't do a thing."

"You can call what's-his-name in Orlando and tell him to get with the program. C'mon Carl, we *need* this money!"

"OK, OK, jeez, I can't believe you're so uptight about this!"

But Carl's OK proved meaningless as a few weeks rolled by with no W-2 forthcoming. When I would remind him about it, I was told I was being a goddamn nag. Considering that I could go the route of 'Married, Filing Separately,' I decided to drop it a while and did, until I received a most surprising phone call from, of all things, Sears.

"Mrs. Ballini, I'm calling to let you know your husband's tax return is ready."

"Huh? Wait, did you say Sears, as in trusty Kenmore and power tools Sears?"

A kind, somewhat amused voice answered, "Oh yes, you know Sears has everything. Including a tax division."

I hesitated only a moment longer before gushing, "Great! I'll be down this afternoon." *That silly goose*, I thought merrily, he was going to surprise me. Or maybe wait until my next nag session and then produce the tax return. I really didn't care, I just wanted to get taxes done. I presented myself at the desk of Ms. Mercedes, the kind lady who'd called. Following her advice to take a quick look at the return before signing, my intended cursory glance suddenly became one of intent study.

"Whoa," I said. "I'm afraid there must be some mistake. This can't be my husband's return. We have no children, and there are two cited here. And my name is not Cynthia." I studied the papers in front of me, finding not one entry that matched anything in my or Carl's lives.

The woman looked puzzled. "Oh, no, there's no mistake. I remember your husband well; he was in here the other day and I remember taking down his information."

A cold knot began to form in my stomach. "Could...could you describe him, please? I don't understand what's been written down here."

"Of course," Ms. Mercedes said, and then proceeded to nail Carl's description down to the rose-colored shirt that he wore with his black suit. "He sure is funny, your husband. And very charming."

I didn't know what to say. How could this woman be wrong and right at the same time? I mumbled an apologetic thank you, saying I'd return later with my husband when he was in town, and scurried out.

Driving home my mind reeled with befuddled, anxious thoughts. Did Carl actually have an entire other family? No freaking way. Well, yes, I supposed he could have one easily enough, with all our time apart...but, no. It made no sense. Why would he make this up though? To hide from the IRS? Carl made no secret of his contempt for that organization. Of course, I couldn't think of one person who thought lovingly of the IRS. I sure didn't. This was just too crazy.

I called Carl the moment I arrived home, asking him to please explain what the hell was going on. I wished I was having this conversation in person rather than over the phone, which I now had to hold away from my ear as I listened to Carl's immediate response:

"That Sears bitch is nothing but a stupid spic! She's lying through her teeth! I have no idea why she'd want to cause trouble like that!"

Dumbfounded, I stared at the phone receiver. "But she knew exactly who you were!"

"She's a lying bitch!"

"Well, let's just go see about that, then," I retaliated.

"No way! I'm not dealing with that incompetent fat-assed idiot. She's gotten my information wrong, and she's trying to cover her tracks."

I considered this. "Well, I do think it could be just a silly mistake—and she seemed perfectly nice to me, by the way—but whatever, we need to get your tax return filed." And before Carl could argue, I said, "Now, that's the bottom line."

After a moment, Carl said simply, "Right you are. OK then."

A few days later with Carl home, I was relieved to see that he put up no further resistance to meeting with Ms. Mercedes. Entering her cubicle, I anticipated with certainty a quick resolution to this weird mistake as well as the completion of a corrected tax return. Ms. Mercedes, obviously anticipating the same charming and funny man she had dealt with earlier, smiled in recognition. Never had I seen a smile disappear so quickly and be replaced by amazed horror, upon hearing the barrage of insults and curses spewing forth from my husband. A similar scene of Carl with Sharon the bartender flashed through my mind.

"You listen here, Ms. Dumbass, I don't know where you got your training, but you obviously missed the class on keeping your information straight."

Ms. Mercedes, initially appearing to gear up for an all-out battle, had now shrunk a dress size and cowered behind her desk. Her face contorted with hurt and confusion as she weighed the options of how to respond to this crazy man.

"You better believe your superiors are going to hear from me about this atrocity! So now your stupid, stupid mistake has got my wife all upset and I can tell you I don't appreciate it one damn bit!"

And on and on. I was appalled and embarrassed, but also felt that Carl might actually be correct, since Ms. Mercedes, having concluded that no rebuttal whatsoever was the wisest strategy, simply sat quietly, her face gone poker. I still wished that Carl's argument, justified or not, had been more civil. But I dared not suggest that, given his apparent rage at the woman's ineptitude.

We stood to leave, Carl exiting hurriedly, while I turned to at least say thanks anyway to this lady. Ms. Mercedes had gone into a sort of Zen state, looking neither defeated nor angry after the verbal beat-down she'd just endured. She turned her head slightly towards me, saying nothing but letting her eyes telegraph her thought: "Oh, I see, you're one of *those* women."

I dropped my own eyes quickly, not caring to elicit further explanation. In mute retreat, I hurried after my husband. Try as I would, I could not shake the woman's unspoken appraisal of me: pity. That expression would haunt me for weeks to come.

The blue eyes looking at me this very moment, though, were dreamy and filled with love. Unfortunately they belonged to one of my cats, the other two otherwise lost in cat-coma. I envied their bliss-ful repose, easy to come by in the silence of the house this evening. Rather than spend the night at home after the disastrous confronta-tion at Sears, Carl had made excuses to return to Auburn, leaving in a huff.

From its holding place deep between the mattresses, I had pulled my nearly ignored journal. It was becoming, I realized, less and less of a safe harbor for me, and more and more like one of those mirrors in the Fun House, which only show distorted versions of the real self. I had even begun to make certain notations in French, as if the beautiful language could somehow mitigate the unpleasantness, or perhaps put a bit more distance between myself and the reality that I was, in fact, in. My pen remained poised above the page a good two minutes before I finally began:

I hate it that my first urge to write is from motivation to tell my fear rather than my content ... Married now two months and seven days, I really don't know if Carl and I will make it. ... the next time we talk will be somewhat of a showdown, I fear. I dread it because if Carl starts try-ing to rationalize what he's doing, it shows that we differ on a very basic principle: honesty—well, or should I say self-esteem, which presupposes honesty. Very, very basic. The thought of getting out of marriage not yet three months old puts a cold chill in the pit of my stomach, but the thought of what I would be ten, fifteen, thirty years from now after compromises over basic principles is even more unappealing. We shall see.

I could hardly believe what I'd written. How could things be going wrong so quickly? My pen rolled to the bedspread, my hand having gone limp as soon as I finished the unhappy entry. I leaned my head back on the pillow as I half-sighed, half-moaned in shame, anger, and fear. What in the world had I gotten myself into? My journal fell to the side as I brought my knees to my chest and huddled morosely. It was nearly midnight and the phone stayed resolutely silent. I turned off the light and tried to sleep half as deeply as my cats.

CHAPTER 17

WHAT? ME WORRY?

At school the next day, I was summoned to the office. *Oh no, not another phone call from that bank...* But I saw three smiling faces of the office aides and my principal who stood behind the counter upon which sat a vase of one and a half dozen yellow roses.

"Awwww, flowers for the bride," cooed the staff.

Relieved, I managed a look of surprise and delight, as I opened the small envelope among the blooms and read the enclosed card. I pretended to blush while putting on my best Southern drawl, "Now, surely you folks aren't expecting me to read what he said...!" I gathered up the arrangement and whooshed from the office, roses bobbing about my head. As soon as I was out of earshot and eyesight of the chuckling staff, my grin disappeared as Carl's 'love note' played through my mind:

So sorry hon. I was an asshole. Don't worry; things will be fine. I love you. - C

Lord. What to do? I popped my head into Vivien's room. "Busy this afternoon after school?" Vivien looked questioningly, shaking her head in the emphatic negative. "Gotta talk."

I crossed the hall, placed the roses on my desk, completely ignoring the raucous shouts of my third period all-male English class and said, "OK, kiddos, today we're starting *Great Expectations* by Charles Dickens."

I turned to pick up my book. The students, rolling their eyes and groaning, didn't notice that I, well aware of the ironic title, was doing the very same thing.

Rather than remain at school the usual two hours after the final bell, I went straight to Vivien's, five minutes away. Despite the pressing discussion about to take place, I couldn't help but laugh as Vivien went about feeding her menagerie of dogs and cats.

"Animals are such funny people," said Vivien.

We took our cups of tea and sat at the kitchen table, our usual location for heart-to-hearts, not to mention the official site for hair-streaking. This painful task, which included the occasional crisis and the obligatory drink, ultimately resulted in salon-quality enhancement of both our Farrah Fawcetts. Today the table top was devoid of the rubber cap, delicate crochet needle, plastic gloves, and other torture tools. Instead of anticipating certain pain to our scalps, we helped ourselves to the plate of cookies, fuel for the upcoming discussion. I filled Vivien in on the Sears fiasco and the matter of Carl's unpaid bills.

"Gosh, do you think that Sears woman could possibly be making a mistake?" Vivien asked without too much hope.

"I'm thinking not a chance," came my mournful reply. I hung my head. "But, Vivien, if you could've been there. I mean Carl was—and still is—*adamant* that she's in the wrong. And, I want so badly for her to be wrong, for her to have made a really stupid mistake and she's afraid to admit it because she really needs her job, or, oh, whatever..." Vivien waited.

"And I *really* wish you'd been in the car on the way home so you could have heard how Carl went on about the nerve of this woman to intrude on the privacy of our marriage, or how he swore he wouldn't let anything like that happen again to threaten the life we were trying to build together... He *made sense* out of the whole fiasco. I mean the man had me ninety-nine percent convinced that the whole thing was a great big mistake."

"You don't sound ninety-nine percent convinced right now," Vivien said.

I took a deep breath. "Well, I am convinced that Carl doesn't have a whole other family. I mean, why? And, how? I just don't buy it." My shoulders slumped as I exhaled heavily. "But I'm not buying that the Sears woman screwed up the info. Which means...Carl made that shit up. Again, why? How? Trust me, I'd like to stick it to the IRS, too, but there's no running and hiding from those folks."

"So, what's Carl's response when you point this out?" Vivien asked.

Now my chin pressed into my chest. "Um, haven't actually done that." Vivien's eyes widened. "Because, if I take this woman's side, I'd be calling my husband—my husband of barely three months, mind you—a freaking bald-faced liar." I grimaced wryly. "Not exactly standin' by yo' man."

"So, what are you going to do?"

"On the one hand I feel like I should cut and run, but—" I looked skyward, "—oh, that would be so embarrassing! And then there's the small factor of my being very much in love with Carl. Which, at the moment, is damned embarrassing in itself!"

"I hear you! That's exactly how I felt with Frank last week, at our..." Vivien's fingers made quote marks, "...*wedding.*"

I clucked my tongue, remembering Vivien's tearful recounting of the wedding that wasn't. Just as she and Frank were exiting the car in the parking lot of the courthouse where they were to be married, Frank had appeared to be having a heart attack which was, in fact, a panic attack. He'd announced to Vivien that he 'couldn't do it...yet.'

Sitting at the table now, Vivien looked at me. "So, yeah, I hear you. Hell, I should've run like the wind out of that parking lot, but he said 'yet.'"

"Kinda the same thing as this." I showed Carl's card to Vivien. "I can't flip this back into his face and give him the ol' 'up yours' because—" I searched for the bottom line, "—I feel like I can make this work, know what I mean?"

We looked at each other with total understanding.

"Any idea on how you're going to go about doing that?"

Now we both snorted.

"Not the foggiest. I'm just going to try to do what Carl says in his card: 'Don't worry.'"

CHAPTER 18

CONMAN AT WORK

When Carl came home the following Sunday evening, not a single word was spoken for nearly an hour, the Sears 'wound' still very raw.

Fresh on both our minds was the heated argument, conducted long-distance, two nights earlier. Not only did Carl never budge an inch from his initial stance that the whole thing was an insanity, his forceful, condescending explanations made my questions sound naïve or plain stupid. While I didn't actually say that some sort of mistake had been made, my resigned comment, that 'the whole affair was just too weird' must have sounded like acquiescence. Indeed, I did eventually accept Carl's repeated assurances that I need not worry; I was tired of arguing.

Later, in my journal, I'd tried to put the matter to rest with the following pronouncement:

A lesson for me to learn is never accuse until absolutely certain!

This evening, I cut through the tension, feeling we absolutely must start communication of some sort.

"Look," I said cautiously, gently, "we're not even going to rehash the Sears stuff..."

A petulant grunt from Carl.

I continued, "I'm sorry giving the loan guy your number put you in hot water, but I gotta tell ya that I'm not going to lie for anybody, even my husband."

"I told you before, you don't have the whole story about what's going on. What's more, your releasing my contact number could result in the bank's talking to my bosses at the restaurant, and that could mean my job, which is a big part of our livelihood. You shouldn't have done that without checking with me first."

I steeled myself. "Look, the bottom line is, you owe money and you're not paying up. I don't respect the way you're handling this. And..." A quizzical look from Carl. "...and I feel a little hypocritical saying 'I love you' to someone who's doing stuff like what you're doing."

Again, no reply from Carl. He went to the kitchen to mix a drink. For the remainder of the evening, he planted himself in front of the TV. I went to bed, leaving a brooding husband in the living room. When I woke the next morning, I saw that he had come to bed at some point. His soft snores carried a stale reminder of the previous night's drinks and cigarettes. I got up and did my morning routine as quietly as possible. I looked in on Carl before leaving, expecting to find him still asleep, but there he was, lying on his back, staring morosely at the ceiling.

"I'm off. I'll just wait until you're ready to talk," I said, neutrally.

Apparently he wasn't ready, so I turned to go. But then, he spoke in a tone which I had never heard; soft, yes, but quite sad.

"I'm a little disappointed to discover that my wife might not love me."

I wasn't about to start an argument since I had to run off tests for my first period class. But I wasn't going to be the non-communicative one. "What you're doing is not helping my love for you grow by leaps and bounds."

"You're wrong."

"No, I'm not."

Stonewall.

I left.

I was in grading mode during my prep period when I was called to the office for a phone call. With great reluctance and not a little irritation—had I not told Carl what a hassle it was for teachers to take phone calls?—I stopped my work, found an empty counselor's office and picked up the phone.

Carl's voice was energetic, not quite a jeer, but sounding as though he'd just discovered something really important. "You know, you probably ought to lay off that goody-two-shoes routine of yours."

"Huh?" my mind was still on the remaining papers to grade.

Carl's inhale told me he'd lit up. Exhaling, he said, "Remember when we went to Penny's and the clerk gave you too much credit for the stuff you were returning and you didn't say anything?"

I felt a twinge of guilt about my lapse of judgment in having failed to bring the twelve-dollar error to the clerk's attention.

Not allowing me to answer, he hurried on, "And, if you're so damned uptight about money, why did you agree to go ahead and *let* me buy stocks, which, if I might remind you, I *discussed* with you beforehand, and now you're saying it was a poor investment."

My acquiescence to Carl's insistence that we invest five hundred dollars—that we really didn't have—based on a hot tip was in an effort to try *not* to come across as a miser; plus, I knew zero about stocks.

"Also," Carl continued, "you didn't seem to have a problem with my buying you a Christmas present a while back. You know, your thriftiness is a lot more like miserliness."

How convenient that Carl had omitted the fact that I had returned the ridiculously expensive pantsuit two weeks later. I started to point this out, but he cut me off, his voice nearly a sneer.

"So, don't think I'm going to let you put the monkey on *my* back." He took a quick breath. "And I sure as hell am not going to live with a woman who doesn't love me." And he hung up.

I stood in the office, phone in hand, dial tone emphatically reminding me that Carl was no longer there. *Well, son of a bitch! What is he thinking? What, is he going to divorce me?! How crazy is that?*

I put myself on automatic pilot for the remainder of the school day. I couldn't believe I was actually trying to process the possibility of divorce at, as an added insult, Carl's initiation. He'd not said the D-word, but what else could he have had in mind? I myself had not really contemplated the Big D as an inescapable and imminent event, even though my own disenchantment with my current lot was undeniable. Nonetheless, faced with the very real possibility of divorce, my disenchantment evaporated and was replaced with embarrassment and fear, but mostly sadness.

I knew that my trust in him—not exactly rock solid to begin with—had suffered a major blow. How was I to continue with someone for whom I had such frail trust? I sensed the importance of this question but, up to this point, I'd not allowed the no-brainer response to enter my head, just as I hadn't dared revisit the teachings of *Atlas Shrugged.* (I could picture Dagny, the book's heroine, shaking her head and tapping her foot.) Rather than contemplate that I might in fact be smack dab in the middle of one of those famous 'breaches of morality,' I chose to tend to the flood of other considerations filling my mind.

First, there was the weighty matter of reluctance. Having waited until I was twenty-nine to get married, having told people all along that I had no intention of settling for somebody simply to say I was married, I was not about to admit that I'd made such a major mistake. But, mistakes could be corrected—sometimes—and I felt the familiar surge of my 'I-can-fix-it!' mentality. Taking on challenges and coming through them successfully was familiar territory.

This marriage, barely off the ground, had already suffered several blows, but I felt it was way too early in the game to give up. *It had so much potential.* I felt it deserved another chance. Furthermore, I believed that, with time, I could *change* some of Carl's bad habits. I had seen his look of satisfaction when his thoughtful gestures like taking out the trash or keeping the ashtrays emptied prompted a response of loving gratitude from me. Surely he would *want* to continue to do things to please me, thereby strengthening the marriage. And then, there was the fact that Carl loved me. Well, he must; hell, he *married* me.

Thoughts such as these swirled through my head all day long, but they finally settled down enough for me to see the bottom line. Yes, as much as all those negative things got on my next-to-last nerve, I knew *without question* that I did *not* want to let go of Carl's positive qualities. I was still electrified by them and I loved them all. I loved him.

I went straight home after school, expecting to find Carl in a horrible mood, but he was sitting on the couch with Sinclair in his lap, looking like the most content man in the world. I was looking at a man in control of his situation, almost smug.

"Hey, hon," he said, as if the earlier phone call had never taken place.

Hearing those words, after having contemplated divorce for the remainder of the school day, completely got away with me. I collapsed on the couch.

"Well," I looked at Carl, eyes brimming with tears, "it occurred to me today that this marriage hangs in the balance of whether or not I love you."

Carl's face was full of kindness and unmasked hope.

"Well, I do." I looked at Carl to watch a visible wave of relief wash over him.

"Oh, thank God!" he said. "Hon, I know things are not perfect right now, but I promise, I am certain, that things are going to be better and we are going to have a fabulous life together. I know I need to curb my temper and take more time to understand where you're coming from and I will because, God knows, I love you more than anything on this earth."

I didn't know if Carl could see the similar wave of relief wash over me, but I sure felt it. Just contemplating divorce, with all the accompanying dynamics, was simply way too confrontational. More than that, though, I plain and simply did not want out. I was in this thing. And now I felt sure Carl was going to come around to giving me, per Joni Mitchell's simple request, that 'little affection and respect' I wanted and deserved. I smiled and breathed a deep sigh.

"I feel so much better."

Carl gently lifted Sinclair off his lap and moved to my side of the couch.

CHAPTER 19

A WIDE BERTH

I clung to my belief that there was not enough working against this marriage to destroy it. Putting my nose to the grindstone to by God make this marriage work, I hardly looked up for the next few months. On the occasions when I did, I found good reason to feel heartened. While not exactly having stared Divorce in the face, Carl and I had certainly taken a brief sideways glance in its direction. We both made quick retreats, taking unspoken vows to maintain a wide berth around it.

Humor—initially on tiptoe but quickly regaining steady and certain footing—was warmly welcomed back into our lives.

For some reason, Carl's chasing me around the house, or scaring the wits out of me, proved entertaining and enjoyable for both of us. On one occasion, a bird had somehow gotten trapped in the house. For two hours, we tried to guide it outside, using brooms or rolled-up newspapers, frantically ducking the occasional kamikaze swoop. Finally, in petrified frenzy, the poor creature rocketed out the front door, leaving a few feathers in its wake.

Nowhere close to having shaken my jitters, I returned to my desk and my paper-grading, eventually managing to gear up all powers of concentration. Unbeknownst to me, Carl had pulled one of the few remaining intact peacock feathers from an arrangement (the others in varying degrees of mutilation, thanks to Sinclair's crazed attacks). Hiding just around the corner from the desk, Carl ever so delicately extended the long sturdy stalk with its feathery tip until it just grazed my neck and cheek.

Like a bullet, I shot from the chair and landed on the other side of the room. Carl fell to the floor in a huddle of wheezing laughter.

"Holy shit, look!" he croaked. "The chair is in exactly the same place! You turned to rubber and slithered out of there!" He bent over again in a paroxysm of giggles.

"You son-of-a-bitch!" I yelled, but then, picturing how funny I must have looked, I couldn't help bursting into laughter while still making a show of pretended anger. It was true. I had totally ejected from the desk and was airborne for easily half the width of the room. Amazing actually. But funny.

Even though Carl usually rolled his eyes at my wide array of ongoing projects, I was certain he secretly admired me for being so passionate about them. Still, he rarely passed up an opportunity to rib me, eye-rolling the interminable macrame mass, or pronouncing an abomination of nature my six-foot Christmas-tree frame of two-by-two's covered in chicken wire, lights, pine cones, walnut bunches, and bows. I would just chuckle and go merrily along with my work.

Once, while sewing a cushy green robe, I sat at the machine, completely nude but for panties. This, to accommodate repeatedly trying it on for fitting, hemming, etc. When a huge flash filled the room, I jerked around to see Carl lowering a camera, devilishly ecstatic to have caught me in such a compromising position.

What began as a tentative, almost reluctant effort on Carl's part was now mild enthusiasm for tennis, as he developed a certain knack for the game. I was nothing short of thrilled to have my husband join in and enjoy something that was so dear to my heart. We even entered a low-level tournament, finishing as runners-up. This could only be a change for the better; of this, I was certain.

Of utmost importance was the growing indication that Carl's work in Auburn was going well after three months on the job. While this was just cause for at least guarded elation, it also generated no small amount of angst on my part.

"Gosh, Carl," I said as we sat on the couch during one of his visits home, "I've barely been in this house two years...you, almost a year...God, I hate the thought of giving it up." I tried not to whine. "Ditto my job!"

Carl was all sympathy. "I know, hon. But things are going great in Auburn. Even so, *damn, I miss you!*" He took a final drag off his cigarette. "Of course, I understand how you feel. But you know, there are plenty of houses and jobs in Auburn." He smushed his cigarette in the ashtray. "Or...we could continue with your living up here and me down there..."

I shook my head. "Nope. I know some couples manage long-distance marriages, but I'm realizing all too quickly that this is not my cup of tea."

Carl nodded almost ferociously. "Mine neither! I do so much better when you're with me." He lit another cigarette and looked at me kindly. "Well, you think about it, hon; it's your decision."

My thinking over the next couple weeks, colored by my deepening determination to make things work, led me to several realizations. Pulling up roots (both long-term and those freshly grounded) and quitting my job would be a solid indication that I was fully invested in my new married life. After all, shouldn't the wife follow the husband who was (usually) the primary breadwinner? I also felt a move to a new place could be the virtual turning over of a new leaf. I wanted to give as much impetus from my part as I could.

To wit, on a Sunday afternoon in early spring, I summoned the courage to bite the bullet and put my beloved home on the market. My real estate agent hammered the For Sale sign in the ground at 3:50 p.m. Within ten minutes there was a knock on the door and at 5:45 p.m., there was a signed contract. So fast! It happened so terribly fast. I tried to feel elated at the ease with which this necessary step had been taken, but I could not escape the feeling that, along with the house, a bit of my soul had been sold for a song.

Thanks to the contract's three-month grace period, I could teach out the school year and maintain other activities. Directing Senior Play practice was great fun, especially when I subbed for an absent student. Attending and studying for an accounting class, enrolled in should I not land a teaching job in Auburn, consumed several evenings. Taking piano lessons proved very satisfying until my full plate forced me to quit in mid April, thus justifying my teacher's misgiving about adult students: "They're so conscientious but Life plays havoc with their schedules." At home, whether concentrating on a bound buttonhole, finishing up a Chinese button macrame knot, or playing my piano I'd realize more often than not that a faint smile had crept across my face. I was happiest when busy and productive.

One evening, the phone rang and I smiled, knowing that Carl was thinking of me.

"So, how're you doin', hon?" using the particular tone of voice that always made my heart do a little flip.

"I'm great! I finished that green robe—you know the one of nekkid picture fame—" Carl's wheezing giggle filled the ear piece. "And play practice was great today. Louise and I think—"

Carl interrupted, saying, "You're going to be here this weekend for signing the contract on the house, right?"

I felt a frisson of anxiety travel through me. I'd spent my spring holiday week in Auburn for a house-hunting spree. We'd found one in the final stages of construction of stone and fresh-smelling cedar, on a cul-de-sac. New and clean, it was completely different from my house. Strong attachment to my first home aside, I couldn't help but be excited about a whole new place that Carl and I would be setting up together.

"How lucky were we, hon, that we snapped that house right up before those other buyers? Jeez, there were so many." Carl chuckled delightedly. "Kinda the same thing with your—our—place in Birmingham. Man, I can't believe that guy jumped on that house so fast," Carl's chuckle of amazement held a touch of derision.

I balked. "This happens to be a fabulous little house, in Forest Park right next to the golf course. So don't be bad-talking my house, Bozo!"

"Yeah, yeah, yeah. So, what time are you getting here Friday?"

"Pretty early since I've taken a sick day in order to do that interview at Opelika High School." If I was feeling any reservations, my voice didn't betray it. Wow, one house sold, another house about to be bought, a new job interview...holy shit, this is really happening!

"I have no doubt you'll nail it as soon as the principal takes one look at your tush and those legs."

"Good to know teachers aren't hired mainly for their subject matter expertise."

"Right, well, you get yourself and your expertise down here, because we have a whole 'nother subject matter to attend to..."

"Spoken like a true dirty old man. We'll expertise each other later but I've got stuff to do right here, right now."

We both laughed and hung up the phone. My smile faded a bit as I noted to myself that I'd not mentioned to anyone at school the reason for this Auburn visit. And I sure as hell hadn't submitted a resignation. Just being cautious, I told myself.

CHAPTER 20

TEAMWORK

One thing about a teaching career, I mused while traveling down Highway 280 to Auburn, is the abundance of school holidays. Hardly fair compensation for the paltry salary, but still, I took advantage of every one of them. Even so, I'd had to draw on my diminishing balance of sick days for this particular visit. I regarded these withdrawals simply as investments in the marriage. One of the more pleasurable aspects of my visits included working as hostess at the restaurant. I found the predominantly college-age clientele lively and, thankfully, well-mannered. One customer turned out to be one of my favorite ex-students, who seemed equally pleased to see me.

"Wow! Is that you, Miss Browning?" A burly but handsome young man towered before me.

"Um, not exactly," I laughed. "Right person, wrong name." I flashed my wedding ring.

"Well, congratulations! At least, I suppose so," he said, mimicking a low, sad groan. He turned to the other guys in his group.

"I—along with half the guys in class—had a huge crush on this lady... even if she was the hardest teacher I ever had. Fair, but hard."

"And you were the only football player who ever actually studied for my class."

He nodded, laughing. "Yeah, you know the first thing Coach said to incoming teams was, 'Whatever you do, do *not* take French. Miss Browning don't cut no slack.'"

"Got that right!" I blushed and laughed at the same time. "Now, sit your derrières down here, 'cause I have to get back to work! Oh yeah, bon appétit, messieurs!"

As I hurried to my welcoming post, I noticed Carl on the other side of the room, nodding his approval at my interaction with the customers. I felt very much a part of a team.

The first order of business, once we returned to the apartment, was to get into comfortable clothes. Then we launched into one of our favorite past times: chase! Like a couple of kids, we darted around the teeny efficiency, vaulting over the one chair, doubling back behind the couch, and finally ending up in the kitchen where Carl cornered me by the refrigerator. Quick as a flash, he opened the door and grabbed a large can of Reddi-Whip. Before I realized what he was doing, he grabbed my robe—my brand new green robe—and sprayed the entire contents through the front opening.

Mouth wide open, I could not believe what had happened. Sputtering with mock anger, searching for an appropriate reaction, remembering that I was one who 'didn't cut nobody no slack,' I flung open my bathrobe, exposing my bare body now completely covered in whipped cream, and I leapt onto Carl, legs circling his butt, arms clamped around his neck. Shrieks of laughter followed the crashing booms and grunts as we hit the floor.

Not all visits were so amusing, however. Two weeks later, in early May, I had no inkling that the beautiful spring evening would turn into a night of dark foreboding. The mood at the restaurant was certainly no indication as everyone seemed high on the weather as well as the excitement that the semester was nearly over. Back at the apartment, Carl and I even did another one of our chase escapades, this time with Carl locking me, wearing the skimpiest of teddies, outside.

"You best be counting your lucky stars there's no one around here!" I exploded back inside, yelling in mock anger, which quickly dissolved into laughter once I saw Carl gasping for breath through his giggles.

Later that night, in bed, I was still smiling about his crazy stunt, when suddenly I heard an emphatic *pow!* followed by glass crunching. Carl shot out of bed, cursing like a madman.

Alarmed, I cried, "What's going on? What's the matter?"

But Carl had dashed outside. I heard men's muffled voices, harsh and angry, the screeching of tires, more yells, and then silence. Before I could get my cream-infused robe on, Carl had come back into the apartment.

"Bastards," Carl muttered. "I'll get 'em."

"Who?"

"I have no idea. A bunch of thugs. Never mind."

He flipped the light switch and began pacing the room in darkness. I lay in bed, wondering who this stranger was. I dared not utter a word, especially to say that the earlier exchanges didn't appear to be between strangers. That tone of voice he'd employed! Had I not gotten a sneak preview of it when he tore into that poor woman at Sears?

Only this was worse: this was a deeper, rougher rage, not frenzied indignation. The closest I had ever been to this level of anger was by sitting safely before a television or movie screen. Now I was shoulder to shoulder with it, since Carl had flung himself back in bed, anger still exuding from his pores. I turned and slowly pulled toward the edge of the bed to give Carl and his rage as much space as possible.

I stared into the blankness, trying to make sense of the past hour's intrusion into our pleasant evening. All sorts of unwelcome intrusions, I was beginning to notice, seemed to be occurring in much greater frequency since...well...since I'd met Carl. That same steel ball that I'd felt in my stomach that day at Sears was back and it was bigger, heavier. A mere six months into the marriage and I was sensing a cold, dead certainty that I'd made a massive mistake.

As I would see the next morning, both the front and back windshields of Carl's brand new Mark VI had been smashed to smithereens. Driving home, I posed one question after another. Why was it *just* Carl's car? Did he know those guys? Did they know him? Why would they do that? Could it possibly have been a random event? I shuddered as I remembered the practically unrecognizable face of my husband as I'd kissed him good-bye.

Contemplation of the recent flirtation with divorce dredged up all the accompanying unpleasant emotions. The strength of these proved enough to push the cold knot down into the depths of my gut. Here I was, married, my home under contract, a possible job offer elsewhere...it was all too much to handle.

I realized I'd been so deep in thought that I'd driven past my exit. I had to drive further before circling back to get home.

Back to work I went with renewed diligence to at least keep up my end of the bargain in being a model partner in the work called marriage. It was actually easy to lose myself in my work, what with those jarring school bells hurtling everyone from one slot in the regimen to the next, relentlessly marching off time. Nightly phone calls varied in mood anywhere from light and affectionate, to heavy and depressed, to judgmental and sullen, all accompanied with the background of ice tinkling against glass. I would hang up the phone, noting that the drinking stuff probably needed to be watched. Then I would quickly resume my busy schedule which, for the most part, provided adequate insulation from reality.

CHAPTER 21

NEVER MIND!

Partly assuaging the worries about the 'window-smashing incident' was this year's spectacular month of May. The city was a fairyland of dogwood blossoms, azaleas, and myriad shades of early greens. Besides the sheer beauty that spring offered, I drew deep peace and joy from its symbolism of fresh, new beginnings. Rather than delve into the darkness that lurked—possibly?—below the surface of my marriage, I chose to transfer the season's positive forces to my renewed determination to keep it afloat.

My immediate future actually held several parallels to the season: a brand new beautiful home that I would enjoy decorating, a new job (most likely, since the interview had gone well) in an excellent school system, a husband successful at and content with his career...yes, I told myself, there were positives galore.

Walking to my car after a hard day of teaching followed by a four-hour dress rehearsal for the senior play, I breathed in the heady perfumes floating about in the soft spring night. Invigorated, I considered squeezing in an hour of study for my cost accounting test coming up in a few days. On second thought, I was bushed. I decided it'd be much more suitable to kick back in a nice hot bath with a Kahlua on the rocks, my favorite toddy. Maybe with a candle or two and the window open so I could hear the night sounds.

Exhaling a contented sigh just thinking about it, I turned the corner onto my street, and was jerked out of my reverie by the appearance of Carl's car—now repaired—parked in front of the house. This was strange. It was a Thursday. I parked and walked past his car, trailing a hand over the hood. Not a trace of warmth. He'd been home some time. I entered the house to find Carl sitting on the couch, drink in one hand, cigarette in the other, a sour expression on his face. He looked at me, shook his head slowly from side to side while doing a thumbs down.

"What's this?" I was frightened.

A second thumbs down.

"What do you mean...you were...let go?" A solemn, rather sullen nod from Carl. "Why on earth...?"

"That stupid son-of-a-bitch says the numbers aren't matching up and he's going to have to close the place. The place isn't showing a profit."

"But...that place is packed to the gills every night! It's right in the middle of University Avenue, great location...I don't understand!"

"I know, it doesn't make a bit of sense to me either. The bastard only gave me two weeks' severance."

My head was swimming. "O. Mi. God. What are we going to do about the house? I mean, the *houses?*" I considered my paycheck. No way could I ever handle two mortgages. We were already stretched to the limit with Carl's just having begun contributing again to our incomes and now taking a huge chunk of it to pay for that goddamned pimp mobile (as Cindi had so appropriately named it). I looked at Carl, my eyes wide with fear.

"Now, hon, don't get your panties all up in a wad. You're always making mountains out of molehills. I've already spoken to the Thomases and they've agreed to refund the earnest money on the house in Auburn. They understand that this was something beyond our control."

"Oh, bless their hearts," I gave a sigh of relief. "I'll call McFarlin tomorrow and ask him if he can see his way to doing the same for us."

On my forty-five-minute prep period the next day, I called McFarlin, the buyer, and broke the news to him that we would not be moving to Auburn, that we really wanted to keep the house, and we hoped he'd follow suit and agree to a refund of his earnest money.

"He certainly wasn't pleased," I reported to Carl that evening, "but he eventually did consent to having his earnest money refunded along with being paid back the four hundred dollars for an inspection."

"Well, that lousy son-of-a-bitch," Carl said.

"I don't think it's such a bad deal," I reasoned. "I've got about two hundred dollars in the Credit Union; surely we can come up with—"

"The hell you say! Why in fuck's name should we pay his unnecessary expense? This house had already been appraised. He didn't *need* to have an inspection done," Carl thundered.

"I suppose that's true, but—"

"Let me handle this," Carl said. Knowing how forceful Carl could be, I decided to let him do just that. I really did not want to lose my house, and surely, surely this man would understand.

A few days later, Carl entered the house, a large envelope in his hand. He gave it to me.

"What's this? But first, did you talk to McFarlin? What'd he say?" I slid a thumb under the envelope's flap.

"No need to worry about McFarlin," Carl said smugly. "I'd say we came to an understanding."

Wanting details, but curious to first see what was in the envelope, I tore off the flap and pulled out what looked like a pre-paid voucher for two round-trip tickets to San Juan. I looked at Carl with rounded eyes.

"I thought we needed a break, hon," Carl said in his best velvety smooth voice. "We've been under such stress."

"And just how do you think we're going to pay for these?"

"Damn, woman! I try to do something nice for you and you have to get all bitchy and judgmental on me. You know I'm hurting from my job being taken away, and damned if you don't turn the knife in the wound."

I looked in disbelief at Carl, a perfect mixture of fury and hurt. His obvious hurt surprised me and I fought back my impulse to blast him for making such an insane purchase. Dang, that job of his had been going so well! I conceded that Carl's pride must be terribly wounded, seeing as he'd been well on his way to assuming the role of *good provider*. Regrouping, I simply said, "OK, OK, sorry. I really do appreciate your thinking of me—of us, I mean—but maybe it'd be better for us to postpone that trip a while until things settle down a bit. What do you think?"

Carl seemed to deflate a bit and appeared to be seriously considering what I said. "I guess you're right," he said. He threw the ticket voucher into the trash can, saying, "Another time."

I lunged towards the trash can to retrieve the tickets, casting a look at Carl that asked if he'd lost his mind. "Jeez! We gotta return these for a refund!"

"Calm down, calm down, I can call the travel agent tomorrow, no problem." Trying to assuage my agitation, Carl's voice softened. "C'mon, hon, don't worry. Everything's going to be fine. Why don't you go take one of those late-night baths of yours and I'll bring you a Kahlua."

"Great minds think alike," I said simply, trying to summon up some levity. A few moments later, my rudely postponed bath was in fact taking place. Grateful and relieved that an explosion had apparently been defused, I leaned back on my bath pillow, sipped my drink, closed my eyes, and tried to concentrate on the untroubled sounds of the night settling into repose. I made myself concentrate on Carl's confident statement that all was going to be fine.

But suddenly I sat up, the bathwater loudly squelching away from my body. It dawned on me that Carl had not explained *how* he'd 'taken care' of things with McFarlin. I stepped out of the tub, wrapped a towel around me and walked to the bedroom, stopping short at the door. There lay Carl on the bed, striking a pose remarkably similar to da Vinci's Vitruvian Man but for the monstrous hard-on looming dead center. Such an inviting sight recalled the most recent of the many cards I had given Carl: on the front of the card, a picture of an open drawbridge; inside, the remark, "Fully erect, it could stop traffic."

I decided I wasn't all that anxious to know the *how* of McFarlin; I was more interested in the *what* of the man lying before me. I weighed the relaxing qualities of a hot bath with Kahlua versus a rollicking, ravaging romp. I smiled. No contest. I let the towel drop to the floor and took a few steps forward in anticipation of sliding down onto my husband. A step or two closer, though, brought me within earshot of his steady snores laden with fumes of booze and cigarettes.

I picked up my towel and headed back to my bath, which had turned an unwelcoming lukewarm. I picked up my glass of watered-down Kahlua and sat on the edge of the tub. "Damn," I said softly.

CHAPTER 22

GONE! NOT GONE!

"So, there's no way we'll be closing on the house on the 16th." As soon as I had found a moment at school the next day, I'd called Virginia, my real estate agent. I explained what had gone down with Carl's job, how we'd been released from the Auburn contract, that McFarlin had given a qualitative consent, and that Carl had said he'd handled everything.

"Oh my, this is too bad! Everything was going like clockwork," said Virginia.

"I know, it's a shame in many ways—you know, I was beginning to like Auburn a lot—but I'm really happier to stay here in Birmingham in my cute little house!" I sighed deeply. "But I wanted to call and thank you for all your help and to say I'm sorry things fell through."

"Oh, you're welcome, and me, too," Virginia said. Then she added, "It's rather odd, though, that I haven't heard from McFarlin yet."

"Oh, I'm sure you'll be hearing from him soon," I said with certainty. "This should all get ironed out quickly."

"I sure hope so," Virginia said, sounding less than certain.

The next few days held no word from McFarlin or Virginia, so I figured that McFarlin had probably decided to hell with the whole thing. Somewhat relieved of that concern, I was able to dive into the remaining weeks of school with all its harried business of exams, final grades, awards ceremonies and graduation. I hardly had time for thoughts of Carl's being at home again. Unemployed. Again.

I returned home late most evenings, grateful to find that Carl had prepared a delicious meal. My smiles of appreciation would often turn to hoots of laughter. With the air of a haughty waiter, towel draped over forearm, and with a sweeping flourish, he'd place my plate down, pronouncing, "Bon appétitties, Your Fine Hiney." Other times, I'd return home to find him still cooking, shirtless, cut-off jeans partially unzipped (to allow for a slightly bulging tummy). He'd turn to face me, spatula in one hand, frying pan in the other and proclaim in an exaggerated gay voice, "Jeez, it's a bitch looking dynamite all day!"

Instead of a home-cooked meal for my birthday, Carl treated me to a real date night at an intimate French restaurant, one of my favorites. Pleased and touched with Carl's thoughtfulness, I decided to mirror Carl's seeming unconcern about his lack of a job.

"To your thirtieth!" Carl raised his glass. "And you still look no older than your students." He looked at me with eyes full of kindness. "And I promise you, for your thirty-first, I'll treat you to a lot more than dinner in a Birmingham restaurant...I'm thinking...Key West?"

"Lawzy mussy, suh, you do treat me so fine!" My silly southern accent always tickled Carl. "So, Key West later...but how about...St. Simon's...now?!" Carl looked at me, puzzled. "Yep, my sister Darrah and Ted asked us to come stay with their kids for two weeks starting the 18th. Great house on a golf course, access to the country club pool and restaurant, beach nearby...whaddaya say?"

"I say, 'not yes, but hell yes!'"

The impromptu vacation was even more fun than expected. My nephew Terence, eight, and niece Brynne, ten, were happy to enjoy more of Carl's wit that they'd encountered at the wedding. Several nights Carl did an expert job of grilling steaks or burgers. They laughed along with me at Carl's hysterical commentary for whatever show was on the TV. Especially funny was Carl's recounting of 'the snake' episode: While vacuuming the living room, both Carl and I were horrified to see a small green snake slither across the hearth and disappear into the fireplace. Despite Carl's comical attacks with the fireplace tools, the snake did not reappear for hours upon end, until it was, we agreed, gone. But not forgotten.

That night, we settled into bed, which was now a mattress on the floor, Carl having complained the bed was too soft. Just before lights out, I was distressed to see a small bug scuttle across the floor. I smashed it with a shoe and resolutely deposited it into the trashcan. After a thorough look around the room, I was satisfied enough to turn the lights off and crawl onto bed. Of course, Carl would not be able to resist, some twenty minutes later, trailing the tip of a sock ever so lightly across my neck.

In a flash, my hands flew to my hair, rummaging through it wildly, then to the mattress, slapping and stamping like a mad woman, followed by completely ejecting from the mattress to a crouched position against the far wall, hand clawing above for the light switch. The room now flooded with light, I saw Carl on all fours, completely naked, convulsed in laughter, gasping for breath.

My expression instantly changed from horror to total disgust. I composed myself, marched across the room and slid under the covers, my back to Carl.

"Very funny," I said.

Carl, afraid he'd perhaps gone too far, said nothing and lowered himself to the mattress. I waited until all was quiet. Then I pounced.

The two fun-filled weeks did wonders for my attitude as I witnessed a glimpse of the life Carl and I could have together...once he got hold of a truly steady job. I had no intention of addressing anything so stressful, though, during this gift vacation. The entire period was fun and lighthearted save for one troubling incident. Darrah and Ted had left two hundred dollars in cash for incidentals or emergencies and I, diligent with all things monetary, was distressed when twenty dollars was unaccounted for.

"I'm sure there was a hundred and forty dollars last time I counted. Now there's only a hundred and twenty. Did you buy something I've forgotten about?"

"Naw, hon, just the coal and lighter fluid we got for the cookout last Tuesday." Carl's surprised look changed to one of slight worry. "You don't think one of the kids could've taken it, do you?"

I scoffed lightly. "Not a chance. They'd never do anything like that."

Instead of readily agreeing, Carl said, "Well, it's just..."

"Just what?"

"...well, it's probably nothing, but I saw Terence walking out of the office the other day, and I kinda wondered why he was in there in the first place..." As if reconsidering, he shook his head. "...Nah, probably nothing." He shrugged as if his thought wasn't worth pursuing. I didn't press him to reveal what he was thinking. I had no further interest in the conversation.

But I couldn't shake the tiny seed of suspicion that Carl had planted. When Terence bounded into the kitchen after a baseball game with some neighborhood kids, I started to ask him about it, but I couldn't quite bring myself to pose a question to this happy, guileless, polite kid. It would be tantamount to an accusation. A totally undeserved accusation. I hated myself for even considering it in the first place. Just forget about the whole thing, I told myself. And I did.

It wasn't until mid-July that I would see how Carl had handled McFarlin. Not well at all, as it turned out, since in the mail came yet another large envelope. No plane tickets this time though. I found myself staring at some sort of legal document. I saw Carl's name, then mine, and was about to figure this was some kind of slick advertising junk mail, but then I saw McFarlin's name. I sat down in the first chair I came to and frantically pored over the legalese, understanding hardly any of it except that ominous phrase, 'breach of contract.'

I could not believe it. This man McFarlin was actually going to sue us and *take the house* from us! Sued?! Holy shit! To me, lawsuits were either for slick criminal defense lawyers or for high-level corporate wheelings and dealings. This kind of crap happened to other people, not me! Hadn't Carl said he'd handled things? Obviously not.

Furious and petrified, I waited at the front door until Carl finally waltzed in. Waving the papers in Carl's face, I shrieked, "What in the hell is this?" I was trembling. "Is this how you *handle things*?!"

Carl only glanced at the shaking papers, not needing to ask what they were. "Aww, looks like McFuckin had to hire some lawyers so he could swing some weight around."

I stood aghast. "What? Throwing weight around, what does that mean?"

Carl said nothing and looked at me as though I just didn't get it. He headed to the kitchen to fix a drink.

"Wait a minute!" I was beside myself. "What do you think this is, some kind of pissing contest?! This is no freaking game!"

Carl halted, sighed, and turned back to me. His apparent lack of concern changed to kind understanding.

"I know that, hon. And I know how upset you must be to maybe be losing the house." He hugged me but backed away as he sensed my tense body. "Look, this is not the only house in the world." Now I looked at Carl like *he* didn't get it. "Remember how excited we were getting about the house in Auburn? Well, we won't be in that house, but you know what? A house is just a house."

Carl's nonchalance, disdain, and half-hearted sympathy proved too much for me. I sank to the floor in sobs, crumpling the papers. A thousand emotions whirled through me so fast that I couldn't dwell on just one. I felt like I'd suddenly been wrenched from the steering wheel of a runaway car and hurled to the back seat.

Carl approached, bent over to pat my shoulder, causing a few drops of his drink to fall on my head. My hand shot to my head, furiously rubbing the offended spot. Then it stiffened upright as my arm extended, signaling Carl had best get out of my sight.

I curled further into myself, still racked with sobs. My arms, crossing and squeezing my rib cage, felt like a vise. *What the hell had happened here? What the hell was going to happen?*

CHAPTER 23

WEIGHT LIFTING

Overriding everything was my unbridled desperation to keep my house, a goal which seemingly held very little value for Carl.

"Can't you please agree to pay him that fee, whatever the hell it was, and, Jesus, anything else that's incurred for that matter...just so we can stay here?!" I pleaded.

"I am not dealing with that asshole," Carl said firmly. He gave a sharp look towards me. "And neither are you."

"Why in the world have you two locked horns?"

"I told you, he's an unreasonable asshole. So, drop it, for chrissakes!"

So unpleasant were such confrontations that I did drop it temporarily, only to run into increasingly heated standoffs each time I brought it up. Why these two men continued this mutual antagonism was beyond me. I could only cling to my idealistic belief and hope that nobody with a shred of decency would go through with something so unfair. Unfair to me, damn it!

I also considered deeply unfair the fact that Carl's efforts to find work were nowhere near as intense as previously. Besides a brief stint of three weeks at a local restaurant, Carl had no irons in the fire. I, on the other hand, had taken on a part-time job along with Vivien and another teacher. We would rise early two or three times a week to clean swimming pools at various apartment complexes. Most sites entailed straightforward labor, e.g., scrubbing the tile rims, vacuuming, backwashing, etc. One site, though, usually involved some sort of disgusting hassle, be it broken beer bottles on the pool deck or underwear caught in the drain. And there was always a dead creature of some sort in the filter baskets. Still, the money was good for work that was usually done by mid-morning.

So it was no small source of irritation for me to find Carl laid out on the couch, cigarette in one hand, coffee—spiked, perhaps?— in the other, watching some idiotic talk show or rerun of *Starsky and Hutch*.

"What's wrong?" I would ask, in bed, my hand resting on Carl's shoulder.

Carl's silence did not fool me. I knew he was still awake. Finally, he responded in what sounded like a barely contained growl. "I don't feel like it."

"Do you think you might be sick?"

"Noo, I'm not sick," he answered, as though replying to a stupid question. After a deep sigh, he said, "Jesus! I'm depressed, can't you see that? Without a job. You know, with nobody hiring. I feel unproductive." His tone took on a hint of mockery. "You're certainly smart enough to figure that out."

Yeah, I'm smart enough to figure out you can't produce a lot from a couch either, I wanted to say, but didn't. Instead, I became frightened that this very strong facet of our marriage was in serious trouble.

"Look, why don't let's give ourselves a little bitty cheap vacation down to Fort Walton? You know, for our nine-month anniversary. I've got some pool money we can use."

I thought Carl might have dropped off to sleep since no answer was forthcoming. Finally I heard a muffled "OK."

The trip did the trick. A depressingly mechanical session the first night was shoved out of mind by a tangled, leg-encircling, bathing-suit-stretching romp in the surf the next day. Later, cocktails and after-dinner drinks bookended a delicious meal. Slightly tipsy, I was amazed and delighted when Carl pulled me onto the dance floor for one or two clumsy, laugh-filled turns. All served as ample foreplay for a final night of much-needed passion.

"I gotta hand it to you," Carl said on the drive home, one hand casually on the steering wheel, the other clasping mine, "this was one of your better ideas."

"I gotta hand it to you," I smiled, "taking me up on my idea was sheer brilliance."

We chuckled into a comfortable silence, both of us sated and lost in our own thoughts.

My hand felt safe and warm in his. I sighed deeply, gazing out the window. At least part of this marriage was still intact.

Not at all intact, however, was Carl's ability to control his drinking. Much to my chagrin and embarrassment, I found myself actually keeping a haphazard tab on Carl's consumption. I could no longer withhold my increasingly frequent admonitions.

"C'mon, Carl, you're drinking like...like half a bottle of scotch a day!"

"What is this, a fucking inquisition? What are you—are you actually *counting* the number of drinks I have? Is that the level of nagging you've fallen to?!"

I wasn't about to admit that I'd been doing just that. "No, dang it, but you cannot tell me that you don't drink a helluva—"

"Oh, and you don't drink at all, I suppose." A sly look settled onto Carl's face. "Seems like I recall your being pretty lit that last night at the beach..."

I checked my next retort, realizing there was tiny truth to Carl's remark. "Right, I was completely out of my mind," I said, not bothering to withhold sarcasm, and I turned on my heel. The irony did not escape me.

"I feel like I've got cinder blocks strapped to my ankles," I said to Vivien as we fussed with pool vacuum hoses, unwieldy boa constrictors. On this late August day of sweltering humidity, we were more than happy to call it our final pool-cleaning chore. I looked forward to the following week's start of school as a troubled ship would a safe harbor. I'd finally unburdened myself of the angst which showed no signs of abating and which I could no longer keep to myself.

"There's all this crap going on and I can't seem to make any headway in resolving it. But when I tell Carl I'm going to speak to McFarlin myself, he first has half a hissy fit, then he tells me communication can only be through the lawyers. We're both listed as defendants on the lawsuit, so we have to behave as a unit, I suppose." I shook my head in dismay while guiding the vacuum back and forth across the pool floor. "Thus my cinder-block anklets."

"Not the must-have accessory," Vivien said. She was on knee pads, scrubbing the scum from the tile rim.

"I keep telling myself I really must wait to put this in perspective and maybe, just maybe down the road I'll laugh about it and take pride in my endurance for fighting for what I believe could be a good marriage." I looked dejected. "But, mark my words: if things don't shape up considerably by our first anniversary, I have no intention of waiting on the second."

"Jeez! I didn't know things had gotten that bad." Vivien pulled up a filter, relieved to find nothing disgusting.

"Hell, I don't know what I think! And the main reason I can't think straight is because I don't know what is going to happen with my house!" Each syllable I uttered gained volume and pitch. "I keep hoping the judge will take pity on us and let us stay in the house if we pay some sort of fine."

"Hate to tell you, but Frank says that's probably not going to happen. They just look at the legality of stuff." Vivien's disgust deepened. "As for your not being able to think straight, my Frank seems to have the same problem." I waited. "He says he can't think about a thing—that would be marrying me, for instance—until he gets this blessed bar exam over and done with."

We both entered the pump room, breathing as shallowly as possible to avoid intake of chlorine fumes.

"Isn't this the second time he's taking it?"

"Yep. I think he flunks it just so he won't have to marry me."

"Uh, boy," I said, flipping the switch to engage backwashing. "What is it with these bad boys?"

"Especially when we girls are so good!"

"Ain't it so!" I nearly shouted. "Well, I tell you what: This girl is about tired of being good all the time...with nothing to show for it." Backwash complete, we exited hurriedly, gulping fresh air.

Vivien was intrigued. "So what are you going to do for your good self?"

I jutted my chin forward. "You know that piano at Marsh I've been drooling over for the past three years?" Vivien nodded excitedly. "And you know we're getting a raise this year?" Another nod.

"Plus, my Master's pay kicks in..." I cast a sly look at Vivien. "...neither of which I've mentioned to Carl." Gathering momentum, I said, "The piano's on sale from ten to six thousand; I figure I'll have another sixty bucks or so a month, I know I can get a loan from the Credit Union—"

"Omigod! You're really going to get it, aren't you?"

"Damn straight."

CHAPTER 24

BACK TO THE GRIND

Relieved to be back at school where I could actually *do* something, I was tickled by my students' humorous butchering of my Italian name—Madame La Balle, Mademoisellini, La Dame de Balles, etc. What didn't tickle me was the sour taste in my mouth as I envisioned my husband—still unemployed—lazing around on the couch—my couch!—with the cats—my cats!—drinking and smoking. All this in my house—my house!

Sitting across from Vivien at the teacher lunch table, I bemoaned my situation, knowing no one could overhear in the lunchroom din.

"You know, I asked myself in my journal why I love Carl, and immediately listed, you know, same ol' same ol', but, I'm not so sure about ambition anymore. God, when I first met him, he came across like some CEO of a major corporation. These days, I'm starting to be afraid that he wants to make a ton of money with very little effort." Then, somewhat sheepishly, "Would you believe he's had four jobs since I've known him?"

Vivien simply nodded, unable to come up with a positive response.

Usually full of back-to-school enthusiasm, my joyous spirit was seriously muted. But I forced myself to participate in some activities—pep rallies, powder puff football and the like—knowing that some semblance of normalcy was of utter necessity to counteract the suffocating malaise at home.

Determined not to be completely downtrodden by this, I made good on my intention previously divulged to Vivien: On Labor Day, in a come-hell-or-high-water state of mind, I entered Marsh Piano and placed my order for my very own baby grand.

Carl scrounged up a couple interviews, one in Atlanta. I wouldn't even contemplate how we might manage living in Atlanta. I knew I wouldn't be moving anywhere until I was positive Carl's job was going to stick. I shrugged when Carl told me someone else—a turkey, no doubt—had been hired. Carl also visited The Cap'n, his dad, now living in St. Pete, Florida, for another one of their 'new venture' discussions—I had a hard time keeping up with them—which proved equally inauspicious.

Suddenly it was October, crispy, clear and colorful. I would not, however, feel the usual shivers of excitement when the smoky scent from wood-fire chimneys pervaded the cool nights. Concern deepened by the day, to the point that I was having second thoughts about my piano purchase, still undisclosed to Carl. How could I have been so rash during such uncertain times? As insult upon injury, Carl came home one evening, his face contorted in pain, his body bent at the waist, one hand on the back of his neck.

"Omigod, what happened? What's wrong?"

Carl spoke in short, anguished breaths. "No idea...something pulled up...hurts like hell...couldn't get to interview..."

Seeing he really was desperately uncomfortable, I made sure to hide any scorn or resentment that had been steadily building up.

"We better get you to the emergency room!"

A pinched nerve was the diagnosis, the pain of which could be mitigated either by surgery (out of the question) or home therapy (more like it). Carl was to sit motionless for thirty minutes three times a day, his head encased in stabilizing straps. Attached to this headgear was another strap which ran through an overhead pulley and then hung midair behind the chair. At the end of the strap, a weight provided steady traction. If ever there was an excuse to put the job search on hold, I was looking at it. Masking my impatience and worry of recent months, I showed concern and kindness in helping my husband overcome this untimely obstacle.

Harder to mask, though, was my urge to laugh out loud at the comical sight of Carl in his compromised posture. Lowering the weight caused the head straps to transform Carl's face: cheeks, eyes and brows scrunched toward his nose; his lips became a pink, fleshy cheerio, which took on various shapes whenever Carl tried to talk. Several times I had to exit the room, rush to the bathroom and flush the toilet to drown out my laughter.

I contained all outbursts of mirth until one day, with Carl in traction and me installed on the couch grading papers, Sinclair, nonchalance personified, strolled past the suspended weight at the end of the strap. Carl, unaware of Sinclair, adjusted his position, causing the weight to move slightly. Intrigued, Sinclair watched the weight tick-tock to a standstill. Sinclair wanted a replay. He lifted his front paw, gave a slight back swing and...whack! Carl let out a howl as his head lurched upwards. His hands clasped the sides of his head, trying to steady it as the weight swung wildly. I ejected from the couch and grabbed the swinging weight, guiding it to a soft stop. But I couldn't stop my giggles.

I doubled over with laughter, which only got louder when I heard Carl mutter, "Fucking hilarious."

Sinclair was nowhere in sight.

Finally, a seeming godsend: In the second week of October, Carl was hired as manager of a classy restaurant, Mountainside, some fifty commutable miles from Birmingham. A very attractive salary gave further cause for celebration, but all we could do was breathe a huge sigh of relief. Tension, so very close to the edge, retreated, but only temporarily.

Now, Carl and I became ships passing in the night with our diametrically opposed schedules. I had to tiptoe around in the early morning as I prepped for work, while Carl had to do the same when he returned after an hour's drive in the wee hours of morning. We had seen more of each other when Carl worked at Auburn, nearly twice as far away. The distance between us seemed to be more than one of miles.

CHAPTER 25

HOME UNSWEET HOME

Barely a week after Carl's re-hiring, the looming lawsuit and trial demanded attention. Believing that having an income would soften Carl's antagonism towards McFarlin, I tried once again to persuade him to settle before the trial took place in early December.

"I'm not about to back down to that little worm and his dishonest bastard of an attorney," said Carl.

I shrieked, "Nasty, no doubt. But dishonest? I don't think so! The sad truth is that their case is rock solid."

"I'll tell you who's at fault! It's the damned real estate company. They should've advised us to put in a contingency clause! What we ought to do is counter sue!"

"Yep, a contingency clause would've been nice, but *we* should've thought of it ourselves, I'm afraid." I wanted to add that we *damn* well should have, based on Carl's lousy employment record, but his anger seemed to be escalating. Seeing Carl's resolute expression, I slumped my shoulders and wailed, "I cannot believe I'm going to get kicked out of my house!"

Instantly Carl retaliated, his head circling in mock repetition, his voice a nah-nahing nasalized whine. "You're always saying '*My* house, it's *my* house!' Hell, I thought we *both* lived in this house. How am I supposed to think your heart's in this marriage when you're always saying 'Mine! Mine! Mine!'?"

"Well, yes, it is my house," I sniffled. "But I was perfectly willing to share it with you."

"So if it's your house, you can pay for the damn house. And you can pay for the damn case as well. It's not my fault McFarlin's being such a hardass. That's only fair."

Appalled, I cried, "That is not fair! If you were to *share* your precious car," I nah-nahed right back, "only for me to drive recklessly and wreck it—you'd damn sure expect me to pay for it." I hesitated, wondering if I should voice my next thought. "But you—you!—are being reckless with my house...I don't even know why we're in this situation...why you and McFarlin seem bent on destroying each other, while I—*me*, damn it!—I'm caught here in the middle!"

Carl's presence became even more domineering, his entire body teeming with pent-up frustration and anger. He snarled, "Oh yeah. I can see it now: We lose the case. Then, for the rest of our lives, you hold it over my head that—*because of my recklessness*—" Carl's voice approaching a sneer now, "you lost your precious fuck-ing house."

No shit Sherlock, I thought, but I chose to keep my mouth shut. Having experienced physical confrontation preceded by an argu-ment much like the current one, I dared not drive an argument to a point that invited blows. Not that I thought for a moment that Carl would actually strike me. Tonight's verbal sparring match frightened and confused me. I'd become the burnt dog who dreads the fire.

As indignant as I was at being called unfair, I simply couldn't grab hold of a convincing point, something that would give me the upper hand in this argument. No matter what I threw at Carl, he twisted it around and threw it back at me. Never had I wished so strongly to be somewhere else, but I knew it would have to be by virtue of some force outside of me, because any remnants of energy and fortitude were evaporating into thin air.

Watching the dramatic deflation of my defiance, Carl's voice softened. "Look, we've said from the beginning that our 'breach of contract' was not intentional; it was due to circumstances beyond our control. Any judge worth his salt will pay attention to that." Having heard no such words of encouragement from our lawyer, my shoulders sagged, reflecting my skepticism. "We're going to trial and we'll have our say then." Carl's hands squeezed my shoulders, signaling the end of the conversation.

I dragged myself to school the next day, promising I would go home immediately afterwards and hit my journal. But, having some time due to an inspirational speaker's disrupting classes, I tore some legal sheets from a pad. Intending to list the many points swirling around about the upcoming lawsuit, I watched my pen as it instead wrote:

Reasons For Divorce

Oh my, there it is in black and white. I sighed. I began, scribbling furiously, to list usual pros and mounting cons (smoking, drinking, laziness, faulty reasoning in arguments, etc., etc., the list seemed interminable...). It didn't take long to see that the negatives far outweighed the positives. Talk about writing on the wall. But I knew there was no way I could act on any of this until the outcome with the house was known. It was all too much to handle.

On a beautiful, crispy November Friday afternoon, my piano was delivered. A beautiful Kawai baby grand, of Brazilian rosewood seemed absolutely meant for its new position in front of the bay window of the small front parlor. I had waited until the previous evening to divulge my purchase.

"Oh boy, that's rich!" Carl had snorted. "You're all over me about finances, and yet, here you go, spending no telling how much money on a stupid piano!" He added, somewhat spitefully, "...that you're never going to be able to play worth a damn."

I refused to be ruffled. "You sell your car and I'll cancel the order."

So exuberant was my mood on delivery day, Carl opted to indulge, seemingly getting a kick out of the long stretch of paper towels I had placed across the keyboard with the message, "Isn't It Gorgeous?!!"

That bright moment may have warded off dark conversations momentarily, but they returned in ferocious fashion as the trial date loomed less than two weeks away. On the night before our one-year anniversary, we lashed out at each other again. I practically demanded that Carl settle with McFarlin before the trial.

"I cannot *believe* you keep bringing this up. Here I am, sweating my brow, driving a hundred and twenty-five miles a day, *trying* to build us a future...for what? This bullshit?!" He rushed on. "You and your striving for Utopia crap! Do you really think there's any solution that can be reached without a trial? You're such a Pollyanna." His look was almost one of pity as he regarded me.

But I still believed there was one—one—chance in hell that I could save my house, and I was the one who would have to take it, seeing as no support was forthcoming from Carl.

Early the next morning, grey with a chilly rain, I found myself on McFarlin's front stoop, waiting a full five minutes before placing a hesitant finger on the doorbell. I knew Carl would explode if he knew I was there, but I was determined to make this last-ditch effort.

McFarlin opened the door, stared in amazement at my trembling figure under the dripping umbrella. After a moment, and with great reluctance, he let me in.

"You know I'm not supposed to communicate with you at all," McFarlin said, totally neutral.

"I know, but I feel like I must come to the source. Listen, I know you and my husband have locked horns for some reason, and I don't even care what that's about. All I care about is my house. I mean, *it's mine*. Surely, surely, there's another house that would suit you. I distinctly remember your telling me, way back when the lawsuit began, that you had had your eye on another one."

For a moment, I thought I detected a shred of pity or acquiescence in this man who dangled my fate on a string, but it passed quickly and was replaced by a stone-cold poker face. "That was then, this is now."

"But—"

"My hands are tied, sorry. Everything is up to the lawyers and the judge now."

"What do you mean your hands are tied?! You're living and breathing aren't you? You've hired the lawyers; can't you un-hire them, for God's sake?"

McFarlin gave a slow but resolute shake of his head.

"Look," I said, desperate now, "I have two hundred and forty-seven dollars in the credit union. You can have every penny and I swear we'll...or I will...make good on that inspection fee." McFarlin's face was set.

Much to my disgust and embarrassment, I began to cry, despite my vow not to do so. I'd hoped to appeal to McFarlin's sense of decency, not his pity. But now, between sobbing hiccups, I said, "Oh, God, please, please don't do this. I know you must not care for Carl but, you know, he is my *husband*, and all this has put a horrible strain on the marriage. I mean, today is our one-year anniversary, and—" I gulped, "—and this may well be the undoing of everything..." More sobs overtook me for a moment until I was able to implore one last time, "Please."

I waited, hoping for a miracle, but heard only McFarlin's empty response. "Like I said, there's nothing I can do. You have to leave." Then, the curt addendum, "Sorry."

Wishing for all the world that I could leave in a flurry of defiance, I couldn't even lift my head from the total defeat that enveloped me. Opening the door myself, I only managed to mutter weakly, "Yeah, you're sorry all right." I pulled the door shut behind me.

I turned, crying softly, having learned two things. I would lose my home. And I would hate lawyers for the rest of my life.

"Where've you been?" Carl asked, as I shook my umbrella and raincoat on the front porch.

"Out. Nowhere, really. Just went for a ride."

Carl cast a dubious look to the sky and the mist encircling the porch. "Great day for it." He didn't press for further explanation. Then, softly, "Oh, by the way, hon, happy anniversary."

I managed a "you, too," and went to my new piano, where I sat until I had to get ready for an anniversary dinner at the country club, a treat from my parents.

In the beautifully appointed dining room, the four of us toasted our milestone and fell into conversation, mainly about the lawsuit.

Because I'd spent over a year mastering the talent, I simply went into auto-pilot.

"Can't you just talk to this guy?" Mama asked as though stating the obvious.

"Nope," I said, my tone unconcerned but not flippant, "there's nothing we can do until the trial. It's the way the legal system works, you know." I was trying my best to ease the deep creases of concern and skepticism on both my parents' faces.

"You know how those lawyers are, Edward," Carl said to Daddy as though sharing a private joke. "Pond scum."

"Can't argue with that," Daddy said. But he didn't smile.

Neither he nor Mama asked a lot of questions, not wanting, I assumed, to appear nosy or belligerently defensive for their daughter's welfare. Whether Carl sensed their restraint from saying 'Something's not adding up here,' I surely did. I dared not look directly at them for fear of seeing a great big 'Are you going to stand for this?'

At the trial two weeks later, the judge—as though on auto-pilot himself—quickly reached his decision to award the house to McFarlin for breach of contract. The current occupants were given three months to vacate the premises.

When was it, exactly, that I donned those blinders?

I direct my question to the sky as bright and clear as my hindsight. They just kinda slipped onto the sides of my head, like on those horses pulling those big-city tourist carriages. Those blinders not only restrict the view ahead, they block out any sense of the whole picture. In those days, I was nowhere close to *getting the picture,* completely missing that so many brush strokes were by the hand of Carl himself.

Those plane tickets to San Juan? Undoubtedly fake and meant to cushion the blow of the imminent legal notice. What I took as head-butting between two testosteronic males was madness of deep method. That lawsuit? Stroke of genius. Losing ownership of my house gave Carl greater ownership of me. I didn't see it, blinder-clad that I was.

I sip on my hot tea, lamenting that its comforting powers are no match for these distasteful recollections.

The two weeks at my sister's when the twenty bucks went missing? My face scrunches up in disgust. That sonofabitch! Of course Carl was the one who took it. Then he planted that seed of doubt. What a nasty little game he was playing! I bet he felt like he'd gotten away with something, *twice.* Shame on you, Rosie-Rose.

No doubt about it, though, the man could make you believe anything. He could tell you to look at the snow, you'd look out the window at a sunny summer day and say, "Oh, isn't it beautiful? I love snow!"

As for our 'funny' games...the chases, the naked pictures, the sneak attacks...OK, those were funny. But isn't it also funny that so many of our 'funnies' revolved around making fun...of me?

Like those apathetic horses, I had lowered my head and focused on the job at hand which, for the most part, was trudging mindlessly along, ignoring (or misreading) any and all distractions.

A long, low sigh slowly escapes as I survey still more journals, calendars and papers to trudge through.

God, what else?

CHAPTER 26

NEXT TO THE NEXT TO THE LAST STRAW

I sat in stunned silence on the luxuriously upholstered seat of Carl's car—a hearse, as far as I was concerned. The verdict—arrived at in staggeringly swift fashion—was just as Harriet's Frank had predicted: by the book. We breached. We fucked up. The only kindness or fairness was in the lengthy grace period for us to find another place to live and move out. I was too shocked to cry. I simply could not believe my house had been stolen from me.

Carl, equally close-mouthed, drove us home from the court-house. Not even a pinprick of light or hope. What was I to do now? Divorce Carl? As belligerent as he had been during the whole house thing, I did not—could not—imagine he'd actually envisioned a consequence such as the one we were in. Plus, if I were to divorce him, how in the hell was I going to afford another house on my salary with real estate having gone through the roof in the past three years? No way could I do it alone. Would I then have to move back in with my parents? And thereby admit defeat after only a year? The idea was anathema to me.

The only clear thought I could summon from the confused glob in my mind was that I needed to find some place to live! And I had to decide if that some place would be lodgings for one or two. Divorcing meant moving to an apartment which would be a huge step backwards in living accommodations and money management. Staying married meant buying a house—quickly; a risky if not downright foolish proposition. Either way, tacked on to the moving expense would be the extra five hundred dollars for moving my piano, suddenly more like an albatross than a treasured, albeit somewhat defiant, gift to myself.

My confused thoughts bounced through my head like pin balls. Had I been forced to bet then and there on the likelihood of this marriage's success, I knew where my chips would have fallen.

But, oh, the massive serving of crow I'd have to consume...I couldn't even go there. No, in my jumbled mind and wounded spirit, I didn't see any other alternative than to hold my head down and fight through this storm.

Within a week after the December 5 court ruling, Carl and I spent a decidedly non-festive Christmas holiday house-hunting... the second time since we were married. While our first bout, in Auburn, was marked by tentative excitement, this time around was a mixture of desperation and half-hearted interest. We chose another almost-constructed home on a dead-end street in a new, nearly empty neighborhood.

I deflected the cautious misgivings voiced by my parents and friends, acknowledging things looked bleak but insisting I wasn't one to run away from a challenge. Not one soul, especially me, pointed out that all these *challenges* could be traced directly to Carl. My response would have been that I was not going to be one of those nagging wives.

Besides, the ocean of anger that roiled within me was directed not at Carl but at McFarlin. He was the son of a bitch who'd kicked me out of my house. He said he had had no choice. But he did. There was nothing I could do about it now.

I told myself Carl and I were now on a new road, still working towards mutual goals. What we'd experienced with my house was a terrible misfortune—an injustice, really—but, hey, life wasn't fair sometimes. Contending with life's knocks was something all couples did, and that's exactly what we were doing. Oh yes, I was in it for the long haul.

My deep grief at losing my cherished home was alleviated somewhat by the bubbling up of my creative juices. I enthused in decorating and building another nest for, yes, two. I dove into the choosing of paint colors, bath and kitchen fixtures, carpets, etc.

Carl, meantime, seemed busy and more content with his work. It was as though we'd both come to a crossroads together, and disliking the challenges of the single-lane side-roads, silently chose to forge on ahead on the double highway, refusing to consider that it, too, could just as well collide into a dead end.

One night, shortly after midnight, I received a phone call.

"Is this Mrs. Ballini?" A man's voice was official, authoritative. My heart sank, somehow knowing this couldn't be good news.

"This is Highway Patrolman Johnson, sorry to inform you your husband, Carl Ballini, has been arrested for driving under the influence."

I sighed.

"His car has been impounded, so he says you'll need to come pick him up."

"And where might that be?" I wondered if the patrolman could hear my teeth gritting.

"Pell City," he said, somewhat apologetically.

I got out of bed, drove the thirty miles to the HP station, picked up Carl (busily chewing gum, so as to lower the reading on the Breathalyzer), and brought him thirty miles back home. When we pulled up to the curb, I uttered the only words spoken during the entire trip. "The drinking stops *now*."

Carl nodded dutifully.

At school the following week, I was notified by the mortgage company that the loan could not be approved unless the deposit was increased from ten to twenty percent. This, they explained, was due to Carl's poor credit rating.

The very next night, a call woke me, this one from the Jefferson County jail, where they'd transported Carl after his involvement in a horrific wreck which totaled his beloved pimp mobile, and severely damaged the pickup truck of the other person involved. Fortunately, no one was killed and injuries were slight, a miracle when I later saw pictures of Carl's car.

"Tell him I'll pick him up tomorrow after I'm done with work," I said, declining to voice my thoughts that the s.o.b. could stay there for all I cared.

After school, I found myself again in the humiliating position of having to pick up my husband in jail. Carl swore he hadn't been drinking and it was the other guy's fault.

Another deathly silent ride home ensued. Finally, Carl broke the silence.

"Can I please borrow your car tomorrow? If I don't show up for work, they might fire me."

Carl's paycheck was critical. I bummed a ride to school for the rest of the week.

This proved to be the proverbial straw.

I did not allow myself to think of anything but getting this ridiculously difficult and unpleasant obstacle out of my life. On the last day of January 1979, I packed a few things, placed my bag next to the front door, and waited for Carl to come home with my means of transportation.

Upon entering the house, Carl first spotted the suitcase and then he saw me seated calmly on the couch. In an instant, he knew what was at stake, and his face was a mixture of disbelief, horror, sorrow and, yes, desperation.

"Aw, c'mon hon, don't do this now! I know I've been fucking up recently but I'm on the right track!"

"So, do you have your own car to travel that right track?" I managed to keep all but a tinge of sarcasm in my voice. I merely was trying to point out only one of the multiple obstacles I no longer cared to contend with: the idiocy of our trying to continue our jobs with one vehicle.

"I'm going to get a good, cheap, used car this weekend! I told you I was going to do that!"

I didn't remember and didn't really care. I simply said, "Carl, I don't see how this is going to work. I keep thinking it can't get any worse, but then it does. I'm sorry, but I can't do this. I can't see any other option for us than divorce. I'm going to stay at Vivien's a few days, you and I will see a lawyer, get the papers drawn up for a no-fault divorce, and just let this be over. This is *not* the way I envisioned married life."

My numbed expression quickly disappeared when the next thing I saw was Carl falling to his knees, in tears, as he earnestly besought me for a full fifteen minutes non-stop.

"Omigod, no. Please. God, I can't even think of how my life would be if I didn't have you in it with me. You gotta quit being such an idealist, hon! There is no perfect marriage, for chrissake, and we are never going to live in Utopia." Carl's face darkened slightly. "You and your *Atlas Shrugged* shit; I knew—"

As though suddenly deciding against this tack, Carl's expression returned to one of pleading. "Please, hon, come out of the clouds and get down to reality. Work with me, hon. You know I love you more than anything. All I want is for us to be happy, but you've just got to help me on this. I can't do it by myself. C'mon, hon, you know, you and me, we're a team. We can make this work." Carl lowered his head to my knee. I watched in amazement as his shoulders shook from ragged sobs.

My resolve dissipated as I considered the consequences to both of us. I did not want to be a cruel, hard woman, and I surely didn't want to destroy Carl. Just as parents don't desert misbehaving kids, wives remain—at least for a while—with irresponsible husbands. Carl had pissed me off royally, but damn it, I still cared for him deeply.

A few moments passed, the only sounds being Carl's jagged breathing and my strangled peeps of indecision. I looked at Carl, an abject huddle at my feet, truly looking like a lost soul. I wondered briefly what he might actually do, should I leave him.

And my heart turned back the other way, toward Carl. My shoulders raised and lowered as I sighed deeply. Carl's earnestness was nearly palpable. Never had I seen his face so open, so pleading. I couldn't do it; I couldn't leave.

"Yes, I do think we are both totally capable of making this work. I repeat, both. This cannot be anything but a total team effort." Feeling drained but oddly proud of my spirit and kindness, I looked deeply into Carl's pleading eyes. "OK?"

"OK," he whispered. He kissed my hands, petted all three cats, got up and fixed himself a glass of...water.

I was too drained to think or see beyond the present minute. When I heard Carl close the bathroom door and turn on the shower, I rose and went to the bedroom, retrieved my journal and placed it in the drawer of my desk in the dining room.

"You coming to bed?" Carl asked softly, leaning against the door frame. I turned my attention from the pile of papers in front of me on the desk surface.

"In a bit," I said, neutral. "Got some more grading to do." I smiled at Carl's nod of understanding and listened to him walk back down the hall. I waited until I heard his unmistakable steady breathing to pull the journal from the drawer. For the next forty-five minutes, I recorded the gamut of my emotions ending with the pride-robbing derailment a few hours earlier. Tilting the chair, I raised my arms so my hands cupped my head as it gently rolled back and forth. Pressed lips accentuated my wry expression as the front legs of the chair returned to the floor with a soft thud. I closed my fitful journaling with one last comment:

January 31, 1979 ... God, if this is happiness, I'd like to trade it for three pounds of fresh shit.

CHAPTER 27

AND THE SHOW MUST GO ON

With shaky determination, I continued packing up the house—an undertaking thoroughly enjoyed by the cats, especially Sinclair, who left no box un-jumped-into! Closing on the new house and moving had to be rescheduled, allowing for Carl's court appearance for his DUI. With very little fuss, Carl and I decided to forego any sort of Valentine's celebration: too much packing and studying was my excuse; a busy night at the restaurant was Carl's. Neither of us wanted to admit that we were still a bit raw from the emotional dispute a mere two weeks earlier.

I awoke extra early the following morning so I could do a quick ride around the neighborhood to find Sinclair, who'd apparently gone on one his escapades. I pulled away from the curb and slowly circled a few blocks, calling occasionally to no avail. Needing to head to school, I rode past my street and made a quick glance toward my house. In the blank space where I had parked, I saw a small mound, tan and black in color.

I screamed. "Oh, God, no! Please, no!" I jerked my car up the street and parked, the tires jumping the curb. Cradling Sinclair's lifeless, limp body, my head flung backwards as I keened a low mournful moan. I recalled that traffic had been rerouted for a few hours the day before for some construction a block over. Sinclair, unused to the heavy traffic flow, must have been hit and knocked back under my car. Thinking that he probably died a slow death all through the night turned my moan primal.

I flew up the steps to the house and entered the bedroom where Carl still slept. My screeching sobs jolted him awake. Looks of aggravation, then confusion, and then utter sorrow swept over Carl's face. He loved that crazy cat almost as much as I did. Joined completely in grief, Carl and I cradled Sinclair into a small box, carried him to our new home, and buried him in back.

I tried not to think that life in our new home would start with a death.

On a brilliant, chilly Friday morning in February, after two postponements, we finally closed on our new home. I wondered why Carl had seemed so nervous during the entire meeting. Holding his hand on the way back to the car, I kidded him for being such a wuss. "You know, people close on houses every day. It's not as frightening as all that."

Carl took a short breath. "Well, it's a little frightening if you've just been fired."

He may as well have hauled off and hit me with a two-by-four. I couldn't even look at him, but said nothing, knowing that anything I said would be full of disgust, rancor, and judgment, and most likely regrettable. I crumpled into tears in the front seat, wanting only to go home and curl up. But there was no home to go to. Today was also moving day.

As scheduled, the moving van sat in front of the house, waiting for our return from the closing. I felt Carl's eyes on me as though in wait for some catastrophic reaction. But I had no energy for any catastrophe other than the one occurring right in front of me. One which, even though I never wanted it, I had indeed chosen. I dried my eyes, got out of the car and gently shut the car door. Looking at Carl, who sat frozen behind the wheel, I said simply, "Just go. To the house. Wherever. I don't care. I'll handle this."

Carl pulled slowly away from the curb. I couldn't decide if the relief on his face was from not having a full-blown argument or from not having to do any work.

Before addressing the three muscular men who were exiting the cab of the truck, I clenched my fist and fought back any brimming tears. For a fleeting moment I considered telling the guys to leave, but then, what would I do with the stuff in the house...the house that was no longer mine? I simply had no other choice than to stay with the current program. Whether I liked it or not, this was one of those times when all one could do was suck it up and carry on.

Squaring my shoulders, I turned and greeted the guys with as sporty a smile as I could muster. "OK, gentlemen, let's get this show on the road." Fearing mightily this show was destined to bomb, I tottered onstage to play my part for now.

After five hours of frenzied loading furniture and boxes into the van, I squeezed into the cab with three sweaty, stinky men. (I hadn't thought about this when I sent Carl away in my car.) I let the guys chat among themselves while I tried to contemplate exactly where in the hell I was going, other than the physical address to which we were headed. Where that was, was a new home with a huge mortgage in both our names. No way in the world could I manage the payment by myself. I felt like a prisoner being led to my cell. I fought back tears as the truck pulled into the driveway of my brand new unhappy home.

I directed the unloading with utmost efficiency, thanks to my having clearly labeled each box with contents and location. Finally, the men brought in the very last item, my prized possession, my brand new piano. I could hardly watch as the men struggled with it, taking great pains to maintain its pristine condition. They removed their belts so no buckles could scratch the surface. I was so nervous I actually found my Kahlua and fixed a drink, wryly musing what Carl would have to say about that. Speaking of whom, I noted, had not shown his face during the entire moving process. For this, I was more relieved than irritated. I wasn't sure I could have handled dealing with the movers and my newly unemployed husband.

About 9 p.m., as I was busily unpacking another box, the front door opened and Carl appeared with bags of fast food. I could hardly look at him, but my eyes fell on the food and I gasped, realizing how famished I was. I mumbled a thank you and the two of us sat on the cold stone hearth, contemplating the scattered piles of boxes and paper before us. In silence, we consumed our first meal at our new home.

Afterwards, I was dimly pleased to see that Carl was trying to make himself useful, carrying out trash, ripping open boxes, arranging his toiletries in his bathroom, and basically staying out of my way. At 1:00 a.m., I fell into bed, utterly exhausted. Carl crawled in on the other side. The two of us lay there until the silence became almost ridiculous.

"You've *got* to get a job," I said finally.

"I know. I know."

CHAPTER 28

AND THE SHIT KEEPS COMING

Certain that Carl knew *in no uncertain terms* that getting a job was paramount, I went about keeping up my side of our bargain to be a team. I dove into making the house a home and found myself becoming the tiniest bit endeared to my new digs. I absolutely adored that everything was new and clean and in perfect working order. I loved living on a dead-end, virtually traffic-free street, and I loved that the backyard was flanked by deep woods. Everything was very private and I could see the house's potential to actually become a romantic retreat.

One evening of the first week, I was unpacking a box of crystal and china when Carl entered the dining room with a small package.

As he handed it to me, he said in a voice shaking with emotion, "This is certainly *not* the housewarming present I wanted to give you."

Almost alarmed, I opened the gift.

It was a plaque, much like the awards given to outstanding students, winning teams, etc. The engraving read,

Sinclair ~ You were one fine pussycat.

"I thought we better let that damn cat know we still miss the hell out of him," Carl said, drawing me close as we both gave way to sobs.

It was the sweetest thing Carl had ever done for me.

When I wasn't busy at home, I was of course deeply involved at work and with accounting classes on Monday and Thursday evenings. I attended the first nine meetings after which I finally accepted that I simply had too much on my plate. I dropped the course, forfeiting the remainder of my tuition fee.

Within a month of losing the managerial job in Gadsden, Carl was able to land a job at a small but popular restaurant by the airport. I tried to be as supportive as I could as Carl set out for his first night on the job.

"True it's no Mountainside, but then again you don't have to drive fifty freaking miles to get there." I tried my best not to sound like a cajoling parent. "A ten-minute commute sounds pretty good to me."

"Whoop-dee-damn-doo," Carl muttered, straightening his tie.

I brushed some cat hair from the lapel and looked at Carl. "You know, you look damn good in a suit."

Carl smiled briefly and headed down the sidewalk, his hands doing that funny little flick at the wrists. I watched him, thinking he'd look even better in a suit if he'd square those shoulders.

A few hours later, I was finally getting around to unpacking the silverware, when I heard Carl trudge up the sidewalk.

"So, how was it?" I asked as brightly as possible without sounding too Pollyanna-ish.

Carl cast an irritated look at me. "Boy, this is going to be one piece of shit job."

My mood lowered quickly. "I'm sorry, Carl, but even a piece of shit job will help pay our piece of shit mortgage, which just so happens to be three times the other one."

"God, there you go! I told you you'd be forever on my case about *your* house. If you think I'm going to grovel on the floor, begging your forgiveness each time you bring that up—"

"Don't be ridiculous," I said, "I was merely pointing out—"

Carl's voice got louder. "Here's what's ridiculous: our staying together." He hesitated, as if testing whether to continue. "I say we get a divorce."

I stared at Carl. Just like that, he'd offered me an out that would put an end to my constant angst. Somewhat dazed, I said, "Fine."

Carl stared back at me, waiting for some kind of discussion, but I'd returned to unpacking.

"Fine, then," he said. "I'll sleep on the couch and be out of here tomorrow."

I lay alone in bed the next morning, wondering when I was ever going to get a good night's sleep. The exchange with Carl the previous night came rushing back into my head, and I groaned. I wondered which unpleasant scene would confront me first. Argument? Unpacking? Packing? I started to roll out of bed, but stopped upon seeing Carl's figure fill the door frame. He held a tray laden with freshly cooked bacon, eggs and toast, and a crystal bud vase holding a single pine needle.

"Obviously," Carl stretched out each syllable, "an evil spirit overtook me last night and said a really stupid thing." I wriggled to an upright position and remained silent. "I don't want a divorce. I want you." Ever so lightly, he placed his hand on mine.

I looked at the breakfast tray, which looked delicious, and then at Carl, who looked as if he'd slept no better than I had, but who looked as earnest and loving as he did on the day we said our wedding vows.

I was so tired.

"No, the idea of divorce does not appeal to me either." I smiled weakly at Carl. "Whereas this breakfast..." I flapped open a napkin and tucked it into my tee shirt.

I heard a whoosh of relief escape Carl's lips. I wondered if he'd noticed I hadn't said I wanted him, too. But, I did. Or did I? I couldn't think about it. I picked up a piece of bacon and sank my teeth into it.

Later that afternoon, I kissed Carl lightly as he left for work, refraining from wishing him well at his piece of shit job. That would be all this fragile peace needed to completely implode.

My favorite time of the week was Sunday morning. Unlike Saturday's errand-filled, project-laden nature with squeezed in-tennis match, Sunday was all about a slow cup of coffee, a leisurely read of the paper, and usually a pleasant outing of some kind. I hoped this Sunday would provide some respite from the stress of the preceding forty-eight hours. I might even try to dwell on this godforsaken domestic dilemma and stop it from swirling around in my head. Maybe Carl and I could discuss things quietly today and, who knows, conclude that divorce was the route to take. No doubt Carl sensed that I wasn't entirely back in the fold.

I rose before Carl, who'd moved back to the bedroom after only one night on the couch, and plodded to the kitchen to feed the cats. Frau Eva rubbed against my legs, happily anticipating her breakfast. I bent down just far enough so that she could stand on her hind legs and bump heads with me. I desperately missed Sinclair, but I still had lots of love for my two remaining cats.

Speaking of which... "So, where's your buddy?" I asked Frau Eva, who had no answer to my ignored question. "Where's Mona Bone?" I called, quietly at first, so as not to disturb Carl. The cat was nowhere in the house so I figured he must've been left outside overnight. "Dang," I muttered, "he's not familiar enough with his new territory."

"What'd you say?" Carl had walked sleepily into the living room.

"Mona Bone's gone. Have you seen him at all?"

"Nope." He went back to the bedroom to change. "Here, you call in the woods; I'll drive around the neighborhood to see if I can find him."

Frantic, I spent the next two hours crashing through the woods, calling constantly for my oldest cat who, I had to admit, probably loved me more than either of the other two. Well, one, now. God, please don't let me lose another cat! Not now!

Sunday dragged on. Neither Carl nor I had any luck. I had no thoughts for anything other than the distraction of my lost cat.

Hardly able to teach the next day, I bolted home immediately after school to continue my search. There was no need. On the couch sat Carl, with Frau Eva on one side, and Mona Bone on the other, looking absolutely no worse for the wear. I collapsed in relief.

"You silly goose!" I cried, grabbing Mona Bone who immediately positioned himself in my lap. "Where in the bloody hell did you go?"

Carl smiled broadly, obviously as happy as I. "Who the hell knows? He probably got holed up in one of these houses under construction." It seemed as good an explanation as any.

That night, Carl and I lay in bed, grateful to have at least one less troubling thought on our minds. With utmost gentleness, Carl lifted the strap of my nightgown and slid his hand across my breast.

Feeling no resistance, he continued. "God, I've missed this," he whispered to me later.

Still bathed in relief about Mona Bone's return, and now, that wonderful sated feeling that Carl knew so well how to provide, I whispered back, "Me, too."

Encouraged that things might actually turn around, I registered for another class for the spring semester figuring I might as well go ahead and get that accounting degree. Couldn't hurt.

Two weeks after he was hired, Carl was fired from the airport job.

"Not that I'm counting," I said dryly, "but this is the sixth job you've had since I've known you."

"Yep, and I've worked under six assholes."

"Even assholes pay money."

"Look, every other interview I go to, they tell me I'm overqualified."

"Maybe you should tell them you're willing to take a pay cut, since at least it includes the word *pay*. You know we do have this thing called a mortgage."

I watched Carl's jaw tighten and face darken as I figured he must be weighing whether to elevate the argument. He did not. With that funny little shake of his hands, he turned and walked to the bathroom.

"I'm in the shower," he said, his voice neutral.

CHAPTER 29

...AND COMING

For the entire next week, we spoke not one word to each other, easy enough to do since I buried myself in school or housework while Carl sat in sullen repose in front of the TV. This was new to me. I'd never encountered such behavior, not even with my parents or siblings when I was a kid. One day, maybe one and a half, was the longest we could last.

"I never knew Hell could be so freaking quiet."

"I know the place well." Vivien was referring again to her former marriage. I sat at her kitchen table, the designated site for hair-streaking and man-bemoaning. I winced as she pierced the streaking cap with a tiny crochet needle, captured several strands of my hair, and slowly, painfully, pulled them through. I decided that very moment my next streak job would be on short hair.

"At least I'm gone a lot," I said. "Even though I've dropped accounting classes *again*," I rolled my eyes on the last word, "I'm still at Senior Play practice every freaking afternoon." I poured myself a drink as Vivien continued to mutilate my scalp. "I swear, I'm too tired to address the crapola on the home front."

A particularly thick bunch of hair had become tangled and Vivien spent nearly ten minutes trying to separate and tame the strands.

"God," I moaned, "can this get any worse?"

Even with tax day looming, several notices from IRS addressed to Carl had remained unopened on the kitchen counter. I could see the Feds appearing at the front door to arrest Carl for tax evasion. Beside myself with frustration, I waved the envelopes in Carl's face. "So! Here we go again! Does this mean another visit to Sears?"

"Well, if it isn't Little Miss Goody Two-Shoes, coming to make sure all is right with the world, like a little cream puff!"

"Damn it, Carl, I'm not getting in a Sears discussion again, but you are going to have to come straight with your taxes."

"Straight? As in honest? As in perfect? Damn, woman, you're still on that idealist crap you found in that *Atlas* book. That is not the real world!" With that, he grabbed a small dish, a wedding present and one of my favorites, and flung it into the fireplace. There would be no gluing back together the countless shards that flew in all directions.

"I'll tell you what's real," my voice started to shake. "You can't keep a freaking job, your attitude sucks, you're back to drinking too much—"

"You'd have a drink every now and then, too, if you had to put up with all—" Carl stopped, realizing I had turned to walk down the hall, ignoring him.

I didn't want to hear it anymore. Enough of this idiocy! I walked to the bedroom, opened the closet and pulled down my mint green Lady Baltimore for the second time. I placed it on the bed and turned to get some underclothes from the dresser. Carl had walked into the room and immediately noticed the suitcase. Unlike the last time, back at the other house, when he'd seen me packed and poised to go, Carl would not resort to begging. Instead, his voice was a low sneer.

"Aw, whassamatter, is she running away again? Can't take it anymore? Are things not the perfect little paradise they should be?"

Startled by this new tactic, I could find no rejoinder. Running along my spine was a faint charge of fear. He was not finished berating me.

"You know you're really not being fair about all this." Carl's voice was strong, stern, totally confident. "Here I am trying my damnedest to find a decent job, despite still being half laid-up with a bad neck—" Carl ignored my quizzical look, "—and you're off gallivanting around with those students for some totally insignificant play, and yet, you're getting on my case."

Seeing I was not going to retaliate and play the yelling match, Carl continued.

"You stand there in judgment of me, saying *I'm* the one who's not holding up my end of the stick. How in the hell can you say that when half the time you're not here, and when you are, you're walking around like some kind of judge? Damn, woman, you've got me on pins and needles."

Carl's arms hung motionless by his sides, but his hands twitched, one, then the other. "I hardly know which way to step or what to say. I'm down here in the trenches fighting like hell, and you're up there on the fence, not wanting to get your fingers dirty, not taking a stand either way, staying above it all, waiting to see if I'm going to fuck up again at which point you're outta here."

Carl regarded me with total disgust, gathering momentum. "Why should I even do anything if you're sitting back with your arms crossed, like some holy bitch?" Carl snorted again. "How can I put faith in you when you're at such a distance from this relationship? I'm killing myself trying to make this work and yet it's for some woman who can hardly bring herself to say 'I love you.' What kind of motivation is that for me?"

"I *do* love you, Carl." My tone was resentful rather than loving. "It's just that I love you some, not as much as I want to."

An incredulous hoot came from Carl, his voice much louder. "Some?! You love me *some?*" Sarcasm slathered the last word. "That's like being partially pregnant! You either are, or you aren't. You either love me, or you don't!" Carl stepped towards me to drive his point. "You know, hon, you're going to have to plunge in here with me or this thing is never going to work."

I had had enough. I finally found my voice and took a step forward. "How in the hell can you say I'm *above* it all when I've been working my ass—"

Suddenly my ass was on the floor. Carl had thrust out his hand and had actually thrown me down. Well, not thrown, actually, more like pushed. Not exactly a gentle push. But not with evil intent. I was sure of it. Just a reaction to my moving forward. I remained on the floor, ascertaining no part of my body was hurt in any way. It wasn't. It really was almost like I'd lost my balance. Wasn't it? I found it absolutely necessary to continue this line of reasoning. I simply could not entertain the thought that I'd gone and hooked up with another jerk—*another Tristan!*—who hit women. Surely, I had *not* married a freaking wife-beater!

Apparently not, as it turned out, since Carl had left the room.

Several moments passed, and I got up and walked to the living room, where Carl sat in the chair, Mona Bone in his lap. His sneer was gone; his face was simply a question, almost a challenge, as to my next move. He saw my face was closed and neither hand held a suit-case. He watched me walk past him, go to the fridge and fix a bowl of ice cream, topped with almonds and Kahlua.

He could see I'd chosen to go with comfort for the time being.

The ice cream was good but its comfort factor was short-lived. I felt like I was in a state of shock as I tried to process what had just happened. I tried to relive each moment of the scene in the bedroom, not half an hour old, but it was a blur. Much clearer to me was the tone Carl had used when he berated me. I supposed I did look laugh-ably self-righteous, pouting down the hallway, yanking down that suitcase the minute the going got rough. Well, thanks to Tristan, I'd learned rough going could lead to rough consequences. Still, I felt a rush of embarrassment that I could be such a weakling.

As for Carl's 'fence' comment...he had a point, really, saying one either loves or one doesn't. My shoulders straightened a moment. *Damn it, I don't feel foolish saying my love is a qualified love.* I loved Carl's admirable traits but his *unadmirable* ones were seriously undercutting unconditional love. But maybe there was some truth to my being too idealistic.

I needed to give all this some more thought, but I was too exhausted.

CHAPTER 30

OOPS! COMPANY!

Another week of strained civility passed with neither of us wanting to wrangle with what lay upon us like a heavy, sticky net. Working (or looking for work, in Carl's case), studying, or inventing various commitments began to lose their power as avoidance tactics. Driving home one Friday afternoon in April, I conceded that casting off this weight was imminent. Sweeping it under the rug was no longer a possibility; there was no more room underneath. Things must be dealt with.

Recalling the recent 'push' scene, I felt the slightest tinge of fright when contemplating the face-off sure to come this weekend. I took a deep breath as I descended the street to our house. *Oh, well, here goes*, I told myself as I pulled into the driveway, barely managing to slam on brakes to avoid hitting another car.

The car belonged to none other than Carl's parents, who'd arrived earlier in the day for a 'surprise' visit. The screeching of my brakes brought Carl, Cap'n and Peggy out onto the porch. All three proceeded down the front sidewalk, each one grinning. Frantically going into reset, I exited the car with what I felt sure was the most forced smile I'd ever produced in my life. I cast a quick glance at Carl, but found no reciprocity for my surprise.

"Look who's here," he chuckled, seemingly not in the least upset. "Our first visitors!"

"Well, hi y'all!" I heard my mouth exclaim. "Welcome to our humble abode!"

"Sorry about leaving our car where we did," Cap'n said. "We weren't thinking, I don't guess."

No shit, Sherlock. "No problem", I said. "I always love to make an entrance!" Smiles all around, especially on Carl's face, which also held appreciation and relief. I was totally in the dark as to why they were here.

I had no aversion to Carl's parents: his dad, part gruff, part charm; his mom, polite enough yet seemingly ill-at-ease, never initiating conversation. I felt like I'd been swooped away from an intense drama moments before the climax and thrown into some wacko comedy for which I was frantically trying to learn my lines. Suddenly I was to assume the role of happy wife and gracious host in our new home, the former with very little experience to draw from, the latter, none at all.

A bizarre charade ensued as the four of us sat on the deck later while Carl grilled steaks (damned expensive ones, I noticed). Drawing on my acting chops from the previous weekend's Senior Play, I regaled the niceties of living in a new house, the crazy weeks beforehand picking out colors, etc. I quickly moved on from that topic lest I arrive at the item about Carl's being fired on closing day. Conversation was not exactly stilted, most responses at least expanding a yes or no, but I wouldn't call it relaxed. Try as I might, I could not push aside the awful scenes of the previous weeks. I wondered if Cap'n and Peggy had any idea of what was going on.

Carl placed beautifully arranged dinner plates before us, and all set about enjoying a good meal and an excuse not to talk. I did my best to put on a good front—forcing a laugh at Carl's jokes, keeping conversation topics superficial, returning to pets and weather often—but I must have failed miserably.

Once everyone finally turned in for the night, I felt Carl tossing and turning on his side of the bed.

"What's wrong?" I asked, figuring it was a bit early for lights out for either one of us.

In an angry whisper, Carl said, "You've got everybody so damn tense around here—"

"Me? Hey, I'm sorry, but their timing for a visit is pretty lousy. I think you ought to be relieved I've held it in like I have!" My whisper was equally angry.

Carl didn't answer. He continued to fidget until he finally rose from the bed. I figured he was going to the bathroom but in the darkness I heard a rustle of clothes, the jangle of a belt buckle, the metallic buzz of a zipper. Next I heard the bedroom door open and close quietly. It took me a moment to realize Carl was gone. What the hell? Could this day get any weirder? I sighed, unable to sleep, wondering what would happen next. Shortly before dawn, I felt Carl ease into bed.

"Where in the world have you been?" I asked, mystified.

"I had to get out of here to breathe."

"Where did you go?"

"Well, what do you think? I had to get waxed."

I had no idea what that expression meant but I didn't want to ask for an explanation. I lay awake, feeling sure Carl was doing the same.

On Saturday morning, Carl fixed breakfast, showing not the slightest hint he'd been *absent* a portion of the night. Once again, we enjoyed a scrumptious breakfast of steak and eggs, cheese grits and oven toast as we sat on the deck on a perfectly beautiful spring morning. It almost appeared like a normal family gathering. Carl's inexplicable disappearance just hours earlier seemed surreal.

"Sorry, y'all," I said, "I have to—I mean *have to*—attend a lunch meeting today for a club, *only* because I got suckered into being an officer, but I'll be home early afternoon and maybe y'all would like to go to the Botanical Gardens." I was doing better at my role today.

For the next three hours then, I left Carl to entertain his parents while I did my civic duty. When I pulled back in the driveway, there was no parked car in it, so I figured all had gone out for a ride, maybe for ice cream. Fine with me, gives me some more time to myself. I entered the living room to find Carl sitting in front of the TV.

"Where is everybody?" I asked. "What the hell's going on?"

Carl seemed not perturbed in the least. "They said they had to go."

"But they just got here..." I tried to act hurt, even though all I felt was relief.

"Cap'n said he had stuff to do and I think Peggy missed the dogs," Carl offered. "They said they were sorry to miss you, but needed to leave in order to avoid rush hour traffic." And then he added, "They send their love."

Totally flummoxed, all I could say was, "That was too weird." I walked to the mailbox to retrieve the mail. Close by, on the curb, rested a pile of dark green grass with fresh roots exposed. Upon closer inspection, I recognized the clumps of monkey grass I'd spent three hours planting along the driveway and sidewalk edges. I stalked back into the house.

"What gives with the monkey grass?"

Carl looked embarrassed. "I'm afraid Cap'n thought it was weeds; he was just trying to do you a favor."

Right, like weeds grow in perfectly identical sizes, meticulously placed apart in a somewhat pleasing fashion. I just shook my head; it'd be easy enough to replant the stuff. But jeez, was everyone in this weird family bent on making my life hard?

"I'm gonna replant it now before the roots dry out," I said and left Carl to his TV.

A few hours later, Carl opened the front door to see I had worked my way up the sidewalk with replanting and was nearly finished.

"You hungry?" Carl's voice was kind, almost hopeful. "There's steak and eggs."

What had this man talked to his parents about while I was gone? Could they possibly have tried to talk some sense into him?

"Sure," I said. "Be there in three more sprigs."

There was something about breakfast for dinner that made me happy and calm. I cast a grateful look towards Carl for the simple, good meal. His expression was vaguely sad.

"I'm sorry about last night," he said suddenly. "I don't know what got into me. All this pressure about work and wanting to make my parents, especially Cap'n, proud of me..." He drifted off, seemingly lost in regret and worry.

I looked at him, feeling a slight wave of sympathy. I certainly understood trying to please one's parents. I probably had been too uptight the last thirty-six hours, simply because I'd been trying so hard to act natural. The visit had been weird, no doubt, but it wasn't terrible or anything. Nowhere close. Except for that monkey grass...

I decided to wait to see if Carl had in fact gotten some sense knocked in him. I noted the vibes between us seemed devoid of static and impending showdown. Now was not the time to revert to the crisis of a mere forty-eight hours ago. Both of us again found different tasks in the house or yard to occupy ourselves.

That night, we lay in bed, well apart. I wanted to sleep, but I sensed Carl's hand sliding across the sheet and then felt his pinky gently curl around mine. Next, I heard his voice, soft, low, and tremulous with emotion.

"I...I look at my parents and your parents and I know—we both know—that neither set of them can claim their marriage was a walk in the park." He paused. "But they're still together." He now held my hand, still speaking to the ceiling, "I want that more than anything. And I want it with you. You gotta believe that."

After a long pause, I said, "I don't know anymore. I don't see how this is going to work—" I paused again, briefly and then, almost half-heartedly said, "—unless we get some sort of counseling."

After the slightest hesitation, Carl said, "OK, fine by me. Anything to make this work. I love you so much, hon."

Truly not knowing how I felt, I remained silent.

I scheduled an appointment for the following week with a Dr. Bralee, per Vivien's glowing recommendation. Expecting to feel relief we were going to get some objective help, I only felt distress and misgiving. *Wow, fifty bucks an hour.* I knew what we were bringing to the counselor's table could not be sorted out in one session, let alone ten. How on God's green earth were we going to pay for that? When I pictured telling Dr. Bralee about the things I'd been putting up with,

I felt like an absolute fool. When I considered saying these things in front of Carl, I grew very apprehensive and worried.

But when I told Carl I'd made an appointment, he showed no resistance. Nor did he press me to respond "I love you," as we lay tangled up after a lovemaking session which could best be described as desperate.

On Tuesday, I was called to the office after second period.

"Look what came for you!" exclaimed an aide, pointing to two dozen red roses on the counter. I felt a warming in my gut. I had to hand it to him, he was making an effort to show me he wanted to turn this thing around. Maybe we could do it on our own. I went into a vacant office and placed a call to Dr. Bralee's office and canceled the appointment.

Even though the next couple days were uneventful, I had the nagging feeling I'd sighted a lovely shell in the surf but it was washed away before I could get my hands on it. I wanted to believe Carl truly wanted to right things, but I dreaded another encounter like that 'push' thing. Could his temper even get worse? My mind took off on horrendous scenarios, including an extremely unlikely one in which Carl pulled his gun from the bedside table and threatened me. When I came home from school a couple days after canceling the appointment with Bralee, I decided—quite suddenly and with no premeditation—that it might be a good idea to hide the gun. So I did.

CHAPTER 31

DETECTIVE ON THE FENCE

Jobs. Booze. Self doubt. Such was the collage of my second year of marriage.

Over the next six months, Carl would have six more jobs, lasting from two weeks to two months, all of them quite a step down from his earlier positions. Each hiring began with a self-fulfilling defeatist attitude, while each firing was met with defiance and depression.

While I was encouraged, not to mention amazed, that Carl somehow continued to get hired almost immediately, it was finally beginning to dawn on me that Carl's seeming ambition was not accompanied by the all-important drive to succeed. He wanted success; he just wasn't willing to work for it.

This was very difficult for me to swallow. The man I'd been attracted to barely three years ago was the picture of energy, can-do-it-ness, and responsibility. I was embarrassed to think it'd taken me all this time to realize I'd mistaken bravado for confidence. It only took Carl's employers a couple weeks.

But I had other bitter pills to swallow. After one of his firings, I had gamely suggested he try another line of work. No, I didn't know exactly what, but with his intelligence, gift of gab, and managerial experience, surely there were other outlets—sales came to mind— in which he could flourish. My suggestions were met with a disinterested shrug from Carl who muttered he *liked* his line of work. Another slow dawning: Carl's reluctance wasn't from being clueless about what else he might enjoy; he didn't want to leave the line of work that supported his drinking habit! Knowing full well what Carl's response would be should I share this new insight, I chose to keep it to myself.

In order to stand up to the vehement denial Carl would throw in my face, I would need iron-clad proof, very specific numbers, to state my case that he indeed had a drinking problem. So, I made it my business to keep a secret record of how much he drank. That I was snooping around was a huge embarrassment. This shame, however, would morph into amazement the more I discovered. Talk about strength in numbers!

First, I simply counted drinks I saw Carl consume, learning instead of the three or four I would have guessed, the actual count was seven or eight. This was in one evening. Then, upon returning home to find Carl passed out in bed, I'd discover an empty bottle that had contained maybe four drinks, plus a new bottle, with only three or four drinks remaining. Perhaps Carl became suspicious I was keeping a closer eye on him because I'd only see one bottle in plain sight. However, I soon discovered hidden bottles, and realized he would sometimes put down a dozen drinks while I was gone. The most jarringly definitive 'evidence' presented itself one day when I wasn't even on the prowl.

One May afternoon, I was pulling weeds in the backyard and noticed Frau Eva chasing a butterfly in the empty, weed-choked lot next door. Enchanted by the cat's grace and athleticism, I approached the edge of the yard to enjoy her performance. I stepped on something smooth and hard, which I figured to be a rock, until I heard the unmistakable sound of glass breaking. I looked down to see a crushed bottle of Popov vodka, Carl's brand. Disgusted he'd be so trashy as to litter, I bent down to pick it up, but then noticed another bottle in the weeds a few feet beyond. This one was streaked with mud as if it had been there a while. I became curious. While Frau-Frau continued her butterfly frolic, I uncovered another half dozen bottles. Holy cow, I thought, I need to get a hefty bag! I retrieved one from the garage and resumed my foraging. *Fifty-two bottles* later, I would finally come to grips that I was married to a full-blown alcoholic. "Holy cow," I repeated, this time aloud.

Still, I did not confront Carl. Our *scuffle* of a few weeks back was still fresh on my mind. Also, Carl's mood swings were on the rise, largely due to his discontent with his latest, lowly position at Baby Doe's, a new popular restaurant. For the time being I chose to keep quiet or, at most, employ a little passive-aggression. Not exactly the picture of trust and love.

Ah yes, the love thing. My inability to reciprocate the phrase 'I love you' at all for a while, and later only as a rote response, turned out to be a huge weapon for Carl in arguments that continually cropped up. These arguments, I noticed, usually occurred just before I was about to turn in after an exhausting day.

"You know, Rosie, this not saying you love me is beginning to wear me down," Carl would tell me, seemingly in a world of hurt. "I'm finding it very difficult to even function under this 'I love you if' shit!" Some flavor of this argument surfaced whenever I made some sideways remark that his drinking was doing nothing but harm to our chances. "There you are, on that fence again. 'Yeah, honey, I love you...*some!*' I don't know how you expect me to dedicate myself to our success with you high up there, all aloof, refusing to plunge in with me..." And so on.

Carl's arguments would plague me on several levels. They mainly infuriated me because I retaliated with nothing greater than a mumbled snide remark. But they did give me pause to consider perhaps there was some truth to Carl's words. That 'aloof' remark caused me considerable unease. Hadn't Warner said nearly the same thing to me? *Cold* was his term. God, could a lot of this mess have been caused by me? My idealism? My coldness? And why in the hell was I holding back from confronting Carl about his drinking? Why could I not seem to fight my way through a paper bag? Was I becoming jaded? Superficial? Hell, was I the one who really needed counseling?

Amidst all my muddled, broken-record interior monologues, I realized one thought didn't unnerve me as it had a few months back: leaving Carl and being alone no longer sent my head—or heart—reeling. (Well, there was that very scary financial aspect...) I was simply becoming indifferent, and therein lay a breakthrough: I began to realize indifference was actually a form of strength.

CHAPTER 32

STORAGE OPTIONS

Spring of 1979 yielded to summer, which I navigated on auto-pilot, a mode usually reserved for school, but now required year-round. I kept occupied in various ways: helping my parents move to a town home, resuming the summer pool-cleaning job, celebrating my parents' fortieth anniversary (with a beautiful meal of Beef Wellington prepared by Carl), joining Highland Racquet Club where my tennis kept improving (not to mention providing an outlet), taking a short trip with my parents to visit Scout (who took pointed notice Carl did not accompany us). I continued in nose-to-the-grindstone mode, enduring one disappointment after another. That earlier pinpoint of a breakthrough would dim, and my indifference would morph into numbness, as evidenced in my muddled journaling:

What is it in me that makes me hold back, that makes me unable to clearly express what I really need to say? I drag this diary from out of its place and then I'll be hanged if I can put into words the feeling that made me go to the trouble.

On one of our few 'dates,' Carl and I attended Vegas Night, a fund-raising event. A large ballroom was transformed into a casino, complete with slot machines, roulette tables, and, Carl's favorite, poker. I thought of our time in the Bahamas when I had sat by Carl's side, as he studied the cards with intense focus. *If only he had that kind of focus on the job...* The large pile of chips in front of him conveyed he was winning. Oh, how fun! I watched Carl's hands as he continually rearranged his cards. Then, mortified, I saw one hand slither imperceptibly down to his jacket pocket, in which he deposited a card.

On that night, I came to grips that, in addition to being a full-blown alcoholic, my husband was a masterful cheat. Legitimately winning wasn't enough; cheating—*and getting away with it*—provided far more thrill.

Arguments, some waxing horrific but never physical, followed this and other incidents (most notably, Carl's futile, shot-in-the-dark attempt to be on Card Sharks), but they never proceeded beyond just that: arguments. All of which I would lose in the face of Carl's angry denials, wicked retorts, and harsh belittlements. No clarity would come my way via journal and pen:

I think I'm in cold storage. One minute I think I love Carl, the next minute I'm totally indifferent. He's just done so much in the last few months to disappoint me. My mind is jammed—I can't write.

Fall meant diving right back into work and accounting classes. Carl's job history had long since become ridiculous, adding another *five* jobs to his illustrious resumé. In late October, Carl landed his *twelfth* managerial position with higher pay and status... in Charleston, S.C.

I didn't care a whit how or from where the household coffers would be replenished; furthermore, I was actually relieved to have Carl out of my hair. Sure enough, his absence gave clarity the foothold it needed to regain a presence in my mind. Some two months later, which included a couple notices of bounced checks and garnishment of wages (Carl had never made good on Goodyear), my journaling reflected a marked change of attitude:

December 11, 1979 - Well, enough of this limbo, uncertainty, disappointment, etc. I filed for divorce today. My stomach is in a knot, I am worried as to how in the hell I will manage, but I know that I am making the right decision. I do have my doubts, but I can quickly dispel them by asking myself which I'm surer of: staying with Carl or making a go of it myself...I pick the latter unflinchingly.
...

Oh, Rosie-Rose, you are getting back on the right track.

I wisely decided to keep my decision to myself until Carl's next visit home, nearly two weeks away, rather than lay this on him in a phone call. I would use the interim not only to sort my thoughts and bolster my resolve but also to study for my upcoming accounting final, upon which I had every intention of making another A. So when Carl showed up the next night (perhaps because he'd sensed my slightly differing tone?), I was woefully unprepared to present my case. Rather than list my complaints in a civil, non-whining manner so they added up to a rock solid justification for my decision, I heard myself blurt out my news at the very first springboard Carl offered. Which he did quickly.

"...so, yeah, Branson Personnel called me to say they were looking around for a more suitable position for me..."

On the job barely two months and he already needs to look around? Why? I decided I was tired of asking and wondering. I took a breath but then faltered slightly, "Well, I suppose that's good, but it really doesn't matter—"

Carl jerked his head to look straight at me. "Huh?"

"—because I filed for divorce yesterday." I held my breath.

Carl's face flipped through surprise, shock, anger, disgust, and then wariness. When he finally spoke, I was relieved to hear a reasonable tone.

"Now, hon, you can't do this to us, not now. Look, the job... OK, OK, not to worry about that! I will *not* be leaving that job for a while—even though it stinks and we're so far apart—but, yes, OK, I'll build up some stability." I managed to keep my expression neutral rather than give the sour look that I'd heard all these lines before.

Carl's tone became more earnest, more persuasive. "C'mon, hon, this job—granted it's not an ideal situation—is bringing money into the household. We'll keep the mortgage current, I'll pay off my bills. Look, you gotta admit it's a step in a positive direction, don't you see? Surely you wouldn't back out of this when we're in forward motion, would you?"

What was it about this man when he talked to me like this? It felt to me like every bit of air in the room moved around him, welcoming his presence, inflating his size, propelling his words, while I shrank into a void.

"I'm sorry, I can't do this anymore." Even I could hear diminished conviction. Carl greedily pressed on.

"Look, hon, I am *begging* you, *please* don't do this now! I simply cannot admit we can't make it. I promise you, on all that's holy to me, I will make good on my part. Please, hon."

In tears now, I barely managed to move my head from side to side.

Now, Carl was quiet. His voice became stern. "I'm sorry you feel that way, because, the bottom line here is—" his voice taking on volume and anger, "—there is no fucking way I'm signing any divorce papers!"

I quaked with fury, but it was all directed to my sniveling self. I had never, ever been a match for Carl's cleverness, wicked comebacks, and power of persuasion. His resolve that we continue together seemed fueled more by desperation than desire, but it was stronger than I'd seen in a while. Could I possibly have jumped the gun here? And, damn it again, the man did seem—despite his nasty attitude at times—to love me. Otherwise, why in the hell did *he* keep hanging in here?

I asked myself again if it wouldn't be better for me to do the same, at least for a while longer, to see if—against all odds—this thing could work. Revisiting the hassles of going the divorce route, I felt my insides curl up and go familiarly fetal. When I was by myself, I could summon up the resolve, but the minute I was in front of Carl, that resolve turned tail and ran like a scalded dog.

Carl stood before me, imploring, "I love you so much. Can't you see that?"

My quaking subsided until I stood stock-still and managed to whisper, "Yeah. I can see that." What I didn't—couldn't—add was that I loved him, too. I simply said, "I gotta study."

I returned to my desk and stared at my notes, so sensible an hour earlier, now an impenetrable jungle, where snipers perched, intent on taking out anyone trying to leave. I sighed and tried to chalk everything up to plain old bad timing.

During the following wintry months, Carl would be fired from the Charleston hotel job and do another one of his short-lived employments at, of all things a car dealership. His followup to these two mini-disasters was to somehow right the ship with what looked like a really good position: a job with Doolins Security, proving his commitment to try a new line of work, one not so prone to turnover as the restaurant business. His seemingly stable employment brought about a cautious calm in me.

Cautious as well, was the encouragement I felt when, early in the new year, Carl resumed tennis, including small tournaments. For the first time, we entertained a few of my nearly ignored friends. I had become a bit of a recluse, so engrossed was I with home-front issues, and I delighted in reconnecting with my many buddies. Other social events—a farewell party for Lucy's move to Augusta, a concert or two, etc.—lessened my sense of apprehension. I welcomed these morsels of proof that I'd not made a horrible mistake and that regarding myself as a sniveling wimp was unfounded.

I'd also become reclusive where my parents were concerned. On one rare visit—almost always solo; easier that way—Daddy and I were digging up young dogwoods for transplanting around their new town home. The late winter day holding the tiniest hint of spring, along with some strenuous shoveling, invigorated me. Daddy and I both laughed at Jimbo as he chased with joyful abandon whatever object caught his attention.

"There's that beautiful smile," Daddy said, his tone waxing nostalgic. "Your mother and I have missed that." Often impenetrable, Daddy's kind, poignant comment caught me completely off guard.

I stopped shoveling, leaning against the handle. "Look, Rosie," he continued, "not to butt in—we realize couples have to work out their own problems—but..." Daddy paused and looked me straight in the eye, "...I want you to know we're willing to buy Carl out. You know, if need be."

I couldn't hold Daddy's gaze, so intent was I on suppressing the sob clamoring to erupt. "True," I said, "it's not been a walk in the park, but things seem to be looking up," I said. Struggling for a light tone, I added, "But thanks. It's...good to know." I grabbed my shovel and resumed digging. The hole wasn't deep enough yet.

Constantly at odds with positive turns of events, though, were several negative incidents. When I noticed a five-dollar bill missing from my purse, I found it in Carl's pocket. He had to give up denying it was the same bill when I pointed to my student's name written on it. When cleaning closets one day, I came across a stack of hard-core porn. Unable to deny ownership, Carl then lashed out at me for being so provincial. When the incessant, sleep-depriving barks of Crissy, the neighbor's dog, suddenly ceased, I had strong but unproven suspicions Carl had enacted a cruel solution.

Given all that had gone down between us by this point, any one of the unhappier incidents could have proved the final straw and served as impetus to call our fragile state of equilibrium what it in fact was: a farce. But both of us, each in our own versions of denial, took great pains to avoid full-blown arguments.

When another incident of my unwillingness to reciprocate an 'I love you' arose, Carl seemed to hold up the white flag. Instead of launching into one of his 'on the fence' attacks, he surprised me with the following concession:

"OK, you win. Call the attorney tomorrow."

But when Carl returned home the next day, he heard me say, "Nope, didn't call the attorney. ... For one thing, it's Saturday, not the best day of the week to be calling attorneys. For another thing..." my voice broke. With a sigh approaching *but still a degree shy of* utter hopelessness, I looked up at Carl, whose shoulders sagged slightly in relief. "...for another thing...I just want so bad to fix this."

My hand fluttered in a circle, as if to encompass everything having to do with the world around us, and then waved to and fro between us, the makers of that world.

That evening, I dragged out my journal, wryly noting it had undergone a depressingly familiar three month lapse. Tonight's entry was nothing short of pathetic:

March 1, 1980 - Well, I'm still married. I'm just a real rock of Gibraltar with nerves of steel and a will of iron.

CHAPTER 33

RISING TO THE OCCASION

It was a fine evening for April Fool's Day. I sat on the deck, enjoying the peace offered by the soft breeze, the delicate colors and aromas of early spring. Frau Eva and Mona Bone were stretched out on the deck railing like two loaves of French bread. Bringing the scene to perfection was a trusty Kahlua in my hand. A few days had passed since the mysterious silencing of Crissy the neighbor's dog. I rationalized any fate trumped that poor, neglected, chained-up animal's predicament. The past several nights of uninterrupted sleep had done wonders for my attitude as well as Carl's. Sleep wasn't all we had done, and I leaned back, faintly smiling while reliving the previous night's tentative return to our nearly forgotten love life. We had been like trains on separate tracks converging briefly in a station.

I knew sex was not the only thing necessary to a good marriage, but it damn sure helped. Still, it would have to be beyond-phenomenal to withstand the trials we'd endured. So much stuff needed to be put in the past, under the bridge, gone, forgotten, forgiven. We needed to move forward, but I knew the footing was still treacherous.

Counseling would be critical, but as yet, I had not moved on making an appointment. The multiple sessions we'd require would be cost-prohibitive. Plus, still holding nebulous attraction was the idea of being able to look back on this and say we'd simply buckled down and worked things out on our own.

I was rudely jerked from my thoughts by a jangling phone. Before I could finish my "hello," I could hear Mama talking a blue streak. All I understood was "dad" and "hospital."

"What?!"

"We were on the deck, having a drink, and suddenly your dad said 'I don't feel so good' and the next thing I knew he fainted. The paramedics have taken him to Brookwood."

I raced to my car and drove straight to the hospital, realizing, in my shocked befuddlement, I'd gone to the wrong one. It was another twenty minutes before I could join Mama at Daddy's bedside in the emergency room. We watched anxiously for any change of expression in his blank face. No doctor or nurse was in the room; I would later learn that, when they had smelled liquor on his breath, they assumed he'd just passed out. I tried to lock gazes with Daddy, but couldn't quite get on the same plane of focus. For one strange, selfish moment, I imagined those deadly eyes were locked upon me, demanding, "Get out! Get away from him!"

Daddy began to convulse and I yelled for help. A doctor and nurse hurried into the room, assessing the situation and quickly bade Mama and me exit. They wasted no time hooking him up to wires and tubes. The paramedic who'd transported Daddy to the hospital was still at the admitting desk.

"Can you please tell me exactly what happened?" I asked.

"Well, he really seemed OK when we got him in the ambulance. His vital signs were normal and he was conscious. When I asked him how he felt, he said 'I feel like hell.'" Those would be Daddy's last words which, I later reflected, he would've loved as an exit line.

Daddy would hang on for four days as doctors performed a couple futile operations to correct or reverse damage due to a cerebral hemorrhage. On the morning of April 4th, 1980, life support was withdrawn and Daddy flat-lined shortly thereafter. He never regained consciousness to witness the presence of Mama, me, or, as it turned out, the most vigilant of all: Carl.

A stalwart of strength and comfort he was during those horrible days. The way Carl rose to the occasion—speaking with the doctors, making funeral arrangements, cooking for family members—was a sight to behold. I was too delirious to react in any way other than grateful acceptance. Oh, how everyone—sister, brother, grandmother, aunt and uncle—appreciated his stepping up to the plate and dealing with the painful behind-the-scenes details. I felt a wobbly swell of pride and hope that now, even in the face of this terrible tragedy, Carl's potential was finally, finally grabbing a foothold, and from here on out he would shine.

"You what?!" I shouted, unable to believe my ears. Home from pool-cleaning, I was soaked in sweat due to the oppressive heat and humidity of late July. I was headed straight to the shower when Carl's bombshell stopped me dead in my tracks.

"I quit Doolins," Carl said, devoid of concern but full of anger and indignation. "They're all idiots over there and are working me to death. And don't start that judgmental shit. For your information, I have an interview tomorrow with another security company."

I sighed. Would we ever, ever have a normal marriage? Could I right now summon the energy for yet another dogfight? I answered my own question by continuing my trudge to the shower.

I turned the water on as hot and hard as I could stand it, wishing it could cleanse me of more than sweat and muck. I could not count the times I'd used showers to drown out the sound of my bawling away like an unhappy child constantly teased with a piece of candy but never receiving it. Not *another* freaking job! This was truly one of those have-to-laugh-to-keep-from-crying moments, but I could summon neither tear nor chuckle. I couldn't summon *anything*.

I turned the hot water back slowly until it became lukewarm, then cool, and finally cold. While my skin felt refreshed, my body and mind remained deep in a mire. I turned the water off, grabbed a towel and wrapped it around my dripping body, savoring for a brief moment the sensation of a soothing hug. I stepped onto the mat to begin my post-shower ritual. I slowly spread lotion all over my tanned body, massaging my tired muscles. Again, I took time to acknowledge the comforting, rejuvenating properties of simple touch. I rolled up a small towel, horse-shoed it around my neck and rubbed vigorously back and forth. I could practically see the waves of tension leaving my body before they evaporated into nothingness.

I was struck by a revelation, at once gentle and strong. The person responsible for this momentary respite, this simple pleasure, this comfort...was me.

I turned to the steam-filled mirror. With my towel, I wiped away a small circle in the middle and gazed at my reflection, feeling older and definitely looking tireder than my thirty-two years. With my hairdryer, I defogged the entire mirror. Wouldn't it be nice if all things could clear up so easily! I couldn't remember the last time I'd really looked at myself.

I thought of another oft-neglected facet of my life: my journal. Encountering either—mirror or journal—demanded a face-to-face, come-to-Jesus I had not been able or ready to handle. Standing naked before my reflection, I felt a tiny shift take place within me. The sensation was almost imperceptible, totally unrecognizable, but undeniably positive.

I grabbed the blow-dryer and made quick work of my short hair (those impractical Farrah locks having recently bit the dust). I cocked my head towards the mirror and said, "So, Rosie-Rose, how much more of this crap are you going to take? I'm just askin'."

In a flash, my reflection answered, "None! Let's get out of this mess!"

I dabbed some Oil of Olay onto my fingertip and smoothed it across my drawn face. I leaned forward to within an inch of the mirror.

"So...any thoughts on how we're going to do this?"

My reflection stared back, eyebrows raised, shoulders shrugged, mouth smirked. "Not a clue."

I pulled on some clean clothes, feeling they reflected a cleaner interior as well. I looked back over my shoulder at the mirror.

"Me neither. At least, not today."

And then, in my best Scah-lett voice, "*But, aftah awl, tuh-mahruh is anuhthuh day...*"

CHAPTER 34

STORM WARNING

While the next day was not *the* day, it was, like many succeeding ones, relatively undramatic. Carl landed the job with another security company. This allowed us to actually enjoy several date-nights, a near rarity in his restaurant-managing days. In October, we celebrated Carl's thirty-eighth birthday, which occurred a few days before the fourth anniversary of our meeting each other. Despite the loosening of tensions, my just-below-the-surface reservations kept me from making a big deal about the occasion. I noted with relief and irony that Carl made no mention of it. I also noted, much more importantly, that Carl seemed content with his new situation.

Just as he'd seemed content with Doolins, which he suddenly quit, my reservations reminded me. While I welcomed the recent heightening of mood, I did not trust it. Even though some two months old, the vision of myself in that foggy mirror had not faded from my mind. Nor had I forgotten the sensation of that faint stirring in my gut. I suspected I was very close to tiring of this train ride called superficiality where I'd been a passenger for so very long. I figured I wouldn't have to wait long before the train would screech to another halt. Whether I would get off at the next stop remained to be seen.

Not long into my third school year as Mrs. Ballini, the next stop loomed into view. A familiar stop, as it turned out, since it had to do with that ever-niggling bit about Carl's unpaid bills. Mortified to find collection notices in the mail, I listened to Carl's adamant declarations all balances had been paid.

The next day, with a mixture of spite and trepidation, I called the collection agency.

"You haven't paid one cent towards reducing this debt!" I slapped a figure-filled sheet on the coffee table.

Ignoring this completely, Carl roared, "How dare you go behind my back like this!"

Livid, I looked directly at Carl and yelled, "I'm *tired* of this shit and I'm going to get to the bottom of this. But not tonight. I am tired."

I didn't tell Carl I was taking the next day off to do just that. I called the agency again, saying I'd like to come down that morning to clear the confusion about Carl's accounts.

"I'm sorry, Mrs. Ballini," the clerk said nervously. "We've been instructed by Mr. Ballini not to give out any information to anyone but him."

I was speechless. What was this? Some kind of sick game? Well, allow me to play! Keeping my voice steady, I said, "Oh, I see. Well, I suppose we both need to come in for an appointment. Let's see, Carl seems to be free on Monday. Do you have an opening?"

"Yes ma'am, at 10:00."

"Perfect." I hung up the phone. Damn him!

"No fucking way am I going to that office if you're there!" Now Carl was livid. I had waited until Monday morning to advise him of the appointment. "What, like I have to be escorted by my mommy or something?" He was sputtering.

I said nothing and finished dressing. I picked up my purse and walked to the front door.

"And just where in the hell do you think you're going?" Carl sneered, perhaps slightly fearing I would demand the meeting myself.

"To see the attorney," I said, and left.

I sat with Mary, my ex-student teacher turned good friend, and now an attorney. Only in her second year of practice, Mary would assist her boss, who would handle the divorce case.

"So, you're *sure* you're going to go through with this, this time around?" Mary smiled slightly, but I knew she didn't want to bother her boss yet again, all for naught. I hung my head, embarrassed I'd been such a vacillating wimp.

"I'm positive," My gaze was the very picture of decisiveness. I headed home, ready to get another show on the road.

"I am NOT giving you a divorce!" Carl screamed, his face contorted with rage. "How can you do this to me? It's lunacy! I refuse to give up on us. This other shit is *nothing, nothing*! Can't you understand that?"

Refusing to be unnerved by this expected rush of rage, I spoke with a calmness that almost surprised me.

"Look, Carl, there is no way now you can convince me you didn't *lie* to me about these bills—" I held up my finger to check Carl's indignant comeback, "—I know you expect me to take your word about this, and anything else for that matter, and that is certainly something which people in love do quite naturally." Carl quietened, waiting to see where I was going. "Well, I *want* to take your word, and I have tried and tried, but something always starts gnawing at me when I do."

"C'mon, that bill to Goodyear—"

"Do you want me to tell you about that bill to Goodyear? You've not paid them a dime since you were in Charleston, and that was a seven-dollar money order. As for Bart Starr, there's been a four-hundred-and-twenty-five dollar balance—"

"OK, OK," Carl shouted, more to silence me than to agree with me.

"Surely you know me well enough, Carl, to know how disgusting I think the state of your credit is." Carl rolled his eyes. "But do you know how little I think of someone who *lies* to me?" Carl looked at me like one of my impudent students. "Wouldn't you? Or will you answer that question honestly?" His disgust was fully visible. "If you answer 'yes,' then you know why I feel I can't stay with you." Carl shot a sideways, almost sly look at me. "And if you answer 'no,' then you know why I can't stay with you."

My voice had remained calm throughout but my heart was fluttering against my chest now. I had so many other things I wanted to say, but I didn't want to incite Carl to escalate tensions further.

Carl's countenance belied the simmering just below the surface. Barely constraining his anger, he said, "I still don't think we're at a point where we throw in the towel." If he intended to plead, he missed the mark entirely as his voice gained volume. "I mean, the laughs, the fun, the sex—"

"Yes, Carl, we have most certainly had that," I agreed, wondering if I was visibly shaking. Determined to state my case, to *reason* with Carl, I continued, "but I want...I need—and intend to have—more than that in a marriage. Basic to a marriage is trust, and we don't have that. You may—you *should*—have it in me, but I don't in you."

Carl was glowering now, his fingers twitching slightly.

Fearing I'd crossed the line and was about to be 'pushed' again, I said, "OK, now, Carl, let's not get physical..."

But Carl made no move forward. He seemed to be studying me, as if calculating what my next move would be. In a quiet but sinister voice, he said with great finality, "No way in hell am I going to give you a divorce." He turned and left.

Utterly drained, I went straight to the bedroom, put on a teeshirt and collapsed in bed. I didn't know, nor did I care where Carl had gone. I was done.

I awoke the next morning to find Carl asleep next to me. I went to school and came straight home and got right back into bed, rising only to get some soup and feed the cats. Carl was nowhere in sight. I was so done.

Just as the previous morning, I awoke to find Carl awake next to me. I got up and began to get ready for school.

"Happy Third Anniversary," Carl said grimly.

I knew full well what the date was but had no intention of bringing it up. I murmured a neutral "mmm" and continued dressing. I fixed myself a quick breakfast, fed the cats, and walked back into the bedroom to get my purse. Carl's eyes were closed, but I knew he was still awake.

Softly, in a neutral voice, I said, "I want you to go to Adam's office and sign those papers."

Silence.

Oddly enough, my day at school went smoothly from the moment I arrived. No one—not even Vivien—saw the slightest indication anything was amiss. I didn't dare bring it up for fear I would completely lose it. Between second and third periods, I was called to the office to see a couple of grinning aides holding a mammoth arrangement of two dozen roses.

"Happy Anniversary!" they squealed, pointing to the envelope with the very same message. I donned an appropriately delighted expression and hurried back to my room with the flowers. Students crowded around my desk, admiring them. I'd removed the envelope so they wouldn't know the occasion. I had to wait until the next period to read Carl's message:

Please, please meet me at Crockmeier's. It's really important.

I sighed, trying to imagine what in the world he would say. Why Crockmeier's, one of our favorite restaurants? To summon up good vibes? To assure me nothing physical could happen in a public place? Perhaps he merely wants to apologize. Right.

With curiosity, doubt and reluctance in ascending amounts, I arrived at Crockmeiers at 7:00, per the P.S. on the note. Carl was already seated, his expression a mixture of anxiety, anticipation, even hope...and not a hint of his mood two nights previous.

"Look," he entreated, "what if I give you post-dated checks to Goodyear and Bart Starr, which will bring both those balances to zero over a four- to six-month period." He fanned the checks, already filled out, on the table. "And, I promise I'll put away two hundred dollars a month for us." I watched him place two more postdated checks at two hundred dollars each on the table. "And..." if Carl was sure he was about to play the trump card, he didn't show it; his expression was nothing but earnestness, "I agree to do counseling."

Damn. We'd never actually *tried* counseling. I'd read many, many accounts of couples coming back from the brink as a result of it. Should I not be absolutely certain I'd left no stone unturned?

Ignoring my gut's exhortation to 'Run! Run like the wind!' I mumbled, "OK."

The next day, Thursday, for what I was sure must be the gazillionth time, I found a private phone in the office and made two phone calls. First, I called Dan Silkwood, a counselor highly recommended by Vivien, saying he'd been helping with Frank's commitment problems. I scheduled three appointments, not allowing myself to think about the cost. Carl and I were to see him separately, then together. My appointment was two days later.

My second call was to Mary, whose disappointment was heavily apparent through the phone line.

"Do you really think counseling is going to do any good?" Mary asked kindly, although I knew she'd rather have asked if I was out of my mind.

"Who knows? I seriously doubt it, but I have to try," I hoped my voice didn't sound as defeated as I felt. "I do know one thing for sure..."

"What's that?"

"I know I don't want you or Adam to toss those divorce papers."

"Gotcha." Mary said. "And, good luck."

CHAPTER 35

DAN SILKWOOD

Two days after our third wedding anniversary, I sat in Dan Silkwood's office, a jumbled disarray of books and papers piled every which-a-where, with dim but warm lighting gleaming off the worn oak desk and comfortable leather chairs. Dan, of bushy beard, long but clean hair, and round-rimmed glasses, looked as though he'd just returned from Woodstock, but the several framed diplomas on the wall reassured me this guy was no fly-by-nighter. Vivien had praised his bedside manner, so to speak, and his ability to cut to the chase with an amazing gentleness.

While my slightly bruised independent streak bristled that, really, I could have managed this crisis myself, the greater part of me seemed to be saying, "Oh, thank God." After introductory pleasantries, Dan listened intently to my summary of the situation, stopping me only a few times. When I told him of my mission to determine how much Carl had been drinking, he asked me why I went to such measures.

I blinked rapidly. "Well, trying to make a point with Carl could be really difficult at times. I'd think I had an iron-clad argument, and it would go up in smoke as soon as he'd start in with his...his reasoning." I searched for more. "I needed to be able to *show* him I wasn't making it up how much he'd actually been drinking."

"But didn't you already have tons of proof he was a heavy drinker?" I nodded. "Were you maybe trying to prove something to yourself, that your admonitions to Carl weren't as crazy and insane as Carl kept telling you they were?" He waited. Then, very gently, "What I'm seeing here is someone who's allowed her spouse to practically convince her *she's* the one who's not seeing things clearly, that she's, you know, kinda crazy."

His words were a tsunami. They blasted into me, knocked me down, whirled me around. But even as my shoulders heaved, sobs wracking my body, I realized these words weren't going to drown me. I knew I could swim. My shoulders quieted as did my sobs. "I suppose I must be a little crazy to stay in this, huh?"

Dan asked me quietly, "So, why do you think you are?"

"Well, because I want...I think...I still want it to work. I want to be sure I've done my part."

"And you don't think you've done that already?"

I bowed my head, then raised it. "I haven't tried counseling."

When I returned home from my appointment, Carl did not ask me how things went. Ignoring it entirely, he approached me in an amorous mood.

"You know, I really can't handle that right now," I said neutrally. "I'm trying to process stuff and would appreciate a little space."

With a show of mocking respect, Carl backed off and busied himself in front of the TV. But the next day, tiring of my continued 'processing,' Carl's method of giving space was to leave altogether, at 11:30 p.m., telling me he could not handle my coldness. After he departed, I actually packed a bag, well aware of the broken-record aspect, but went no further than closing the clasp. I was not going to leave the house at this hour. I was plain and simply too tired. It didn't take Carl long to return.

"Sorry, I'm just upset," he mumbled.

Carl's turn to see Dan individually was set for the week after Thanksgiving. He canceled, claiming he felt terrible, possibly with the flu, but he did schedule a make-up appointment for two weeks away. Before that one, however, we attended our joint appointment. The session began with my reiterating several points from my earlier session. All the while, I felt Carl's gaze drilling into me. Although his face was poker-set, I sensed a contained rage and indignation.

In due time, the subject of Carl's drinking was discussed. I mentioned the fifty-two bottles along with the ones filled with water to appear full of vodka. Now Carl's gaze enveloped me like a steel clamp. With total neutrality, Dan asked Carl if he felt his drinking was an integral part of our problem.

Carl's voice was laden with rationality, laced with charm. "Oh, no doubt it has caused problems in the past, but I *know* I've cut back on my consumption level...even though I certainly don't think I need to do the tea-totaling thing. Every now and then, a drink can just be a nice way to relax. How about you, Dan, do you take the occasional drink?" Dan nodded in the affirmative.

Carl's voice took on a somewhat less charming tone. "Uh-huh, and like you, I feel a need to relieve the everyday stress, you know? You see, Dan, here I am under terrible pressure trying to hang on to a job that doesn't fulfill me nearly as much as my former career, and I've got this wife, who's supposed to be my love and support, but who's checking around behind my back, picky as hell. Now, how am I supposed to feel all warm and fuzzy and full of trust with that shit going on?"

I didn't even hear Dan's answer, so jammed was my mind at hearing Carl's oh-so-familiar tactic of twisting an argument such that any blame was deflected from him and deposited squarely onto my shoulders. I felt tears sliding down my cheeks, wondering if counseling was a good idea. I tried not to think about how we were going to pay for something that might not even provide a solution.

In an effort to cling to at least some small symbol of holiday merriment, I hauled up the Christmas tree from the basement and wrestled it into its stand. As I unwrapped the ornaments, I drew faint joy from ones holding a particular memory. All the while, Carl sat quietly, almost sullenly, smoking and watching, his expression noting the irony of the situation.

"I do regret the way things are right now," I offered, with some kindness.

"Me, too," Carl said. He did not join me in decorating the tree.

Nor did he join me for any festivities, including a couple parties and music at the church (I had never missed it; not for its religious aspect, but for its sheer beauty). It was as if I sent a shell of myself to these activities. I could not remove myself from the pins and needles upon which I was treading, in anticipation of Carl's upcoming individual appointment with Dan and the progress that would hopefully, miraculously follow.

On Wednesday, a week before Christmas, I came home to find Carl asleep and not at the scheduled appointment. He awoke in a horrible mood.

"What do you mean you didn't go? When did you cancel?"

"I didn't call him."

"You mean you just didn't show? Oh, great, we're probably going to have to pay fo—"

"Shut the fuck up!" He stalked off and fixed himself a drink. I started to protest but thought better of it. I'd never seen Carl's face so dark with anger.

Things were none improved the next morning. As we were dressing for work, Carl yanked on his clothes, jerking at his tie, muttering and cursing under his breath.

"What's wrong now?" I dared to ask.

Carl stood there, head lowered as if trying to come to grips with some hidden secret. "Hell, what do you think? I'm sexually frustrated!" he screamed. "Trying to maintain some sort of normalcy when I'm lying next to the cold bitch you've become...it's insane!"

I expelled a short but cautious laugh, remembering how Carl had withheld sex nearly the entire previous summer when he was *depressed.*

"I really don't think sex is the root of our problem."

With that, Carl took a couple quick steps toward me, his right arm angling up as if in preparation to strike a blow. But he checked the movement and simply lowered his hand to the dresser. He grabbed his keys and slammed the door behind him.

Rattled, I made my way to school, where, thank heavens, unit tests were on tap for every one of my classes. My entire day was spent grading the previous class's papers, and getting all scores recorded so I at least wouldn't be faced with that chore over the holiday break, which would begin the next afternoon.

I arrived home late to an empty house. I sent a silent thank you to the gods for allowing me a few moments of peace that I fully anticipated being destroyed once Carl came home. If he came home.

I rather hoped he didn't. I went to the basement and was rummaging about for boxes to mail gifts when I heard a terrible racket upstairs. Thinking maybe the cats had knocked something over—but no, they had of course followed me downstairs—I rushed upstairs and realized it was Carl pounding on the front door, furious because he couldn't find his key.

He bolted into the room, giving me an accusatory look as though I was responsible for losing his key. Seeing the slight shrug of my shoulders which seemed to say, 'Hey, not my problem, asshole,' he stopped dead in his tracks and whirled around to launch into a litany of complaints, sneering as he yelled: "Oh, right, you'd *never* do anything so stupid as misplace your fucking keys. Only your stupid-ass husband would do that!"

A sixth sense in me told me not to move, and, for God's sake, not to say one single solitary word to antagonize Carl further. With every bit of self-control I could muster, I stood stock still, forbidding my neutral expression to morph into fear.

Carl regarded me, snorted in disgust, and continued. "You're so fucking perfect, aren't you? You know, you never get mad. You probably think that's being strong, but you know damn well it's because you're a fucking doormat." His eyes—bleary with drink, I could tell in a heartbeat—surveyed the room as though in search of another complaint. Both hands twitched uneasily. "And this counseling shit! This, of course, has gotten us nowhere...as I suspected. But noooo, I said I'd do it to appease you. You, so reasonable, sooo earnest."

Carl nearly choked with rage. "I knew counseling was a crock and now you've got it in your head it's our only hope. You've had the gall to tell me I've got stuff in my head that needs to be dealt with. Well, try dealing with a marriage partner who second-guesses your every move!"

He paced around in a small circle, stopping a little closer to me. He stuck a finger out, inches from my nose. "I tell you what would solve this situation: a good, hard fuck, that's what. But, noooo, you have no intention of doing what normal married couples do. You intend to remain a cold, dead fish until you deem we're...what? Rehabilitated! Fuck that!"

His hand swooped to his side, making me flinch. "Well, I can tell you I'm not living under these circumstances anymore!" And with that, his arm lunged past my head and grabbed the Christmas tree. He lugged it to the back door, fumbled a frustrating moment with the lock, and then hurled the entire mass out onto the deck. Looking as though he'd just conquered a mountain lion, he glared at me, daring me to oppose him in any way.

Horrified, I tried to keep as calm as I could, lowering my eyes, as one is advised to do when confronted with a gorilla, to show I had no intention of taking up the dare. Why did this man even want to stay in what he'd just described? Could he not see our few common goals or interests were flailing in the onslaught of our differences?

The two of us stood apart, Carl breathing heavily, me hardly at all. And then, as though thoroughly disgusted with the whole predicament, Carl turned on his heel, stomped down the hallway, hands still flicking from the wrists, and slammed the bedroom door.

I all but collapsed as I allowed my pent-up tension and fear to release in a jagged exhale. Not about to enter the bedroom, I tried to busy myself in the sewing room, wrapping a few presents and being as quiet as I could.

Finally, I heard Carl fall into bed in a drunken slumber. I felt sure our nights together in bed were numbered.

CHAPTER 36

GAME'S UP!

I awoke—or, rather, arose, since sleep had been out of the question—
an hour earlier than usual so I could leave—or rather, escape—for
the last day of school before the Christmas holiday. Carl, still in
passed-out stupor, never budged.

Normally a fun day of craziness and celebration, even my
French students' skit of "The Night Before Christmas"—en français,
bien sûr!—had no power to dispel my mood of foreboding. I knew
eighty percent of Carl's hellacious behavior the night before had
been alcohol-infused, but I also knew there would still be plenty
residual anger and resentment once he sobered up. I dreaded our
next encounter.

I also dreaded my next session with Dan—an individual one—
scheduled for that evening. Dan had called me that morning at work,
during my prep period.

"Just wanted to confirm our appointment tonight, since, you
know, Carl never showed up for his."

Embarrassed, I said, "I know. I'm so sorry. But I'll be there."

As soon as I hung up from Dan, I called Mary at Adam's office.

"So, what's going on? It's been nearly a month!" Mary asked, far more concerned than irritated that I had virtually disappeared since our last conversation.

I snorted. "Took a little detour." Mary waited. "Just calling to make sure you still have the papers."

"I'm looking at them, right over there on my desk."

"Good to know. Gotta go."

At 6:00 p.m., I entered Dan's office. I was an absolute wreck.

Dan studied me and then said, "I wanted to be sure you came tonight so I could tell you my observations from when you and Carl were here together. If you hadn't come, I was going to call you."

I regarded Dan with sardonic anticipation. "Uh boy, can't wait to hear this," I said, and steeled myself.

"You didn't see it, but when you started to cry, Carl gloated." I knew Dan was speaking the truth. "You see, as soon as he saw you break down, he knew he had you under his control again."

Control. How did this gentle counselor-man know *exactly* the word to use to knock some sense into me? I looked at Dan, imploring him to continue.

He did, watching me carefully so as to gauge the level of firmness needed. "You have spent this entire time with him, telling yourself you're wrong, that you're the one who really needs to steer this ship, that if you toe the line, things will work and you will not have made a gross mistake."

As Dan spoke, tears flowed down my cheeks, but this time they were tears of relief at hearing—finally!—somebody pronounce these words to me. It had been as though I could not come up with them on my own, my internal resources having shut down early on. I had to have this external, objective and totally rational pronouncement of what a farce my marriage was, and how I'd practically driven myself crazy trying to keep it going. So these words, rather than blasting me with tsunami force, felt more like one of my own showers, where I'd often taken refuge and found comfort. And come clean.

Dan remained silent, allowing my tears to dissipate and for me to gather myself. Then, his voice became firmer.

"This man is a con-man, one of the worst—or should I say best—I have ever seen. By con-man, I mean manipulative, controlling, self-serving. He has done nothing but disrespect you during your entire time together. Every time you give in to him, he remains the same and has no intention of changing. Yes, people can change—although I highly doubt Carl can. And he will never change if you continue to stay with him. Every day you do is another day he has won what is a very unfair battle."

I sniffled into a Kleenex. "I know."

"So, what are you going to do about it?"

"I have to leave him."

"Right."

CHAPTER 37

SHIT AND FAN TIME!

I drove home slowly, contemplating the challenge before me. Unlike other times—there had been so many!—I felt girded to follow through with what I now knew unequivocally I had to do. I considered my choices: either become my own person—which absolutely meant leaving Carl, which most likely meant a highly volatile confrontation, which also meant an unpleasant aftermath what with divorce expense and, oh God, enduring far more publicly the embarrassment of having made such a horrible choice; or...remain with Carl, which meant more exhausting, mind-numbing spells of keeping up appearances/stiffening upper lip/staying the good soldier route, all of which meant falling under Carl's power yet again. Gee, sure *looked* like a no-brainer.

But I didn't kid myself that what I was about to do was going to be easy. Rather than run home to my parents or bother Vivien, who was attending a gala event with Frank that evening, I decided I'd check into a hotel, damn the charges! I'd sneak my cats inside, and sit in a nice, quiet, safe place to gather my thoughts and write a firm

'Dear John' letter, being as kind as possible and avoiding all incendiary language. It would be the decent thing to do.

Growing more resolute by the minute, I pulled into the garage, sending out another message of gratitude the house was empty. I went upstairs, pulled down my suitcase—still packed from the most recent foiled escape attempt—carried it down to the car, and placed it in the trunk. From the garage shelf, I retrieved two cardboard cat carriers and went back up the stairs, calling the cats as I went. I turned right at the top of the steps to head through the living room towards the kitchen and ran smack into Carl's chest, much as I'd done four years ago at that Halloween party.

Only, tonight was way different.

Carl had entered silently through the front door (apparently having located his key), and he now stood like a six-foot tall human impasse of granite. I pulled up short, cat carriers still in my hands. Damn, had he been lying in wait for me to come home? Trying not to look as wary as I felt, I studied Carl's face, ascertaining he was not nearly as drunk as he'd been the previous night. But he sure as hell wasn't stone cold sober.

"And what the hell do you think you're doing?" Carl taunted, not at all in the fashion he'd addressed me at our first collision. This was not the gentle, humorous, sexy 'Whoa, lady.'

Knowing I must look like the kid at the cookie jar, I raised my eyes to Carl and said simply, "Carl, sit down. Please. I need to say something to you."

Carl's expression slid from sarcastic curiosity to disgust. "Aw, shit man, what kind of crap did that fag of a counselor cram into your head?"

"Whatever he said, my head already knew it," I said steadily. "Look, this is not working and will never work if we stay together. You—"

"What do you mean 'not working'?! All this is is a bad patch! Look, we *love* each other, you told—"

"—you are going to have to come to grips with some of the stuff you've done that's pretty much destroyed this marriage." I paused, then added, "And if I told you recently I loved you, it was probably just to keep the peace."

Carl jumped on my words. "Oh, so you were lying. And yet you say *I'm* the dishonest one around here. One big reason we're having problems is *you're* the one who's—you're the hypocrite! All you've been doing is 'faking it'!" Carl threw out this insult at me as though relishing how weak my defense would be.

I simply looked at him and sighed. "Yeah, if you want to call it that. I suppose I was, as you say, 'faking it.'" Carl balked, but I raised my hand. "I'm not saying I'm blameless, that's for sure, but it's obvious neither of us is going to deal with our faults so long as we stay together. It's entirely too fraught with tension."

"I can't believe you've let somebody else twist your mind like this!" he exploded.

"Look, Carl, there is absolutely nothing else to argue about." I could see he was itching to do just that. "At least not while we're this upset."

I saw this reasonable comment fly straight over Carl's head. He continued to look at me as if every syllable I spoke was stupid, wrong, and full of deceit. With all my might, I kept my voice steady, not daring to say the D-word. "Look, we should take some time here and separ—get away from each other for...a while...to think things through. We just need time."

Carl stood motionless, incredulous. Determined not to be guilty of offering false hope, I continued. "I frankly don't think even time will help, but I'm willing to be a good soldier about this."

"Good soldier, my ass!" Carl snarled, taking a step towards me.

Sensing my next move should be to allow him some space, I tried my best to turn calmly, go back through the door I'd just come through, and retrace my steps leading down to the garage.

I heard a quick rush behind me and suddenly all went dark and bright and loud in the same instant as I felt my head being slammed between the door and the door frame. I screamed as Carl grabbed my neck, pulling me back into the hallway. I stumbled, feeling one of my shoes fall off, but I wrestled away from Carl's grasp. There was no getting past him, so I kicked off my other shoe and ran to the room at the end of the hall, reaching for the phone. Carl lunged over me, yanking the phone from the wall. I swayed in front of him, unable to get my balance. As I started to scream at Carl to stop, his fist plowed into my left eye. Just like in the cartoons, I saw stars. I fell back onto the daybed, head crashing into the wall. Dazed, I lay there in a crumpled heap, and saw Carl hulk out of the room.

I wanted to just lie there, to cradle my aching head, but my gut, so long repressed, refused to remain silent and urged, "Leave! Now!"

I pulled myself up to stark attention, trying to figure out what to do. Where was Carl? Where had he gone? I bolted clumsily down the hallway into the living room and saw the front door was still open. Had he gone that way? Was he going to ambush me? I turned, went through the still slightly open hallway door to the basement and took the steps two at a time. I'd have to leave the cats for now, I knew, and pray Carl wouldn't hurt them out of spite.

I saw the car door was open—had I left it open?—and then I was horrified to see Carl's feet and knees scrabbling about on the garage floor while he'd flung himself over the driver's seat, frantically pulling at wires from under the dash. Unfortunately, my loud stomps down the steps had alerted Carl, and his face, livid with rage, appeared in the car door window. I turned and scrambled up the stairs with Carl in crazed pursuit. As I reached the top stair, I felt Carl's death grip around my ankle, causing me to free fall to the hallway floor, knocking the breath out of me for an instant.

I kicked with all my might to free myself, lurched upright, and fled through the living room to the back door, which was now closer than the front door. I rushed out onto the deck. I was met with a freezing cold blast of air and misting rain. I hesitated a moment, thinking for a split second how I really needed shoes and a coat, but then realized this was not the time for comfort. That split second was just enough time for Carl to catapult through the back door and grab me, not from the back, but from the front, his hands clamping down onto my small breasts. Small they were, but they provided enough purchase for Carl to hurl me back into the living room. I felt as though my entire torso had been ripped from my body.

Petrified beyond bounds, I tried to reach the front door, but again was intercepted by Carl. This time, he screamed at me, "So you want to leave, do you? How about this for an exit?" And with that, he hoisted me up and threw my entire body out the front door. I was completely airborne for a moment and would have stayed that way until hitting the ground, but for the railing, which brought my flight to a crushing halt, as I heard my ribs crack against it.

"You bitch," Carl screamed. "Where's the fucking gun?" He drew back from the door opening and turned on his heel, headed down the hallway to retrieve the gun that, I thanked my stars, was still safely hidden away.

I didn't wait to hear his screams of frustration when he'd make that discovery. Barefoot, I tore across the soggy, half frozen front yard, ribs screaming. Up the steep street I struggled, listening for Carl's pursuit, until I reached the preacher's house at the top. I stumbled to the front door, grateful the porch light was as dim as it was, and knocked on the door. A young boy, perhaps eight years old, opened the door and stared at me in horror.

CHAPTER 38

SHELTER

The child stood stock-still staring at the frightening apparition that was me. Shoeless, blouse half-ripped baring one shoulder, blood dripping from a ragged cut extending from my brow and disappearing into my scalp. Hair tousled, matted with more blood. Eyes crazed, desperate. Even as I quaked in complete disarray, I strained to repress the tone that should match this image as I whispered in a trembling voice, "Hello sweetie, please don't be frightened. Could you please go get your grandmother? Tell her it's Rosie from down the street. Tell her I need a little help."

My eyes darted furtively back down the street, searching for sight or sound of Carl. Even in my craziness, I felt a fleeting dash of comfort, figuring Carl would be far too lazy to run up the street after me. But I had to get out of sight.

The preacher's wife, Marlene, appeared at the door, her expression changing from questioning to horror to disbelief. She extended her hand, pulling me inside, enveloping my shaking body with a gentle but firm hug.

"Come in, sweetheart. It's going to be OK."

Marlene led me to a bathroom where she pressed a washrag to my forehead and helped me adjust my clothes. She noticed me wince as I lifted my arm to untwist the blouse's sleeve. "Honey, you probably need to get to the emergency room. I'm so sorry, but I don't drive and my husband isn't home."

Still shaking, I said, "Oh, please, I don't want you to feel you have to do one other thing for me. I'm so embarrassed to put you out like this. I know I must've scared the wits out of your grandson. If I could borrow your phone for a minute, I'll call my best friend, and she'll come get me, I'm sure."

"Honey, you don't have a thing to be embarrassed about," Marlene said as she handed me the phone. My shaking fingers dialed Vivien's number, and I prayed she would answer. After six rings, I was about to hang up, wondering why she wasn't home. But then I heard a breathless, slightly aggravated "Hello?"

I tried to speak but couldn't get past the boulder in my throat.

"Hello? Hello?"

"'s...'sme," I managed between a choke and a sob.

"Rosie? Rosie, is that you?"

"He beat me up."

Silence. "I'll be right there."

Thirty minutes later, Vivien pulled into the preacher's driveway, having turned off her headlights per my instructions. She found me waiting with Marlene by the garage door. Vivien and Marlene helped me into the back seat where I struggled to a reclining position, stifling a cry of pain as my ribs protested. Vivien, dressed in evening clothes, said, "Thank God you called me when you did. I was two minutes from being out the door."

My whole being swirled with pain and humiliation. "Omigod, that's right, tonight was that highfalutin wing-ding you and Frank were going to. Jeez, Vivien, I can't believe I called you. I wasn't thinking straight."

Vivien looked at me as though I'd said the stupidest thing ever. "Well, gee, can't imagine why!" Then her expression turned to concern. "What in the hell did he do to you?"

I tried to relate the events of the last two hours—*God, had it just been two hours? It seemed like two days!*—breaking into tears but checking them because it was entirely too painful. "I think Marlene and I heard him zoom up the street in the car and drive back by slowly. I'm not even going to think of what he would've done to me if he'd found me."

We reached the emergency room where we stayed for the next couple hours, waiting until I was finally called in for an examination, which showed my ribs were not broken but were severely bruised and slightly cracked. The scalp laceration was closed with several stitches. A deep blue and black bruise had been slowly spreading from my right temple to my jawbone; Carl had just missed connecting squarely with my eye. With stitched, bruised scalp and wrapped midriff, I eased back into Vivien's car.

"How would you like some company tonight?" Tears began once again to trickle down my cheeks.

"You bet," Vivien said.

Half an hour later, I was wrapped in Vivien's warm, fuzzy robe, her 'wubby' as she called it. My hands cradled a cup of hot chicken noodle soup, the number one comfort food of all time.

"I've got to get back over there and get the cats. I cannot believe I left them there with that monster. But I couldn't go back in the house to get them; I really think he would've killed me. I heard him say 'gun' and I knew I had to get the hell out of there. But, oh, if he does anything to those cats, I swear, I'll..." I broke into tears, once again pulling up short with a painful grimace.

"I don't think he's going to hurt Frau Eva and Mona Bone. All he's interested in getting his hands on right now is you. We'll go back over there tomorrow and get some of your stuff and the cats. And we'll go with the police."

While sleepless nights had been becoming more commonplace in the last year of my marriage, none matched the misery of this one, fraught with fear, anxiety and pain. What would Carl do to me if he found me at Vivien's? Would he harm the cats? Would he harm the piano? Each time I made to toss and turn, intense pain arrested me mid-motion. *This was all so incredibly unfair.*

The following morning I entered my house, sandwiched between two policemen. Vivien had remained at home, agreeing with me it might keep Carl from discovering my whereabouts. Carl stood in the middle of the living room, his face a livid mixture of fury and indignation. Then he gave a soft and engaging chuckle.

"Well, officers, I hardly think this is necessary. My wife can certainly come into our home without a police escort. I promise you, she's in no danger whatsoever."

The officer looked from Carl to my stitched forehead and slightly bent posture due to my wrapped ribs. "With all due respect, sir, your wife doesn't feel that's the case. She'll just be getting a few things and then we'll be out of here."

"Now, just a damn minute—"

"Please, sir, we don't want any trouble. I'd advise you to step aside."

And Carl stood aside, his eyes searing into me as I walked past him. I let out a quick sob of relief as I saw Frau Eva and Mona Bone, seemingly no worse for the wear. I gathered them up, one by one, willing my ribs to withstand the pain, and coaxed them into their carriers. Oddly, as if wanting to help their mistress, they displayed none of their usual resistance. The second policeman took them to my car in the basement. He'd already checked to see if the car would run, since I had expressed my fear Carl may have screwed things up.

"There doesn't seem to be anything wrong with it," said Officer Williams. He looked at me with kindness and concern. "It started up without a hitch. All the wires looked like they'd been jumbled about, but nothing was disconnected. He must've not known what he was doing."

"Wouldn't be the first time," I muttered.

Carl was instructed to not even think about following us out of there. One officer drove my car while I sat in the backseat with the cats.

"Can you tell if he's following us?"

"No ma'am, the coast is clear." He looked at me in the rear-view mirror. "You did real well back there, ma'am; I mean, not letting him hook you into an argument. I'd think, now that he sees you mean business, he'll come on around and, you know, face the music."

I looked out the window. "Yeah, you'd think, wouldn't you?"

The unfinished basement at Vivien's ran the entire length of the house, providing an excellent hiding place in the far corner for my car. We covered it with an old bedspread—me grimacing at the effort but determined to help—and placed a few odds and ends including a floor lamp and a coat rack around it as an extra measure of camouflage.

"I can't believe I'm having to do this shit," I muttered. I looked at Vivien. "Bet you can't, either."

Upstairs, I made my way to the guest bedroom, my new home for the holidays. It did not escape me the last four Christmases had been pretty lousy, all for the same reason. Wanting nothing more than to take a long nap, I knew there still remained one other pressing task. I moaned as I removed both cats from my lap where they'd taken refuge from their strange surroundings.

"Gotta call Darrah," I told Vivien. "This being Mama's first Christmas without Daddy, Darrah thought it'd be a good idea to get her away from her empty house. I need to give Darrah a heads-up on what's going on, so they won't call me at home." I rolled my eyes. "The last thing Mama needs to know right now is that her other daughter is going through a divorce."

"Right, good idea."

I dialed the number and waited several rings before Darrah answered with an extremely wary "Hello."

I began, "Darr—"

"What in the hell is going on?" I couldn't tell if I was hearing concern or anger. She continued, "Carl has called here at least half a dozen times. At first he said he just wanted to say Merry Christmas, but then he wanted to know if we'd spoken with you, which I thought was odd, and then he finally admitted y'all had had a little tiff of some kind—"

I snorted. "Tiff! Yeah, the cracked-ribs-stitches-in-forehead kind of tiff."

"What?"

I gave a brief summary of how the last twenty-four hours had gone down.

"Oh my lord!"

"Hey, can Mama hear you? I really don't want her to know about this yet."

And then, much to my amazement, I heard Darrah's tone turn to one of frustration and sarcasm. "Well, you're a little late on that one!"

"Oh no, has Carl talked to Mama?"

"No, but she knows he's been calling like a madman. She knows something's up."

"Well, don't tell her he beat me up. She doesn't need to know that right now."

A moment of silence from Darrah, and then: "Boy, what a sense of timing you've got! I mean, Mother's as fragile as a newborn right now, and yet you choose *right now* to leave Carl! I mean, how selfish can you get?"

I was stunned. "Um, I didn't exactly *choose* last night..." I began to cry but cut it short because the pain in my ribs was unbearable. Darrah didn't reply, perhaps considering she'd come on a bit too strong.

"Look, I'll call in a couple days. I'm at Vivien's but, whatever you do, don't tell Carl. Tell him I called from a pay phone and wouldn't give y'all any info. I'm planning on being at Lucy's in Atlanta for a few days to, you know, give Vivien a breather."

"Jeez. OK." Darrah said, the venom having disappeared. "Hey, just be sure you're not going to go back to him."

"Nope. The boy crossed the line this time."

I hung up the phone and relayed the conversation to Vivien. "God, she's right, you know. This crap has been going on for *two—make that three—frigging years!* I probably could've timed this a bit better..."

Vivien looked at me as though I'd lost my mind. "No, your sister isn't right. Your sister's a bitch."

Now I looked at Vivien as though she'd lost her mind. I wanted to protest but I was too consumed by two suffocating emotions: guilt, that I was causing everyone problems; and humiliation I'd been such a fool. I lowered my face into my hands and moaned, "Nooo, no."

Now that I had my cats, I stood a much better chance of getting at least some sleep. Not that the cats would sleep any better though. While I was a cat person, Vivien was a cat *and* a dog person. A big dog person. For the next two weeks, Mendy, an English sheepdog, would be a hunking furry obstacle in the hallway, body trembling in anticipation and curiosity, nose scrunched under the crack in the door, blowing like a dragon, trying for all she was worth to get to whatever was on the other side. Frau Eva and Mona Bone remained transfixed in wonder and horror as they contemplated the gray, snorting snout flattened underneath the door. On this first night of togetherness, though, the threesome—Frau Eva, Mona Bone and I—provided each other with comfort enough to finally drift off into much-needed sleep.

I spring straight up off the glider. Rotating my head, circling my shoulders, shaking out my arms, then my legs, I try to shed the tension that has invaded my body. That I'd not lent conscious thought to these memories in, what, *decades*, would partly account for my visceral reaction. To virtually relive that horrific night—my body completely consumed by terror and pain *inflicted on me by another human being*—has dredged up a mass of emotion. My lips reverberate as several short, forceful exhalations escape. I have to walk this off!

A thirty-minute tromp through some trails in the back woods proves somewhat calming. I reclaim my seat. While that most offensive memory has faded somewhat, others remain for further and final contemplation.

Considering all the times I might have ended things but for some distraction, I'm struck that one—Daddy's death—occurred without Carl's lifting one scheming finger. Carl probably looked like some evil cricket, rubbing his hands together in glee at this timely stroke of luck. He could not have missed that Daddy's opinion of him had lowered significantly, his patience wearing thin as he watched his daughter change from a happy, free spirit to a stressed, closed robot. But the sticky obstacle of a disgruntled father-in-law had up and removed itself of its own accord. Carl must have felt an amazing surge of empowerment as he watched his wife and mother-in-law succumb to grief. Stepping into the role of hero, he must've felt invincible. I sputter in disgust. Fortune might favor the brave, but all too often it lends an undeserved hand to assholes.

Thoughts of Mama remind me of the 'heads-up' phone call to Darrah, eliciting Vivien's caustic remark. I give a gentle 'Wow! I coulda had a V8!' smack to my brow. I'd totally forgotten about that! So completely out of character for my kind, funny, generous sister. I suspect she was pretty much at her own wits' end that night. Not her finest moment, to be sure, but then—I regard the journals scattered about me—who doesn't have a suitcase full of 'wish I hadn't dunnit/saidits'?

Opening the next journal, I'm somewhat heartened, figuring regrets are on the wane.

CHAPTER 39

LEGAL AID

By the next afternoon, Carl was banging on Vivien's front door, demanding to see me. Vivien, with a strong calmness belying her petite frame, refused to open the door. She claimed no knowledge of my whereabouts and told Carl she would call the police if he didn't leave. Amazingly, he did. We knew we hadn't heard the last from him.

Early Monday morning I sat across from Mary and her boss, Adam Alexander Hamilton. Exceptionally intelligent, Mary had landed a job with the city's top criminal attorney. "Divorce is not Adam's expertise," she'd told me, "but he's willing to take on your case, since you're my friend, and since this ought to be pretty cut-and-dried." Figuring my cause for divorce was about as just as they came, I had agreed with Mary.

The law office was deserted except for us, everyone else having taken off for the two remaining days before Christmas.

"Oh, Adam, Mary," I said, trying not to gush, "I can't thank y'all enough for coming in today." From my briefcase, I pulled several official documents. "Whatever I can do to get this divorce on the fast track, just say the word."

"Let's see what you have here," Adam said, taking the deed to the house, mortgage contract, check stubs, tax returns, etc. (These items I'd retrieved the day before on my second police-escorted visit to the house, having been far too rattled by Carl's ominous glare the first time around to think straight. This time, the house was blessedly vacant, everything seemingly intact. No axed piano, no shattered china or crystal; silver still safely hidden from two weeks earlier. I'd lowered my head in solemn gratitude for small miracles.) Adam flipped through the documents, jotting down a few figures. "So," he said, "who's in the house right now?"

"Carl," I said. I patted my rib cage and pulled back my hair to reveal the stitches at my brow. "Didn't seem like a good idea to stick aroun—"

We all heard a door open in the adjoining lobby. Halting my attempt at humor, I cast wide, frightened eyes in the direction of the sound, certain it was Carl. Adam, seeing me stiffen in fear, rose from his chair, exited the office and intercepted the intruder.

Mary and I couldn't make out what was being said, but I knew the other voice belonged to Carl. His tone ranged from charming to aggressive. After a seemingly interminable five minutes, we heard the front door close and lock, and Adam reentered the office, alone. Before Adam could speak, I said, "I have nothing to say to him, and he has nothing to say that I need to listen to."

"Well, the man seemed pretty contrite; he left you this letter."

I steeled myself as I took the letter from Adam. I did not want to touch anything that had been in Carl's hands, thinking it might be a trap. I laughed at my paranoia—good grief, I was in my attorney's office!—and opened the envelope. Mary pulled up a chair next to me to read along. Adam continued perusing my papers.

Rosie,

I would like to tell you about Friday, not as an excuse, but a reason.

I lost three sales, lost my commission on a fourth because of a screw-up on Slade's part. This bothered me but because of Thursday night, despite the fact that we argued I thought that you still cared. I got the same impression Friday morning and I kept this thought all day. I came home and found out my mother is not doing to well. I started to put the tinsel back on the tree. I had picked up roast beef & hoped we could have a quick sandwich & go to the mall & maybe just walk around. You came home and proceeded to tell me you were "faking it."

What happened after that I will live with for the rest of my life.

You are the most important person in my life. I have never felt so happy and peaceful about being in love with someone, that's why I married you. I have never felt that in return from you. That is my insecurity and it's because I've always been afraid of losing you because of something I had done or would do. I concealed things from you for that reason—Foolish!

Love needs honesty—not the nit-picking honesty that keeps account of every flaw, but the deeper honesty of the heart that lets us share what is most genuine in ourselves, imperfections and all.

I looked sideways at Mary. "This is rich."

When we are not brave enough to do this, it is often because we feel unworthy of love. We're afraid our past mistakes and habits cannot stand the scrutiny of a lovers eyes.

People need time to appreciate or understand one another's differentness, to share, understand and deal with them. If you and I had married ten years ago I would not have made the mistakes I have made.

Back then I was much the same as you are now. Compared to a lifetime 3 years is really not that long. With each day and with each problem we see and have we can do nothing but strengthen our marriage—if we deal with it. I truly regret that you have to deal with the more visible signs, but I am dealing with things that are not always visible. My greatest fear has been that before I can correct or improve on these flaws you will discover them and then I would lose you.

My brow furrowed. *What the hell is he talking about? Does he have a Big Secret or something?*

Love needs words to make it real. Without words, quarrels can't be resolved, resentments can't come to the surface, we lose the power to share the meaning of our lives. So many times we have used words to hurt each other. The two of us can hurt each other very deeply with the words we use.

Love is not a single act, or ten acts, it is a lifetime venture on which we are always learning, discovering, growing. It is not destroyed by numbered failures or won by numbered carress's.

Noting the spelling error, I also noticed the handwriting had changed. *Had he gotten tired of writing and had to go beddy-bye? Or have a drink? Or...was someone else writing this letter for him?*

I love you Rosie, the way the last 24 hours have gone more than life itself. Whatever is left in you—hope for the future or maybe the wish that it could be the way the feelings were 3 1/2 or 4 years ago—would you please reach down inside yourself and grab onto it. You said today that you "owe me no favors." I'm asking for one—don't leave me now—I need you Rosie, I don't want to be without you. This is a very lonely house without you and a very lonely, —— person.

[the scratched-through word looked to be 'lost']

We both had the same dreams & hopes not to very long ago, didn't we? The love we had for each other made both of us feel higher and higher.

Oh, please. Spare me!

You said Saturday that you don't owe me anything. You don't , but maybe because of that feeling that I was able to give to you, you'll at least talk to me before any decision is made that would be irrevocable.

This is the time of year for love, understanding and maybe a little compassion and forgiveness.

Maybe what we need is some time apart. There are alternatives available to us, but we need to discuss them. I care about you, I care about us, and I care about our future. I know I have expected too much from you recently. I wanted things to move too quickly, that might have been wrong—

Might have?? 'Scuse me, now whose fault was this?!

—but it was unfair. I know I hurt you but maybe more importantly I hurt us. If there were any way to erase Friday and make it go away I know we would both wish for that. I can never make up for what happened, but I will not stop trying.

One of my fears now is that you will take this letter as words and not honest feelings.

The letter ended abruptly. No closing, no signature.

"Wow," Mary said. "He's pretty good with words, isn't he? He's really shooting for your heartstrings."

I sighed and lowered the letter in my lap. "It doesn't matter." Resolute, I looked at Mary and Adam. "I am done."

To my amazement, Adam said, "I'd advise you to call him, though. Cutting him off like this may antagonize him." Adam had made no indication he considered reconciliation an option, so at least we were square on that. But I wondered if he fully appreciated my emotionally wiped-out, hurting state.

With great reluctance, I called Carl later that day from a pay phone. So far, Carl wasn't positive I was at Vivien's and I was trying my best to keep it that way. Guilt was beginning to take hold of me. It was bad enough I had the nightmare of dealing with Carl; what made it even worse was that I was apparently going to drag a boat-load of folks down with me.

"Sweetheart," Carl cried, "Oh hon, are you OK? I'm so sorry! I just went crazy thinking I was going to lose you. I love you so much! Surely, because of that, because there is so much love in me to give you, surely, surely, we can work this out. God, please!"

"I'm sorry, Carl, but it is over," my voice was surprisingly neutral. "You need to sign the papers and we'll get on with our lives. We tried and we tried—" *well, 'we' is a stretch*, "—and we just didn't make it. I'm sorry, but this is the way it has to be."

I waited for a response. The silence stretched until I heard the click of his hanging up.

CHAPTER 40

OF POT PARTIES AND POOP

For the next couple days, I holed up with my cats in Vivien's guest room. The constant ringing of the phone was followed by the immediate lifting and lowering of the receiver. Making no headway with Vivien in demanding my whereabouts, Carl employed nastier tactics. He told Vivien what a fool she was to stay with Frank, because Carl had just seen him at a restaurant, infatuated with a brunette.

"My, my, for someone who knows so much, you don't know shit," Vivien said with complete aplomb.

She hung up and whirled around towards me. "Oh, no! Do you think the brunette was Carla, Frank's ex? Or, should I say, supposed ex?"

I regarded my friend's face, full of pain and disbelief. "Probably not. Carl's just making junk up to try to get you rattled."

"But how does he know Carla is a brunette?"

"Lucky guess, maybe?"

Vivien, unable to come up with a better explanation, looked at me. "Boy. Carl is mean."

"Yep."

On Christmas Eve morning, I joined Vivien in the final stages of tree decorating. We—Vivien a wisp, me an invalid mummy—had had to struggle with the set-up the day before, since Frank had claimed bruised pride when Vivien confronted him with Carl's 'brunette' tidbit. "How hurtful," he had claimed, that Vivien would believe something like that about him. He'd suggested they stay apart a few days to let things cool down a bit, give them both time to think more clearly.

The tree made Charlie Brown's look like something out of *Southern Living*. It stood at a decided slant which we tried to right by stretching a string from mid-trunk to the clasp of a nearby window. Upon plugging in the lights, Vivien and I had to jump to safety as sparks shot from the outlet.

"Been meaning to get that fixed," Vivien muttered. She located a bright orange extension cord and stretched it from the tree across the room to a working outlet. "Stunning, don't you think?" We stood in mock admiration of our efforts.

"Merry Shitty Christmas," I offered, with a half-chuckle, half-sob.

Later that evening, as we sat in comfortable chairs, wrapped in humongous robes, drinking hot chocolate, the darkened Christmas tree mirrored our moods.

"At least it's quiet now," Vivien noted with sarcasm. "The phone hasn't rung for three hours."

A sharp rapping at the front door shattered the silence. We riveted to petrified attention, Vivien standing while I scuttled and ducked behind the chair, lest Carl might peer through windows. Gathering herself, Vivien walked to the door.

"Who is it?" she asked, trying to keep her voice as firm as possible.

"Police."

Vivien turned to see my head shaking back and forth since I was positive it was Carl in cop's clothing. With due caution, Vivien peered through the peep hole and looked at me again.

"It *is* the police! Two of them!"

Vivien opened the door and the officers entered the room. The first one said, "We've had a complaint from a gentleman that his daughter is at a pot party at this address and—" he stopped short, now taking a second, closer look at Vivien. "Is that you, Ms. Hazelton?" Then, his gaze moved to me as I rose from behind the chair, a trembling apparition of fluffy blue material, clutching a mug, eyes round with fright. "Miss Browning?" The policeman removed his hat.

Vivien and I screamed. "Gabe Parrish! Oh, is it good to see you!" Vivien wrapped her arms around him as I crept forward to do the same. Gabe had been a model student in my French class, and had also, truth be told, had a huge crush on me (his being a Senior in my first year of teaching). He started to pick me up and twirl me around, but stopped abruptly upon hearing panicked cries of protest. He looked at his ex-teachers, completely flummoxed.

"What the hell is going on?" And to me, "And what the hell has happened to you?" And to both of us, "And where's the pot?"

Gabe and his partner gladly accepted the offer of hot chocolate and cookies ("Sorry, we're out of pot," Vivien had joked) on this cold Christmas eve. They listened spellbound as we filled them in on the ongoing nightmare.

"So," Gabe said. "What we've got here is a crazy man. Right?" Somber nods from each of us. "Well, I suspect he's done for the evening. Don't worry though, we'll be patrolling the area for the rest of our watch."

They handed empty mugs and plates to Vivien, thanking her. Gabe looked at me then, remnants of his former crush evident as he said, "And you. You call me *anytime*. I mean it."

With tears brimming, I thanked him. The policemen left, primed to bust the next out-of-control party should they get whiff of one.

I turned to Vivien. "Well, Merry maybe-not-quite-so-Shitty Christmas," I smirked.

We sat in silence, contemplating our own dilemmas. Finally, we rose, cleaned up the kitchen, and headed to our bedrooms.

Lights hadn't been out an hour before there was some commotion on the front porch followed immediately by Mendy's frantic barks and howls. Vivien was at the door in a flash while I limped in warm pursuit. Our hands were over our ears to protect them from Mendy's ear-splitting yelps. Nudging the curtain from the sidelights, Vivien could see two figures running towards the upper corner of her front yard. She cracked the door open to get a clearer look.

"They look young," she said, yelling so I could hear over Mendy. "Students maybe? To roll the yard?"

Mendy's head was half-way through the slight opening, straining to give chase to the marauders. "I can't let her out! What if they hurt her?"

Just then we heard a barrage of curses coming from the shrubs at the corner. Vivien burst into laughter. I simply stared at her, not following the sudden mood change. She looked absolutely delighted.

"Those bad boys just discovered the spot where Mendy does her business every afternoon."

The cursing continued, accompanied by stomps and swipes on the pavement, until finally all racket faded into the distance.

I curbed my restrained laughter to ask Vivien, "Do you think Carl could have hired them to hassle us in some way?"

Not discounting my supposition, Vivien said, "Well, if he did, he'll have to pay them double now."

CHAPTER 41

CLOAK AND DAGGER CHRISTMAS

In stark contrast to Vivien's fire-hazard of a crippled Christmas tree was the glorious display of festive joy at her mother's, or Maw-Maw's, who lived right next door. Sharing a scrumptious holiday feast with Vivien's entire family, my troubled spirit savored the warmth, caring and safety abundant at this unpredicted Christmas gathering.

Although Vivien's beneficence was open-ended, I knew she needed some space, mainly to deal with Frank. I would now impose upon the other two Inner Circle members, Louise and Lucy. Later Christmas day, Louise pulled up to Vivien's house, as planned.

I removed all camouflage from The Merry and backed her out of Vivien's garage. I followed Louise to the northeast area of the city where Louise's mother, Jane, lived. I was positive Carl would never in a million years figure out where I had stashed my car now. I tried to reassure Jane she was in no danger.

"Don't worry, Carl has no idea what your last name is and, anyway, I have my phone book. You really don't have anything to worry about." I feigned as much confidence as I could.

"If you say so," said Jane, unconvinced. The phone rang. It was Vivien. Louise gave the phone to me and I listened incredulously to Vivien's alarmed voice.

"Lucy just called and said Carl *knows* you're going over to Atlanta to see her, and he's coming to get you. He says he's going to follow you over there and 'run you off the fucking road' if he has to."

Aghast, I hung up the phone, looked at Louise, and said in a voice Jane couldn't hear, "I think I need to call the Highway Patrol." Louise helped me look up the number and dialed it.

After giving as brief an explanation as possible, I asked the officer, "Would it be possible to get an escort of some kind, at least for part of the way out of town?" I could hardly believe I was making such a request. This was all too unreal.

"Sorry, Mrs. Ballini, but I'm afraid we're short-handed because there's that really dangerous escaped convict, a cop-killer, on the loose and nearly all our manpower is trying to track him down."

En route to Atlanta in Louise's car, I felt the heavy weight of guilt pressing harder onto my shoulders. "God, I thought a divorce was between two people, three if you count the lawyer. 'Scuse me, make that fuckinglawyer...one word, donchaknow." Louise grinned. "So let's see, so far, it's Vivien, her mom, you, your mom, my sister, my mom, the freaking police, Lucy, the freaking *highway patrol*... God, who's next?" I exhaled in exasperation.

Louise, never one to shrink from adversity, said simply, "Don't sweat it. We all love you."

As it turned out, we didn't need a personal escort. Our first fifty miles were ablaze with flashing blue lights atop cop cars, the convict hunt at fevered pitch. "I should've given the cop Carl's description and license number," I said. "For, I dunno, Operation Asshole Roundup."

I constantly checked the rear view mirrors. It was unnerving to know dangerous people—at least two—lurked nearby.

Three hours later, Louise and I pulled into the driveway of Lucy's family home, where her mom, Minnie, and brother, Jimmy, still lived. Lucy opened the back door, her eyes wide and scared. "He keeps calling. He's called here at least half a dozen times, saying crazy things!" She hurried us inside, locking the door behind her. We sat in the kitchen where all curtains were drawn.

"What kind of crazies was he saying?" No sooner had I spoken than the phone rang.

"Well," said Lucy, still nervous, "listen for yourself." We all huddled around the phone's receiver.

In an exasperated tone, Lucy answered. "Hello?!"

Carl's voice hissed like a snake. "I *know* Rosie's over there!"

Lucy's voice betrayed none of her fear. Looking straight at me, she calmly replied, "Rosie's not here, I'm telling you. Besides, why in the world would she be here with me instead of there with you?"

Carl's voice lowered slightly. "We had a little spat. I need to talk to her."

"A *spat*, you say?" Lucy was careful to pursue it no further. She had no intention of locking horns with her former boss, and she simply said, "Well, she's not here."

Anger returned to Carl's tone. "Yes, she is, too, goddamn it!" Then, coaxing, "Look, I just want to give her her Christmas present... so if you'll give me directions to—"

Lucy bristled. "Look, Carl, there is absolutely no reason for you to come here, but if you do, trust me, either the police will meet you at the end of the driveway...or my brother will. With a gun." She slammed the phone down, just as a flash of headlights streaked across the curtains. "Speaking of whom..." Lucy said, in obvious relief.

Jimmy was a bit of a wayward son only in that he imbibed a bit too much. His heart was of gold; he loved his sister and he loved her friends, especially me. Moments after he arrived, the phone jangled again. Jimmy yanked up the receiver.

"You listen here, you cowardly little son of a bitch. Trust me, you set one foot on this property and it's the last step you'll ever take. If you've got half a brain, you'll stay away from here." He hung up the phone and gazed at the three women staring at him as if at The Terminator. "That ought to do it," he sniffed.

Jimmy was correct, as the remainder of the evening proved uneventful, more like a subdued spend-the-night party. The entire crew plopped on Minnie's huge antique bed. Leaning against an intricately carved headboard, I updated everyone on the events of the past few days. I ended with my head in my hands, engulfed once again in humiliation and grief that I was bringing so much trouble down on so many of my friends and family.

"I can't believe I've been so stupid," I moaned.

Louise and Lucy looked at each other and slowly slid off the bed to stand directly in front of me. "We hate to say it and we're only going to say it this once but..." with wagging fingers and sing-song voices, they chimed, "...we told you so!"

"I get it, I get it," I said, patting my ribs. "Don't make me laugh."

The next day, exactly one week since the *spat*, the four of us set out to join the crazies for the day-after-Christmas bargains. Trussed up in my rib brace, I kept close to our tight little group until suddenly I had to pull up short. I approached the nearest wall and leaned against it. Eyebrows furrowed toward the bridge of my nose, eyes squinting, mouth half opened into a grimace, I emitted a bark-like shout and slowly collapsed. My friends rushed to the heap on the floor that was me, their faces horror-stricken, questioning.

"Had to sneeze," I gasped. "Been needing to do that for a week. Couldn't hold it any longer." I made to hug my ribs, but stopped in pain. "God, that hurt."

Back at Lucy's, we were in the midst of a Scrabble game when the doorbell rang. Jimmy picked up the rifle that he'd retrieved from the shed where it had been for years. "Hope I don't have to fire this thing," he said. "No telling which end the bullet's coming out of." Dubiously armed, Jimmy stood to the side of the front door. "Who is it?" he said sharply.

"Telegram," came the answer.

And it was.

PAPERS NOT SERVED YET STOP IF YOU WANT NO CONTEST CALL ME NOW STOP 205-956-5283 FDALE WAS LEADING PINSON VALLEY @ HALFTIME CARL STOP 10:22PM

"Lord, what next?" we all said. The phone rang. "Holy shit," we chorused.

"Hello!" Jimmy shouted into the receiver. "Oh—hi. Just a minute." He handed the phone to Louise. "It's Jane."

Louise took the phone and held it away from her ear. Apparently, Jane was yelling. "Yes ma'am. Yes ma'am." Louise hung up the phone and looked at me. "Mother says your car is leaking oil and is stinking up the whole house and she's on crutches and can't get downstairs to see what's going on. She says for us to get our butts home asap and do something about it. She's scared the house is going to blow up or something." I looked at her mournfully. "We gotta go," Louise said.

The following Monday, I received word from Mary that Carl had finally been served papers while taking out the trash at the house. "Something poetic in that, I'd think," I said ruefully. Grateful for that small amount of progress, I tried to come out of the stupor I'd been in since the attack, ten days prior.

One thing I needed to do was to have Mama's car serviced before she returned from Darrah's. Per previous arrangement, Mama's neighbor, Bonnie, was to help in car shuffling. While finalizing arrangements, I gave Bonnie a brief account of how my holiday had gone.

"He's still in the house—our house; no, I mean *my* house—but would you and Gimpy (I never could say the name of Bonnie's hysterical husband without a giggle) please keep an eye on Mama's place. There's no telling what this crazy man might do next." Thinking it might be wise, I gave Bonnie Vivien's phone number.

On Wednesday afternoon of New Year's Eve, I sat at the attorney's office and, again, Carl appeared. Again, I refused to see him. I heard him arguing with Adam, just outside the office.

"Look," I heard him cajole, "this is all one great big mistake. A divorce is not the answer here; it's crazy! I just need to talk to her, reason with her."

"I'm afraid there's no more reasoning to be done in this," Adam said firmly. "I'm going to have to ask you to please leave." I heard some muttered cursing and the slamming of a door. Adam reentered the office.

"You're positive you're not planning on getting back together with this bozo, right?" he asked, apparently unwilling to go to bat for someone who might prove too fainthearted to stay the course.

"Not a chance in hell," I said, one hundred percent sure, and wondering again why in the hell people kept asking me that question. Returning to my car in the parking lot, I made a three-sixty survey of the surroundings, seeing nothing suspicious. Still, once in the car and moving, I invented yet another ridiculously circuitous route before finally easing Merry into her cache at Vivien's.

Upstairs, we sat at the kitchen table to eat the burgers and fries I had picked up. Vivien's hair was in rollers, in preparation for a New Year's Eve out on the town with Frank, who'd apparently come to his senses, and had convinced Vivien that any dealings with his ex-wife were simply follow-ups to the divorce settlement.

With hope in her voice Vivien said, "So the man looks like he keeps on choosing me."

"Well, it'd certainly be the smart choice," I said and then pondered a minute. "Whereas Carl The Asshole had a chance to choose wisely and instead did what he did. Kinda like ol' General Woundwort in *Watership Down*." We nodded knowingly, smiling at the reference to one of our all-time favorite books, largely because it was told through the viewpoint of rabbits. Woundwort's character embodied the futility of control over those desiring freedom. "Yep, the do-do head is still fighting to keep me. Why, I'd like to know."

"Could be you're actually a pretty good meal ticket for the boy."

This brought on a howl from both of us. "Oh, for sure," I snorted. "I can hear it now: 'Man, I gotta find me a good woman with lotsa money. I know! I'll marry a teacher! From Alabama!'" As laughter subsided, I drew a deep breath. "Well, like the bad wabbit Woundwort, Carl's still fighting. But he will lose."

Snuggled in bed that evening with the cats and journal in my lap, I could almost ignore the pain and stress, as I happily contemplated a New Year which would not include Carl. The divorce trial date being a mere six weeks away, I felt sure better times were on the way.

Not so fast.

CHAPTER 42

IS CIRCUMSTANTIAL A FOUR-LETTER WORD?

New Year's Day began at Vivien's at 6:45 a.m. with a particularly shrill telephone ring. It was Bonnie and Gimpy.

"Your mother's house has been robbed. You better get over here."

Gimpy met me as I pulled into Mama's driveway. "I thought you might want a manly man to escort you into the house," Gimpy chirped. Gimpy was all of five feet, a veritable human apple, and undoubtedly one of the funniest people I had ever met. He and Bonnie had endeared themselves to Mama such that Gimpy took this break-in as a personal affront.

"Bastard," he spat. "Josephine's first Christmas without Edward, you'd think the bastard would have had a little more compassion." Gimpy had already concluded Carl was the culprit. His saying so, while confirming my suspicion, only troubled me further.

I stepped inside the townhouse, expecting complete bedlam, but saw only a few things out of order. The doors of a small china cabinet were open, revealing empty shelves where two dozen silver goblets had been housed, along with other small serving pieces.

Several kitchen drawers were open, the contents jumbled about, but, as far as I could tell, not much was missing, certainly not anything of real value.

"When the police were here," Gimpy was saying, "they said it didn't look like a normal robbery since so little was taken. They said it looked more like an attempt to merely hassle or frighten somebody. Also, there were no signs of forced entry. They must have had a key."

I tried to think whether I had extra keys to Mama's house lying around, but I couldn't think straight. God, would Carl actually do something like this to Mama? How evil! How cruel! How scary!

Assured now, though, the house was safe, I thanked Gimpy, saying I'd call him if I needed him, but for now, he should go back home to help Bonnie prepare New Year's fixings for a football party. I locked the door behind him and, steeling myself, headed upstairs to the office. The desk drawer was ajar, its contents also having been rifled through but left behind. I sat down at the desk, trying to decide when and how I was going to break this news to Mama.

I dreaded the jolt I was about to inflict upon her. Our relationship had not been what I would describe as close, but we had become closer since Daddy's death. I had called and visited several times each week, trying to help her adjust to her new and uninvited circumstances. By summertime, a few months after the funeral, Mama had actually shown signs of grabbing hold to the new normal, but her hold, tenuous at best, had probably slipped during this first holiday. What should have proved a warm and reassuring bandage from sadness was going to be further ripped away by the violence and chaos that had erupted at home. I wondered if it all was going to be too much for her.

My head was about to burst and I lowered it to the desk, feeling a sob working its way up my throat. Two inches away from my head, the phone rang, nearly ejecting me from the chair. Oh God, it's Carl! How in God's green earth does he know I'm here? I held my hands together refusing to answer the phone. The ringing continued, piercing the quiet. That bastard! Enough! I grabbed the receiver and shouted into it, "Carl?!"

A voice, unlike any I'd ever heard, came over the line. Crackled and old, wheezing and high-pitched, words stuttered out as though spoken through a mouthful of spit. "Heh— heh— hello?" it said.

Could this be Carl playing some kind of nasty joke? "Who is this?" I demanded.

More stuttering, spluttering and hesitation. "I'm Mr. Pope!"

"What? Who? Who's Mr. Pope? I don't know any Mr. Pope. I think you must have the wrong number."

Quickly, the helium-filled voice spoke again. "I'd like to speak to Edward Browning."

My heart stopped. What kind of cruelty joke was this? "Who is this! What do you want?"

I heard several quick intakes and expulsions of breath, followed by the voice, now highly nervous and excited. "...wallet...got credit cards inside...found pillow...picking up cans...lots of glasses...... golden rule!" I strained to make sense of what I was hearing.

"Wait a minute. You're telling me your name's Mr. Pope, and you found my dad's, I mean, Edward Browning's wallet inside a pillow case full of silver goblets outside the Golden Rule restaurant?"

"Yesh, yesh!" the voice spurted with great relief.

"And where are you right now, Mr. Pope?" I asked as gently and normally as I could, trying not to excite this person anymore than he already was. His voice grew faint several times and I feared he was getting ready to hang up."

"At my housh. Here in Arndale's where my housh izzat."

For the next few dizzying moments, I was finally able to obtain the address from the high-strung gentleman and to make tentative arrangements for retrieving the stolen goods and wallet.

I hung up and immediately dialed the number on the card the policeman had left with Gimpy. "Mr. Browning?" how odd a name, I thought as I addressed him. "This is Rosie Balli—Rosie Browning, Josephine Browning's daughter. My mother's place was robbed and you were here this morning."

"Well, Happy New Year," he said wryly.

Fortunately, New Year's Day morning is typically a quiet time, seeing as most folks are nursing hangovers from the previous night's celebration. Detective Browning met me at Mr. Pope's little house in the older section of Irondale (Arndale, per Mr. Pope), just across the highway from my neighborhood. We knocked and, within seconds, the door opened to reveal what I was sure was Ichabod Crane's older brother. Thin as spaghetti, head wobbling on a noodle neck, eyes magnified behind thick lenses, the man pumped my hand, and spoke excitedly while sending out a spray of spit that hit both me and the detective.

"Pleashed to meeshu! Pleash come inshide!" He motioned us into his small, cluttered living room. There on the floor was a pillowcase bulging with silver goblets, footed dessert dishes, bonbon bowls and the like. I could hardly believe I would not have to tell Mama these little treasures were gone forever. I would have been more gleeful had I not taken another look at the pillow case. The purple fleur-de-lis border was eerily familiar. This was not my mother's pillowcase. It was mine.

Detective Browning picked up the pillow case. "I'm sorry, Mrs. Ballini, but I'll have to take this in to the station to be filed as evidence. You can pick it up in a couple days as soon as everything is documented."

I nodded, taking one more look at the items strewn across the floor. A strange-looking object caught my eye.

"What the heck is this?" I picked the piece up, confirming immediately it was not silver.

Detective Browning studied it. "Looks to me like a hubcap." He turned it over. "Yep, look at this." I looked. Engraved on the surface was an outline of an animal of some sort. A cougar.

"Guess what kind of car my husband has," I tried to sound sarcastic, but my voice was barely audible. Up to this point, I'd tried to tell myself this was some fantastic coincidence, that Carl would not strike out at anyone as innocent and vulnerable as my mother. But here was undeniable proof he had done just that.

"Hate to tell you," Browning said, "but they'll classify this as 'circumstantial evidence.'"

I looked up at him, my eyes saying 'you got to be kidding.' Then I said, "You got to be kidding."

CHAPTER 43

HAPPY DIFFERENT NEW YEAR

My utmost priority was to get Carl out of the house, so I could get back in it. The house payment was due on the second of the month which was that very day, in fact. My hand trembled with anger as I wrote the check. I had no intention of paying for a roof over Carl's head. I called the power company and requested a disconnect. Next, I called Gabe—the ex-student policeman of pot party fame—and asked him to accompany me to the house. I was really worried about my piano. There was no telling what I might find.

What I found was that Carl had changed the locks. Foiled, I headed to the police station to pick up my pillowcase and Mama's silver only to find the detective division was still closed for the holiday. So frustrating! All I wanted to do was to get this over with! I wanted normalcy! I wanted my ribs to quit hurting.

At 6:00 that evening, I entered Dan Silkwood's office.

"I see things have changed since I last saw you," Dan's voice was gentle rather than sarcastic.

I collapsed carefully into the chair. I looked at Dan, unable to speak, not knowing how to condense the last eleven days into forty-five minutes. His gentle gaze fell over me like a soft blanket.

"You're strong, you know. You wouldn't be here unless you were. You've stood up to the worst danger you'll probably have to face. Now, you simply need to stick to your guns, and, I'm here to tell you, that will take every ounce of focus you have. I've seen many a con-man in my practice but, like I said, this guy...this guy is one of the best. But you are strong and you have right on your side. You just need to believe it and keep believing it."

The following night, I drew upon every ounce of courage I had to spend my first night alone at Mama's. In hopes of outwitting Carl, I'd parked The Merry two blocks away. Bonnie and Gimpy, right next door, and with whom I'd stayed the night before, urged me to stay with them again, but I stood my ground. It was time to stand on my own two feet and face the music, no matter how discordant.

"I can't give Carl the satisfaction of seeing me running scared."

I assured them I would call no matter what the time if I became frightened in the least. Swallowing a huge sob of fear, I entered my mother's home, alone but for my cats. For the first time in two weeks, I was in total solitude.

I built a fire, made some tea, and nestled under a huge afghan with my journal and the cats, who were confused with yet another location, but who settled into their familiar positions against me. I turned on the stereo and tried to draw what peace I could from Rachmaninoff and Chopin.

Even though my nerves jangled at every creak the house made, even though I didn't dare walk in front of a window for fear Carl would be out there and see me, even though I knew this whole mess was far from over, I was certain I had done what was right for me.

As if to confirm that, I pulled from my journal two sheets of legal pad paper and re-read what I'd written at Vivien's on New Year's Eve. A wry smile crept across my face as I read my words:

Here's to the New Year! ... finally made a decision ... only took me three years and three times to the attorney. What, me vacillate? ... absolute conviction that, baby, I tried everything! ... it took having a counselor to actually say the word "con man" ... to bring me out of my stupor, my limbo world, my disgusting, degrading vacillation and say do something!

I closed my eyes and felt a tear escape. I wiped it away and straightened as the refrain of Dan Silkwood's proclamation looped through my head: '*You're strong.*' His words, along with my own phoenix-like journal entries, would provide powerful reminders to stay on course in the face of whatever lay ahead.

I recalled my own self-description: *Tharn no more!* This phrase I'd yowled to Vivien, during our recent *Watership Down* allusions. *Tharn*, the rabbit rendition of "deer caught in the headlights," was exactly how I had felt nearly the entire duration of my marriage. I'd been paralyzed by doubt, inertia, and fear.

OK, enough of Wallow World. Looking over the resolutions I'd written two nights earlier, I observed, for the first time in four years, they stood a chance of being realized.

New Year's Resolutions - 1981
1. One final thrust at A's in accounting - you can do it
2 Get back in super shape by beginning of summer
3. Get back into tennis

4. *Start jazz lessons*

5. *Play piano more*

6. *Get myself financially settled with house: either with a part-time job of at least $400 more a month, or with 2 livable roommates at $250 each*

7. *Read more good books -*

8. *Dress better*

9. *Do crafts for Christmas presents next year*

10. *Get my head back on straight—mind you, it's not that cockeyed!*

When I caught myself nodding off, I made my way upstairs to the guest bedroom, the cats close behind. Willing every thought from my mind, keeping only the refrains of the beautiful music, I pulled up the covers and said, "OK, pusseroonies, let's get some sleep."

Had I heard the front door open? I couldn't pull myself out of the deep sleep I'd fallen into. A creak on the stairs now? My eyelids, seemingly glued together, finally separated enough to look towards the bedroom door. A shadowy outline? Try as I might, I could not fight through my grog, even as I was aware of my pounding heart. Now, omigod, I felt pressure on my chest! I sickened as I made out Carl's face coming toward me, a wicked grin smeared across it. My heart raced but I remained maddeningly immobile. And now, the flash of a knife, held lightly on my throat... My body felt like it was in damp, rapidly setting concrete. I must, must, fight against it before it trapped me! Carl's sneering, smirking face swam before me, delighting in my terror. I felt more pressure on my throat. Finally engaging my numb muscles, straining mightily, I lurched awake and screamed as I felt the weight on my chest fall away. My arm flailed out in front of me to push Carl away, but it came in contact with nothing but air.

I lunged for the lamp, commanding my fingers to twist the knob, flooding the room in light. No one! Nothing! Just the cats, startled and somewhat annoyed by my rude ejecting them from their slumber on my chest. I soothed them while adjusting their jeweled collars.

I sucked in several deep breaths, trying to gather my wits. I smelled an odd, acrid aroma. Adrenalin, I determined. Holy shit, I'd had a real, live nightmare! I was alive! I was OK! Sobs of relief overcame me as I remained upright in bed. I couldn't remember ever having experienced such stark relief.

In the morning, I rose, dressed, and went to work. My holiday was over.

CHAPTER 44

FAULTY HEARING

"Awww, look!" chortled the student aide in the front office. "Somebody must really love you!"

A bouquet of sixteen red roses stood on the counter, its opulence obstinate, futile and unimpressive.

"Thank you," I smiled weakly and lugged the roses upstairs. I entered Vivien's classroom. "Want something to brighten up your house?"

"What on earth is this man thinking?" Vivien voiced my thoughts.

"I don't care. Here." I thrust the roses at Vivien, turned and went to my classroom.

As soon as the bell rang, I rushed to the county police department to pick up the pillowcase of silver. As warned, Detective Browning confirmed the hubcap was merely circumstantial evidence.

"No one saw your husband enter or leave your mother's house. Someone else could have been driving his car. Someone else could have a Cougar just like your husband's."

I could not believe what I was hearing. "But surely the most likely—make that the *only*—explanation is..." I counted off the logical steps on my fingers, "...he threw the pillowcase of silver in the trunk, and when gathering it up to leave it behind the Golden Rule for somebody else to pick up, he inadvertently included the hubcap which he'd previously thrown in the trunk. Where's the hole in that argument?"

"I'm sorry, ma'am. It's just not strong enough evidence to arrest him."

"But...can't someone—a policeman or somebody—at least go see if his car is missing a hubcap?"

"Not unless you file charges and we get a warrant for his arrest."

That, I knew, was not going to happen. I could see it now: Carl gets arrested, gets out on bail, and comes after me, royally pissed off.

"So, y'all can't do anything unless I go through the hassle of some sort of legal wrangling which, in your opinion, won't be worth the trouble. Is that what you're saying?"

"Pretty much the size of it."

Fighting every impulse to scream, I hurried to my next appointment, a quick stop at Birmingham-Southern College to register for the interim term. Next, I zoomed to the airport, arriving in time to pick up Mama. I was determined to shield her from as much of this hassle as possible. There was, of course, the slight detail that I would be living at her house......

"My God, what in the world has been going on?" Mama huffed and puffed. "Why in the world did Carl keep calling up at Darrah's? It was non-stop!"

"Well, he's a bit upset I'm leaving him, I suppose."

"Thank God for that. It's about time."

"Yep." I lowered my head, guilt tightening its grip on me as I posed the question, "Will it be OK with you if I stay at your place a while? Carl refuses to leave the house."

"Of course, sweetheart. This will all be over soon."

We entered Mama's house, Frau Eva and Mona Bone greeting us. Also greeting us was the ringing of the phone. I picked up the receiver and hung it up. "He's been pretty annoying."

But I didn't always instantly hang up. I followed Adam's advice to talk to Carl now and then, theoretically containing his level of frustration below the boiling point. I decided to call him one afternoon when I'd returned to Mama's finding her exhausted from an hour-long rambling conversation with Carl. *Just another straw on my pile of guilt.*

But before I dialed Carl's number—my number, damn it!—I had a small order of business to attend to. From a small Radio Shack bag, I pulled that afternoon's purchase: a short, thin cable with a single prong connector on one end and what looked like a rubbery suction-cup on the other. I took a measure of satisfaction as I linked it between the phone and a cassette player. I looked at Mama, saying, "This just might come in handy." Then I called Carl. The following forty minutes consisted of convoluted conversation filled with Carl's interruptions, repetitions and reinventions all leading to the same dead-end.

"Carl, did you tell Mother you were going to give me the divorce?"

"You win."

"Then will you meet me tomorrow at Mary and Adam's?"

"No, I can't."

...

"Rosie, are you sure this is what you want?"

"I am absolutely positive, Carl."

...

"I love you hon. I was so fucking wrong. Do you really not love me at all?"

"No, I don't."

"Not at all?"

"Not at all."

"But hon, I'm a different damn person than I was..."

...

"I'm sure it's going to be better for both of us. It's going to be hard...well, it's going to be harder for you, but you'll find that when you face this—"

"Don't fucking preach to me, I don't need that."

...

"Don't you think that if we could just—"

"No. No—"

"walk and talk—"

"No, no—"

"and see each other on occasion..."

...

"Hon, I love you."

"Well, I don't love you."

"I saw it in your eyes in front of your attorney's office."

"Oh, you were seeing crazy, Carl."

"No, I saw the *wish* for it."

...

"If you're so damn convinced that it's over with, why can't we see each other?"

"Carl, listen to the paradox in that statement."

"What is to be lost? What is to be lost?"

"Doing something I don't want to do. I'm not going to do it."

"What is to be gained?"

"Doing what I want to do."

"What is to be gained?"

...

"What are you afraid of?"

"It's not fear, Carl, it is absolute indifference."

"It was indifference four years ago."

"It's a different kind of indifference."

A small laugh from Carl.

...

"Hon, you know, deep down—and Lord knows it's gotta be way deep down—that the touch, the feel—"

"That does nothing to me, Carl."

"I know that. You didn't love me in October when we met."

"I know. And then I did love you and now I don't love you again."

"But what generated that damn love four years ago, that basis is still there."

...

"You don't care."

...

I hung up. *Holy screaming chromininicles! That was insane!*

I stared at the phone, stupefied by Carl's pigheaded, futile contrivances to regain the upper hand over me. I shook my shoulders as though to rid myself of some bothersome gnat. The phone rang. I raised and lowered the receiver. This silly song and dance repeated itself nearly a dozen more times.

CHAPTER 45

STRIVING FOR NORMALCY

Living at Mama's was disorienting in itself, but the incessant phone calls from Carl—made from the home in which I should be housed—added an extra degree or ten of stress. Lulls on the work front were non-existent, of course; from the time I arrived at 7:00 a.m. to my 5:00 p.m. departure, I hurtled through the day, coming up for the briefest respites between the clanging of bells.

In keeping with my New Year's resolution to get in better shape, I formed an after-school exercise class. Much to my amazement, thirty teachers showed up! Determined to continue my studies in accounting, I had registered for both an Interim project and one other course, hoping I'd be able to focus strongly enough to maintain my A-average. Early into the term, I blew my first big exam in the course, forcing me to drop the Interim project.

It became apparent that a trip to France with my students, on the books for nearly a year, would be ill-timed. Luckily, Louise was more than willing to take over chaperone duties in return for a free trip. (On my Hallmark calendar, I scratched out 'LEAVE FOR

FRANCE!!' and wrote, 'Forget it. Thanks, Carl.') Besides wasting even more time ascertaining the hubcap was indeed useless 'evidence,' I also had to take a day off in late January to attend a court hearing for possession of the house. Carl was ordered to vacate the premises after two more weeks. I allowed him, via Adam, an extra day, after Carl's wounded insistence he had absolutely nowhere to go.

"So, we're on the right track," Mary encouraged me one cold February evening at a dinner meet-up to celebrate regaining possession. "The trial will take place on the 24th of this month. That's soon! Things ought to settle down once a judge tells Carl it is over and done with."

I wasn't inclined to agree. "I'm not so sure Carl's going to fade away," I said.

At that very moment, I caught a glimpse of Carl in the adjoining section of the restaurant. "Oh, no! Speaking of the devil! He's right over there!" Mary twisted in her seat to look. Carl was nowhere in sight.

Nor was he anywhere in sight in the parking lot, through which we cautiously walked to our cars, both our heads doing three-sixties. My relief at not seeing him was quickly overcome by my anxious wondering, *How in the stinking hell does he keep finding me?*

"I think I'll scrap my plan to take possession of the house tonight," I said. Mary's nod stated her approval of my wise move.

On the following sunny, bright afternoon, I approached my house for the first time in nearly two months, feeling no hint of warm fuzzies upon returning to my nest. I looked up and down the street, even peering across to neighbors' front and back yards to see if Carl was waiting a block over. Only then did I exit my car, fling open the garage door, jump back in my car, pull in, yank the garage door back down, and lock it tight. *Gotta get a garage door opener, that's for sure!*

Legal possessor or not, I knew full well it would be a while yet before I'd feel safe to sleep here every night

I ascended the steps to the living room and stood in place a moment, trying to sense anything awry. Detecting no danger, my tensed muscles loosened. 'Home Sweet Home' would surely remain a misnomer until cats lazed up to greet me. I hated to deny them their digs even longer, but they were comfortable enough at Mama's. (At least there was no Mendy to keep them on edge.) Carl probably wouldn't harm them, but I was taking no chances.

I made it my first order of business to lift the very nice crystal ashtray from the coffee table and, with huge joy and relief, toss it into the garbage. Next, I yanked Carl's few articles of clothing, shoes, toiletries—anything that hinted of him—and threw them in a box to take to Adam's for Carl's pick-up. I fixed a cup of hot tea and called Mama to check in. She answered, her tone exasperated and exhausted. "My Lord, Carl has kept me on the phone for over an hour!"

That familiar blanket of guilt became heavier, wetter. "God, I'm so sorry. What did he have to say this time?"

"He says he's dead certain the two of you can still make it."

I resumed nest-reclaiming. I would never feel the same way about this house as I had my first home, but I did detect vestiges of pride that it was now all mine. Of course, it would all belong to the bank within months if I couldn't figure out how to pay for it. Musing on how I would go about finding a roommate, I was jolted into the present by a sharp knock on the door.

"I must've left my beeper in the house," came Carl's voice. "I can't find it anywhere."

He didn't sound threatening, but I wasn't about to let him in. Through the closed door I said, "It's not here, Carl. I've been cleaning house all day and there's no sign of it. If I find it, I'll put it with your clothes at Adam's—"

"What in the hell gave you the right to mess with my clothes?" Carl yelled.

Ignoring this absurdity, I said, "You are not supposed to be here. Please leave or I'm going to call the police."

Cursing, Carl stalked down the sidewalk.

Ten minutes later, the phone rang.

"Look," he said, "you and I need to discuss some things about this divorce."

"Fine. Anything you need to tell me you can tell me in front of Mary and Adam."

"No. What is wrong—"

"Or you can tell me over the phone, but I am not going to meet you—"

"Who is coaching you, Rosie?"

"Coaching? You mean, like, in a game? This is not a game, Carl."

"I mean like some quack counselor, or one of your stupid friends—"

"Nope, Carl. Nobody but me's doing the talking here. Every word I've ever said to you is my own, even though you keep insinuating they've been planted in me by someone else."

"When did I ever say that?" A quick pause. "Aside from just now?"

"Well, how about the night when I came home December 19th and you told me I was crazy, that I was getting all this stuff from outside sources..."

"Now, you and I, or...I had about as much sense going to a marriage counselor with you when I was drinking as trying to perform brain surgery."

I was not going to continue this useless conversation. "I have to go. Good-bye." I hung up quickly and took the phone off the hook.

To my complaints about these pointless, interminable phone conversations, Adam only reiterated his advice that I meet Carl somewhere public. He pointed out that by agreeing to meet him, whether anything was actually discussed or settled, I could show a judge I'd indeed tried to communicate with Carl. Contacting him, however was easier said than done, seeing as he could no longer lay claim to a permanent residence. I figured I'd be hearing from him soon enough.

CHAPTER 46

OF COPS, ROBBERS AND BALLS

After school the next day, I dropped by my house to get Mama's vacuum cleaner—borrowed because mine was broken, due more likely to Carl's clumsiness than malice. As I pulled into the driveway, my rear-view mirror filled with the image of Carl's car. As if dropped from the sky, it landed in the driveway, blocking my exit. Seeing the next-door neighbor's kids playing in their yard, I figured Carl wouldn't pull any stunt, so I exited my car.

"I've been trying to call you," I said.

"Liar," he said, exiting his own car.

"Look, I'll meet you at Denny's to discuss whatever it is on your mind."

"Let's go inside." Carl quickly moved to within a few feet of me.

"I am not going inside the house with you."

He grabbed my arm and I jerked it back and cried out, "Don't you dare!"

Carl immediately backed off, yanking my purse from my grasp as he went. He threw it in his car. I leaped back into The Merry. Carl hurried around to the front of it and tried to open the hood, ineptly searching for the latch, apparently aiming to disengage some vital motor part. Once again I blessed his being a total mechanical klutz. Carl started for the back door of the house, perhaps thinking it was unlocked. No chance of that, I knew, but there was a huge chance he'd not turned over all keys at the possession hearing.

I noticed the two neighbor kids, no longer playing but simply watching the scenario develop. Carl was rounding the back corner of the house, scowling at having found no entry. I cracked my window and, trying to keep my voice as steady as possible, spoke to the kids: "Hey guys, how about going inside and ask your mom to call the police?"

"You don't need to do that," Carl yelled immediately returning to my side of the car. "Rosie's just being crazy. She's nuts!"

"Mama, Mama!" they screamed as they ran inside. "Call the cops! Rosie's locked inside her car and there's a robber outside!"

How Carl did not break the window, I didn't know. The torrent of curses flooding from his twisted, sneering mouth sent a wave of terror through me forceful enough, I feared, to either make me throw up or have an accident right there in The Merry. He ranted and raved another few minutes, but then backed off. I wondered what his next move would be when I saw lights flashing in my periphery. The police, bless their hearts, had arrived within minutes.

I exited the car, wondering if Carl, who still stood so close I could hear his jerky breathing, would slam the door back on me. I hurried towards the policemen. "He grabbed me," I said, trying not to go totally melodramatic, "and I was frightened as to what he'd do next."

"She's lying," Carl hissed, as he walked towards his car. "She invited me over here." I reached into Carl's car to retrieve my purse, once again coming within inches of him. As I passed him, he directed a low growl in my direction. "I'm going to kill you."

"He just said he was going to kill me," I struggled to keep from crying.

"You're under arrest for contempt of court, sir. You are not supposed to be here." The policeman slapped handcuffs on Carl's wrists and shoved him into the back of their car. As it pulled away, Carl cast a dark look towards me through the back window while the fingers of one of his cuffed hands took on the shape of a cocked gun. No way could I hide the fear coursing through my body as I beheld Carl's menacing stare while, in the same moment, his lips mouthed the word 'Pow!'

I turned and tried not to run to my front door. In the neighbor's doorway, the kids stood encircled by the protective arms of their mother, all agape. I quickly gave them an assuring thumbs-up, while shaking my head and rolling my eyes in mock disgust, that this was really no big deal. Once inside, I collapsed.

I tried to let my pulse return to normal. *What kind of trailer-trash scenario was that? God, would Carl go so far as to kill me?* Every fiber in my body told me he was more than capable. I shuddered. *At least he's in jail for the night, so I'm safe for a bit.*

After a very long while, I rose, straightened a few more things around the house, rewound the cord on Mama's vacuum cleaner, and hefted it to the front porch. I stepped outside and locked the door behind me. I turned around to see the police car pulling to the curb. The back door opened and Carl got out. His expression could not have been more smug. But, as soon as the policeman exited the car, Carl walked straight to his own (which the policeman had moved to the street), got in, and drove slowly off.

"Why is he out?!" I almost wailed.

"We couldn't hold him for going against what was really a warning, not an actual court order. Judge Burnham—you know, the city attorney for Irondale—suggests you get a TRO."

"What's a TRO?"

"Temporary Restraining Order," said the policeman. "It has more bite than a warning from the court."

"But, this man is dangerous! Can't anybody see that?"

"I'm sorry, ma'am, that we can't do any more for you than that. It's the way the law works. We can't keep somebody in jail because he grabbed somebody. You know, he also gave Judge Burnham the line that you'd invited him over." The officer let out a little laugh. "Judge Burnham didn't believe a syllable of it, but he said, 'Never mind. You deal with her *only* through attorneys.'"

The officer looked at me as I shook my head in disbelief and defeat. "Look," he said, "if it makes you feel any better, I can tell you, in my experience with divorce cases, most of the guys who seem so tough and dangerous are basically blowhards. Their egos are bruised big time and their normal way to deal with that is to throw out threats left and right. But, usually they don't mean anything. Just a bunch of hot air."

"Hot air or not," I said, not in the least calmed by the officer's kind words, "I'm still scared to death. Could one of you please follow me to my mother's? I need to return her vacuum cleaner."

"No problem," he smiled and got in his car, turning off the flashing lights.

I walked into Mama's house, less ruffled on the outside as I still was on the inside. At least I could shield her from having to deal with this particular episode. She rushed into the living room, her eyes wide with fright and concern.

"Carl has called three times, screaming every time I pick up the phone. He says he's furious with you and he hates you as much as you hate him!"

"And yet," said I, deadpan, "he's 'certain we can still make it.'"

Mama rushed on, "Oh! He said the trial was going to be postponed; is that right?"

This puzzled me. "A postponement? Mary didn't say anything about that. Does he know something I don't know?" I didn't even want to go there.

Mama added, "He said something about trying his best to keep up his end of the bargain, to not make these proceedings any worse than they have to be. So he left the check for the Cougar in the front door of your house."

My Lord. The man has balls the size of church bells!

CHAPTER 47

JUST FOR THE RECORD

While the TRO had slightly more power than a judge's warning, it had no effect whatsoever in halting Carl's incessant phone calls. Mary suggested filing a Rule NiSi, supposedly a restraining order with sharper, longer teeth but, since it also required a bit more legal maneuvering, I was hesitant to set things in motion. With the trial only days away, I felt this might be an unnecessary hassle. Plus, both Mama and I figured the imminent divorce decree would put an end to the phone calls. Most times, a simple pick-up and hang-up of the receiver proved the best method of handling these annoyances. On one of the few times I did listen, I picked up the phone after letting it ring for four minutes, and waited to hear what Carl had to say. His voice was low and threatening:

"What we need to do is burn the house down. ... And if *we* don't, *I* will."

I told Mary to go right ahead with the Rule NiSi.

I was counting on the divorce trial itself to abate my level of fear as well. I'd come to keen understanding of the quote about 'nothing to fear but fear itself.' I had no idea what Carl would do next, but I didn't put a lot of faith in that officer's reassurance that Carl was nothing but a bunch of hot air. I knew he was capable of maiming me badly, if not killing me. Surely—surely!—the finality of a divorce decree would bring about an end to Carl's crazed efforts to control me.

Early on the morning of the trial, Mary called me with the bad news that the case had indeed been continued to March 3, a little over a week away. Mary had been able, however, to retain that same date for the Rule NiSi hearing, required before the rule could go into effect.

When I arrived home from school, Mama told me Carl had called and wanted me to call him. I wondered if he—or, he and his lawyer—had somehow orchestrated the postponement. *Hell, I'll just ask him.* I turned on the recorder and dialed the number he'd left with Mama. As soon as Carl picked up, though, he gave me no chance to ask my question.

"Listen, Rosie, I have a simple solution to this whole thing."

"And what is your simple solution?"

"Well, that maybe you and I could talk and at least get a couple things squared away."

"I'm talking."

"No, not over the phone, Rosie."

...

"Well, I...I don't understand the conflict."

"Well, I'm sorry, Carl, that you don't understand this. You don't understand a lot of things. For you to keep on like this shows me you don't understand I have made up my mind."

"No, I understand that."

"Well, then, why don't you deal with it and get it over with?"

"Because, Rosie, it's not as simple as you might think it is."

"Anything complicated about this divorce can be discussed at Adam's. I'm not meeting you anywhere and that is final."

"Hey, hey, hey, hey, wait a second. Why are you shouting?"

"I'm not shouting. There's noth—"

"I asked— I asked you— be- by— I— then, let me talk to you on the phone, OK?"

"Then talk."

"Were you ever happier?"

I hung up.

The next couple days passed with nary a peep from Carl, an extreme rarity. I got in some excellent studying in the afternoon at Birmingham-Southern College and later in the evening at Mama's. After work the next day, I returned to Mama's—I still wasn't ready to go it alone at home—who told me I had a call from Mary.

"You're not going to believe this!" Mary said. "Carl was arrested last night."

I was dumbfounded.

Mary continued, "Yep, at Bennigan's in Homewood. He was charged with—"

"Drunkenness and disorderly conduct, I bet!" I was almost gleeful.

"—with illegal possession of credit cards, fraudulent use of credit cards and second degree burglary." Mary paused, apparently checking her notes. "The burglary charge was because of some stuff in the trunk of Carl's car. It belonged to the mother-in-law of Slade,

Carl's ex-partner from McLane Security." Mary allowed several moments for this to sink in. Then she added, "Can you believe it?"

Finally, I spoke. "Well, yeah, I suppose so, based on how he's behaved in the last few months. I mean, this man's waxing certifiable nuts. Of course, what I can't—I mean CAN NOT—believe is that I used to be married to this...this...lunatic!"

Both Mary and I contemplated that last statement. I said, "Well, at least I know now why he never called yesterday. And to think I thought maybe he was in church."

The next day, I had to study for my upcoming exam. Concentrating on accounting principles, in light of the previous evening's news racing through my head, was trying indeed. The phone rang, decimating whatever focus I'd achieved. Momentarily aggravated, I remembered it couldn't be Carl, because, oh yeah, he was *in jail*. I answered, coming to full attention when I heard a stern voice introduce itself as Detective Sargeant Thacker of the Homewood Police.

"I'm calling," he said, "to see if you can shed any light on last night's, uh, incident."

I hung my head, in wretched embarrassment. Once again, I found myself trying to condense the nightmare of the past three months to an officer of the law. It did not escape me that I'd now spoken with three such authorities from Jefferson County, Irondale, and now, Homewood. I guessed this was what all wives of criminals went through. I hoped I didn't sound as guilty as I felt.

"No sir," I began in an unsteady voice, "I can promise you I had no idea of Carl's whereabouts or doings. The only reason I was able to study hassle-free the other night is because, unbeknownst to me, he was in jail. Where he probably needs to be for quite a while," I added.

"Mr. Ballini is no longer in the Homewood jail; he's been transferred to Jefferson County."

"Omigod. I can't believe this is happening."

"Well, it's not really all that surprising, based on his police record."

I froze. "Scuse me, you're saying he has a police record?"

Sergeant Thacker, having concluded I was on the right side of the law, softened his tone. "You could say that," he chuckled quietly. "Ma'am, he has an FBI record. He has a number of *aliases*."

Of all the numbskull acts I'd committed since birth, I knew in that moment that my marrying Carl Ballini would forever hold the PFC Award (that would be *P* for Poor, *C* for Choice, and *F* for, well...). Nothing would inflict greater, more withering embarrassment than to hear a listing of my husband's aka's and prison sentences.

"Please stop," I said, my voice croaking like a sick frog. My humiliation was suffocating. "I don't think I can handle any more of this."

Sergeant Thacker did not sound unkind. He simply wanted me to know what I was dealing with.

Three days later, Carl's attorney posted bail for the three counts incurred in Homewood. He was transported from the Jefferson County jail to another one in Montgomery where he was booked on two other charges. Apparently the goods in his car were stolen from a Montgomery residence. Before going to bed, I called the Montgomery jail and was relieved to learn Carl was indeed still incarcerated with a $500 bond on two charges. *At least I'm safe tonight.*

On the morning before the *second* trial date, Mary called to report the judge himself had had to continue the trial to a couple weeks away, March 13. A Friday.

"Please tell me no!" I moaned. "Wait, could this be happening because Carl is *in jail* and can't make the freaking trial? Do you think his fucking lawyer—sorry Mary, but a lot of them suck, as you well know—could have *bribed* the judge?!"

Mary didn't answer immediately, perhaps contemplating the likelihood of my supposition. "Well, I don't know. But, stranger things have happened."

CHAPTER 48

STRANGER HAPPENINGS

Figuring that Carl was still holed up in the Montgomery jail, I felt almost lighthearted walking through the beautiful campus in the late afternoon sun. I crisscrossed the quadrangle framed by stately, columned buildings which faced the bell tower at its center. Several students surrounded the tower, chatting quietly or studying on benches. I was reminded of my days at the University of Alabama, where its own quadrangle, four times the size of this one, was a similar picture of peace.

I reached the edge of the quad and began my descent down two steep flights of steps—the bane of many students—to the parking lot at the bottom. I opened The Merry's door, threw my books on the shotgun seat, and plopped down behind the steering wheel. I pulled out of my parking place and made my way down the row of parked cars.

Suddenly, a strange car loomed in my rear-view mirror, drew broadside, and then lurched slightly ahead of my car at an angle, forcing me to slam on the brakes. From the driver's side, Carl emerged, his face clouded with frustration. My sense of peace shattered in an instant, replaced by that all too familiar wrecking ball of fear, more powerful now that I was privy to the addition to Carl's resumé: *convicted felon*. I grasped and punched the lock on my door as I watched Carl swagger around the front of his car. What, was he going to try (again) to smash my window in? As he came even with the corner of his car and the front left fender of The Merry, I realized there might be just enough space between Carl's car and the one parked to the right. I edged forward.

"Oh no you don't!" Carl slapped the hood of my car as if to stop it but the forward motion knocked him slightly off balance. He was jostled backwards as I, teeth gritted and eyes wide with terror, continued to inch my way forward. Carl's chest was now pressed against my window as the space between our two cars became tighter and tighter. With his neck at an odd angle, Carl's face suddenly appeared in my side window. I looked in horror at the dark, threatening mass of facial features. He screamed through the glass, "You're gonna talk to me one way or another, goddamn it!" He had to shift his position because I, keeping my eyes peeled straight ahead, continued edging forward. Still screaming, "You think you're so high and mighty—Awww—Owwww! Carl's cursing turned to a howl of pain. Gyahhhhhh!" His left hand reached to extricate his left leg, his right hand beating on the roof of the car. "You fucking bitch! My knee! Owww!"

Another couple feet, and—yes!—I was free! I screeched off. The last thing I saw was Carl, hobbling back around his car, shaking his fist and screaming to the heavens every curse known to a sailor.

The trial was continued another four weeks, this time because, according to Carl's attorney, Carl's dad was having open heart surgery.

I tried, but couldn't locate Cap'n in any St. Pete hospital. I called his work number, and he answered, sounding perfectly normal.

"Wha...why...um, how can you be at work today?" I asked.

"Sorry?" he sounded confused.

"You know, if you're having open heart surgery in the morning, how can you be working today?"

Hesitation followed by a slight chuckle. "Having sur—?" Then, quickly, "Oh, my insurance won't cover the day before, only after."

"So...you are having the operation tomorrow?"

"Yes." Silence. Then, "Sorry, I'm at work and I have to go."

Rendered speechless by Carl's father's bald-faced lie, I next heard a click, followed by a resolute, in-your-face dial tone. A cold chill spread throughout my entire being. Omigod, this whole family is fubar.

Also totally effed up beyond all recognition was that, on the following day, Friday the 13th, I found myself seated in my advanced accounting class for the final exam. Because of the trial postponement, I no longer required a make-up date. Considering the disjointed studying I'd managed over the past few weeks, I could only hope for a B-minus. Encouraged the first few problems were on familiar material, I quickly deflated as I came upon one that rang no bell whatsoever. I leaned my head back in my hands, searching my brain for something pertaining to the material in question.

I opened my eyes and they fell upon the skinny vertical window of the classroom door. I could not see out into the hallway, though, because it was blocked by a scowling face, staring menacingly straight at me. I tried to snuff out my cry of terror by pretending I was having a coughing fit. Not wanting to disturb the other test-takers, I managed to quieten myself. I strained to look calm and raised my eyes to the window. There was nothing to be seen but the hallway. I looked back down to my test and watched my tears turn the insoluble problem into an indistinguishable blur. I waited at my seat until several students finished about the same time; I rose to join them, handing my unfinished, slightly damp test to the teacher while muttering a tearful "Sorry." I kept close to the small group of students on the way to the parking lot, my head doing the Exorcist three-sixty. There was no sign of Carl.

So far, the day known for bad luck was living up to its reputation, with its miserable unfolding thus far. However, the Rule NiSi hearing did go ahead as scheduled at Irondale City Hall with Judge Burnham presiding. Mary and I arrived before Carl, who shuffled in on crutches, his face full of pain and accusation.

Mary reiterated to the judge my justification for requesting such a ruling, giving him a condensed version of the 'spat' and Carl's subsequent harassment tactics, including the recent car chase and more recent exam appearance. At this revelation, Judge Burnham broke his attention to eye Carl's crutches and the thick wrap on his knee. "Humph," was his only comment, which, for all its brevity, sent the message that Carl had gotten exactly what he deserved. The judge turned back to Mary. "And how much would you say is the weight of your client?"

"About one hundred, your honor."

"And that of the defendant?"

"About two hundred, your honor."

Judge Burnham turned to Carl. "You are now ordered by the Court of Jefferson County to never come within a mile of the plaintiff. The only manner in which you are to communicate with the plaintiff is through attorneys. This means no phone calls, no letters, etc. Is that understood?"

"Yes, your honor." Carl's face was a poker mask.

And that was that.

Any comfort I might have drawn from this firm ruling straight from the judge's mouth quickly evaporated as soon as I entered Mama's house, where the phone was ringing off the hook. I picked up the receiver and heard not Carl but a woman.

"Hey, bitch," came a wheedling, high-pitched, drunken voice.

I was in no mood for pranks. "Who is this?"

"Why, this is Sherry," the woman mocked. "You know, the Sherry that Carl's been with forever, for a really long time. Says he needs a real woman." She paused to let the insult inflict deep pain. Then, as the final whammy, "We've got a child."

I snorted, almost relieved. "What, and you think that's supposed to make me jealous?" I laughed again. "Honey, you can have him. Take him. Please."

My bravado lasted long enough to spout those words before hanging up. *Who were these freaking people?* Why would anyone even want to do that for somebody else? How could Carl know these kinds of people while I didn't have the slightest indication? What kind of world does he operate in?

Not ten minutes later the phone rang again. This time it was Carl. I could envision his sneer through gritted teeth:

"You better be careful, girl. You better be looking over your shoulder every minute of the day."

I hung up the phone. So much for moving back home.

CHAPTER 49

MARCH MADNESS

But I did move back in, that very weekend in fact. As petrified as I was by the 'look over your shoulder' comment, I knew it was high time I deal with it, whatever 'it' might be. Three months at my mother's had been beyond plenty for both of us. Perhaps because she was so ready for me to move out, Mama agreed to stay all day Saturday and overnight with me. We worked in the yard—me looking over my shoulder as surreptitiously as possible—and passed an uneventful night before she returned home Sunday.

Still not quite brave enough to go solo, I entreated Vivien to spend Sunday night. We sat at the dining room table, grading papers. Nearly every time the phone rang, usually five minutes apart, I simply picked it up and hung up. On one pickup, I held the receiver midair, waiting to hear what Carl so desperately needed to say this time around.

"I will blow your ass away," Carl's voice was stone cold. "I will beat you until death."

I hung up. I would have screamed in fear except for one thing: I looked at the dandy little recording gadget that had dutifully kept track of every conversation since I'd been at Mama's. I punched the buttons on the recorder and Vivien and I shuddered while the unnerving threat replayed. Carl's earlier calls were mind-numbing mumbo-jumbo, but these recent ones? I decided it was time to share. With shaking but determined fingers, I dialed the Irondale police, who were now on familiar terms with me. Within minutes, Officer Williams arrived. I promised him he wouldn't have long to wait before the phone rang again. No sooner had the words left my mouth than a ring pierced the air. Williams picked up the phone.

"Hello?" he barked.

And with that, Vivien and I watched his expression change as he listened to the torrent of curses and threats gushing from Carl. A full two minutes passed before he hung up the phone and looked at us. "That guy's crazy as a loon," he whispered, damn near awestruck.

The next day, I carried my cassette player to the city hall for more sharing, this time with Judge Burnham. He listened attentively to Carl's threats and appeared equally in awe that the man would so flagrantly disobey the NiSi ruling. He issued a warrant for Carl's arrest.

On the same day, Don Bingham, the gruff but lovable mountain of a man and the assistant principal at school, came over to change locks on the doors. While he worked, the phone rang several times, each time causing me to nearly eject from the chair.

"My God," he said. "You are a basket case."

Vivien stayed over two more nights. I simply could not summon the courage to stay by myself.

On March 17, I took the recordings to Mary and Adam's office. Surely this would be proof to a judge that I should not only be divorced from this man but should be awarded at least some amount for pain and suffering.

On March 18, I checked my grade for Advanced Accounting: D; this, the result of the exam's containing more tears than answers. I had never in my life received anything less than a B. I spoke with a counselor and was able to have it changed to an Incomplete, meaning I could retake (and pay again for) the course to keep the D off my record.

On March 19, I called the postmaster to report Carl for stealing mail from the mailbox. The postmaster told me I really didn't have much of an argument if the mail was addressed to Carl.

"Yes, I understand that," I said, invoking my dwindling supply of patience. After again explaining I dutifully delivered Carl's mail to my attorney's office for his pickup, I said, "But what about *my* mail?"

"Well, you'll have to have proof he took it."

"Oh yeah, right. The evidence thing. Never mind the obvious," I said grimly.

"Sorry, ma'am."

"Not your fault."

As insult upon injury, an envelope addressed to Carl arrived several days later. It was from the IRS. His refund. (Ever since the Sears fiasco, I had prolonged my dance around the beast by opting for Married-Filing Separately and hoping to hell the IRS wouldn't catch whatever discrepancies or oddities Carl's returns might hold. Such a risky act definitely required a larger rug for sweeping-under.) That Carl was actually receiving a refund to which I had no access was maddening. I wasn't sure how I was going to make the next mortgage payment. Should I not, I knew the bank would waste no time in delivering a collection notice, which would be a source of huge embarrassment to me. And yet, here was this...this *criminal* receiving money from the government for what was most likely another falsified tax return. The utter irony was laughable.

Within a week of moving back into the house, I steeled my jangled nerves to go it alone; I was not going to let Carl keep me from that. Further imposition on my mother was out of the question. That went for me and the cats. We needed to be with each other. I would have to bite the bullet and risk leaving them alone while I was at work. I would have to suppress scenarios of Carl's breaking in and hurting or stealing them. I still didn't think Carl could hurt the cats. But he'd have no problem doing a number—not a musical one—on the piano.

More than anything, I simply could not believe I was still in this hellhole! To live in fear like this, to be talking to detectives and lawyers and jail house clerks...this was a world in which I wanted no part and yet, for the life of me, I could not extricate myself from it. And the legal system! That supposed symbol of justice and support for the downtrodden...all they'd done so far was enable Carl's prolonged terrorizing.

Knowing Carl had zero respect for the Rule NiSi, I remained fearful he would come to the house. Taking a shower was particularly stressful: the bathroom floor wound up half flooded because I kept the curtain open with an ear bent to any unfamiliar noise inside or outside the house. Whenever I took a bath—no longer a spa-like retreat—I'd run the water before getting in the tub. Relaxing on the bath pillow was futile since my gaze, directed to the sink counter, rested upon the gun I'd so wisely hidden a few months earlier.

On March 20, I conceded to call Carl, whose calls had remained incessant, to say he really needed to give me some of that refund so I could pay the mortgage.

"I don't know why you're so worried about it. You know, you've got a rich mother."

Maybe not quite so much since you robbed her, I wanted to say, but refrained, having heard the tense sarcasm in his tone. But I figured it was safe enough to ask, "So, speaking of parents, how's your dad doing after his open heart surgery?"

Carl chuckled as though dealing with some naïve child who'd finally caught on to a riddle.

"Turns out he didn't need it after all." With barely muted glee he added, "Yeah, we were all so relieved and grateful."

By now, I had begun keeping a log of harassing calls, per the instructions of the phone company, which was still a decade away from introducing Caller ID. Relief would come only through changing numbers, a hassle neither I nor Mama entertained. We simply put up with them. Because most calls were hang-uppers, I surmised Carl was finding it somewhat dodgy to remain in town what with the outstanding Rule NiSi arrest warrant, not to mention the scarcity of employment opportunities. Carl's reputation had spread beyond his many short stints.

While I considered positively brilliant my strategy of forwarding all calls to the police, I had been instructed in adamant terms that this would simply not do. So, I opted for Dial-A-Prayer. Throughout most nights, my sleep would suffer only the mildest of interruptions from the phone's intermittent solitary chirps, signaling Carl was being channeled over to holier grounds. More amused than irritated, I would smile sleepily, wondering what God might have to say to the asshole.

At 6:00 p.m. on the last Wednesday of March, I walked into Dan Silkwood's office. A look of concern spread over his countenance upon seeing my shrunken frame and lined face.

"Please don't tell me you've gone back to him," he said, half joking, half pleading. "When you canceled last month's appointment, I was a bit worried."

"No, no, trust me, that's not going to happen." I refrained from telling him I simply hadn't been able to come up with fifty bucks. "But I'm definitely feeling like I've stepped from that frying pan into the fires of pure hell." I exhaled deeply and for the next fifteen minutes gave Dan a rundown of the past three months since the 'spat.'

"I'm hardly surprised. His behavior is typically sociopathic, practically devoid of social conscience. And, of course, he does *not* like losing control of someone he apparently had in his clutches."

"Is this supposed to make me feel better? That I married not just a wife beater, not just a criminal, but a certified psycho?"

Jim laughed gently. "Guess not, but what's important here is that you are no longer playing—I should say, allowing yourself to be a part of—his game. More importantly, you are beginning to reclaim your inner strength, your own personal compass, that got buried deep, deep down."

I nodded my head. "I hope one of these days I'll figure out why I ever let that happen." I looked at him and smiled weakly. "But I suspect that's a great big story that would take many more sessions with you than my wallet can handle at the moment."

"Well, for now, I can tell you that you are on the right track."

CHAPTER 50

APRIL ANGST

I placed great trust in the recuperative, regenerative, and revitalizing powers of that Spring of 1981. True to form, the beauty of my favorite season burst forth, first in the delicate pinks of tulip trees and red buds, then the creamy whites of dogwoods, with the myriad shades of azaleas and the riot of annuals planted in yards, malls and office parks. One of the things I loved about Birmingham was its four distinct seasons, each a metaphor on its own, but I was partial to Spring's reminder that 'this, too, shall pass.'

I leaned heavily on the brightness of the days and the softness of the evenings to shore up my resistance to the unceasing darkness Carl seemed intent on rendering upon my life. Dial-A-Prayer went into overtime during the first two weeks of April, averaging, as best I could guess, around eight calls a week.

Hang-uppers and call-forwarding chirps were fairly reliable indicators Carl was not in town. I curbed my basket-case mindset and enjoyed a Sunday afternoon helping Mama in her yard. I was gratified I could in some way repay her for the three months of lodging and continued hassle.

Back home later that evening, I was in usual Sunday-evening protocol, kissing my weekend goodbye so as to ready myself for another week of school. The phone began ringing, incessantly. I took the receiver off the hook. Peace lasted about thirty minutes, broken by the buzzing of the front doorbell. Carl was on my front porch. This, despite Rule NiSi! Not about to open the door, I called the Irondale police for what seemed the gazillionth time. They arrived while Carl was still on the porch, still ringing the doorbell. They hauled him off.

Immediately after school Monday, I arrived at the police station for an update. Officer Williams, now my good buddy, had some bad news and good news and bad news.

"Yeah, his attorney paid his bail, so he's not here anymore." Officer Williams shook his head in mutual disgust. "Funny thing, though..." I looked up quickly, not knowing what to expect. "...while he was here last night, he tried to feign a heart attack."

"No! What won't this man try next?"

"Yeah, he was screaming, 'You gotta get me to a hospital! To a hospital! Now!'" Williams leaned in his chair, hands behind his head, enjoying the replay. "So I told him we could transfer him down to Jefferson County Jail where there's a medical staff on hand."

"And what did he say?"

"'Aw, to hell with it!'" We both laughed, shaking our heads at this man's machinations.

"And I say to hell with him!" I made to leave, but Officer Williams checked my exit.

"Well, he may be going to hell, but first he's going to be back here at 5:00."

I did a double-take. "Huh?"

"Yep, you don't mess with Rule NiSi. Judge Burnham called a hearing *today*."

"Yowza! That's forty-five minutes from now! I'll be right back, promise!"

I made record time to Mama's. I wanted her to attend the hearing, lest further attesting of Carl's hassles might be required. In forty-four minutes, we rushed into the courtroom. Carl was already seated with his attorney, Don Black.

"Now, Mrs. Ballini," Judge Burnham began, "am I to understand you in fact had invited Mr. Ballini over last evening?"

Before I could answer, I heard a "That's outrageous!" blurted out by Mama. With the slightest amusement breaking through his stern facade, Judge Burnham looked at Mama, then back at me.

"And may I ask who this lady is who has accompanied you today?"

"That is my mother, your honor. Mrs. Browning."

"I see," the judge acknowledged the introduction, nodding slowly in Mama's direction, much as a parent might to a child being a bit too noisy in church. He returned to me, awaiting my answer.

"No, your honor, I no more invited him over last evening than I did a while back, the other time I had to call the cops—the police."

Mama, unable to contain herself, cried, "He *beat her up*, you know!"

Judge Burnham lightly tapped his gavel and looked directly at her. "Ma'am, I'll have to ask you to refrain from speaking unless spoken to."

Not one to disrespect authority, Mama offered a meek, "Yes, your honor."

"And how do you plead, Mr. Ballini?"

Carl stood to answer, in an air of absolute conviction, "Not guilty, your honor."

"Nonetheless, the court finds you guilty in flagrant disobedience of Rule NiSi. You are hereby fined one hundred and fifty dollars plus fourteen dollars court cost, plus a two-week jail sentence, plus thirty days community service."

Carl's attorney stood immediately. "My client appeals, your honor."

And, as justice would have it, an appeal meant Carl was free to go.

I thanked the judge, and walked Mama, still sputtering, to the car. "'Thirty days community service'?" She snorted. "That'll be the day."

I smiled. "Yeah, and if it entails hard labor, the community can forget it."

Mama offered to spend the night. I thought it might not be a bad idea.

When Mary called the day before the April 16 trial, I took the bad news as no real surprise.

"The judge says he's caught up trying another case and—"

I really didn't give a flying rat's ass about the reason. "So when's the next possibility?"

"June 2." Mary waited for me to say something. "I'm really sorry, Rosie."

Fully expecting a snarky call from Carl to gloat about the postponement, I forwarded my calls before turning out the lights. I was still awake at 2:00 a.m. when I heard the bright little chirp from my phone. Why, thank you, God, for taking that call.

On Friday, April 17, I received a letter from the Alabama Department of Public Safety saying my license and tags were to be suspended. Because my signature was on the loan for Carl's Cougar, I was liable for all the shenanigans it was involved in, including wrecks, robberies and impoundments. Fortunately, Mary's efforts put a quick stop to ADPS's unfair targeting of me. Finally, a little justice on my side.

A week later, I received a response from a notice I'd put up on the bulletin boards at the music departments of the area colleges, requesting a roommate. Four days later, Shu-ling Yang, from Taiwan, appeared at my doorstep. She was slight in size, with thick, long black hair that curled around her face. Her dark eyes were intelligent and bright, and they lit up considerably more with her wide, two-hundred-watt smile.

"...so, I was thinking you could practice or teach your students during the day while I'm at school so we wouldn't, you know, get in each other's hair."

Shu-ling, whose command of English was a long way from *full*, looked confused. "Get in hair?"

I silently scolded myself, a teacher of language. Of course, keeping abreast of idioms was one of the most difficult parts of mastering a language. "I mean *disturb* each other."

Shu-ling nodded enthusiastically. "No, no, not disturb! I rike peace and quiet, too!"

Tickled by her pronunciation of *like*, I said, "Yeah, well, there is peace and quiet around here a lot of the time," I willed the phone to silence, "but I need to tell you I am in the middle of a divorce—" Shu-ling's face showed concern. "—and sometimes it can get a little... disturbing."

"Awww, divorce not good. Not happy."

"Well, I can promise you I'll be a lot happier when I get this divorce!" I hoped no desperation appeared in my tone.

That same evening, I received a call from a Sergeant Isaacs of Mountain Brook: "Sorry to tell you this, Mrs. Ballini, but I'm pretty sure your husband was involved in a Doolins Security-related burglary yesterday."

"What?! another one? Different from when he robbed my mother?" What kind of balls is this fool toting? I wanted to shout, but opted for strained propriety.

"I'm afraid I don't know about that one. This robbery is different from when he was picked up in Homewood with the stolen credit cards."

"You said Doolins, right? I ask, because the last place where I know he worked was McLane, a different security company."

Hearing my exhale of disbelief, Sergeant Isaacs added, "There's another suspect, another ex-Doolins guy, name of George Peer, a tall curly blond. Do you know him?"

"No idea." Why in the hell should I have any idea? I did not— *did not*—belong to the world of cops and robbers. "I also have no idea how my hus—soon to be ex-husband, may I point out—how Carl got hired by a *second* security company!" No explanation from Isaacs forthcoming, I continued, full of sarcasm. "Well, what better way to case a joint, make a copy of a key, and then rob it sometime later? He did bar/restaurant jobs to support his alcoholism; security work is perfect for his criminal side! Brilliant, don't you think? I mean, ya gotta give the guy credit; he finds jobs that support his, ah, proclivities."

"Yes ma'am, brilliant," chuckled the sergeant. "Not that I'd call these two guys brilliant."

CHAPTER 51

MAY MAYHEM

"Now, I'm here to tell you: it is some kind of weird to see a *mug shot of your huzzb'n!*"

I leaned over the table, nearly tipping over my wine, as I concluded my tale of meeting with the Mountain Brook Police Sergeant and seeing Carl's mugshot. My light tone belied the suffocating humiliation within. I was with Cindi and another good friend, Sandra Gilchrist. Gilly, as we called her, was another beauty like Cindi, successful owner of a high-end interior decorating firm, and whose hoity-toity-ness soon succumbed to the down-to-earth demeanors of her two friends. Her tone usually dripped with sarcasm, coupled with rolling eyeballs and perfectly manicured fingernails fanned out to emphasize her point.

We had met at our favorite watering hole, Duggan's, a warm and comfortable sports bar with rich-looking wood paneling throughout, low lights, and comfortable, high-backed booths. I had barely seen Cindi at all during my entire ordeal—this due in great part to my preference to curl under my rock. Now I was unloading one story after another to the two spellbound women.

"I mean, not only did I not—having waited, mind you, until age twenty-nine to do so—I repeat, *not only* did I *not* get the rose, I didn't even get the weed. What I got was the cow patty that nurtured the weed." Laughter all around as I added, "Yes, ladies, I have been through some shee-ut."

And then, in a manner only Gilly could cop as she eyed my shrunken frame and dark, baggy eyes, she said, "Well, obviously because, my God, Rosie, you *look* like shee-ut!"

"Yep, living in frustration and fear...ah, that's the life!" came my comeback, as we clinked glasses.

Carl's whereabouts following the Doolins-related incident were questionable. Evidently he'd left town immediately, leaving his buddy to be arrested by police, even though, Sargeant Isaacs had said, the case was a weak one. Which left me to wonder: *What in the hell makes a strong case?*

Continued hang-uppers rather than just-sit-there-and-breathers served as theoretical proof that Carl was not a man about town. Not only was he avoiding long-distance charges, he probably suspected by now I was recording calls. Still, at 10:00 one evening, I lifted the receiver to hear: "I miss you, hon." I hung up. Six phone calls followed and, on the seventh, I picked up and just listened:

"Hon, you are the first thing I think about when I wake up and the last thing I think about before going to bed at night. I just wonder how you're doing and wish to hell I had a way of knowing."

His comment, meant to needle, did. Upon returning from an out-of-town wedding a couple weekends earlier, I got one of Carl's calls. "Welcome back," he'd cooed. Another time, a shopping spree with Vivien prompted his subsequent phone inquiry: "So, how was the mall today?"

But knowing now what I did about Carl, I was loath to confront or accuse. Hell, the man scared me.

Towards the end of May, I welcomed Shu-ling into my home. Even as the two of us lugged stuff into the house, the phone was ringing off the hook. Shu-ling looked at me questionably when I merely picked up and hung up the receiver.

"I told you I'm trying to divorce myself from a crazy man," I pleaded. "The divorce trial is coming up in less than two weeks so I'm sure things will calm down after that. He's trying to make me call off the divorce but, trust me, that ain't gonna happen."

After she'd had time to settle in, I begged Shu-ling to play something on the piano and was immediately mesmerized by the Liszt Hungarian Rhapsody. Then the two of us tried a Bizet duet, something I had played long ago with Cindi at a recital. We both laughed at my mistakes, and I promised I would practice. Two hours whizzed by, during every minute of which I could feel—what was it? Joy? Yes!—joy welling up inside of me as I felt engaged with beautiful music and a brand new friend.

I was having such a good time, I'd completely forgotten to check the mailbox where lay another letter from Carl. I decided I'd read it later, once Shu-ling had retired for the night. Should the letter upset me, I'd just as soon keep my anxiety to myself.

"OK, pusseroos, let's see what the asshole has to say..." I pulled both cats to either side of me on the bed. "...and then I'll tell you what I think about it." I opened the envelope, unfolded a couple legal sheets and began to read out loud to my less-than-rapt feline audience:

Rosie,

Since we can't talk on the phone or see each other before our divorce I thought I would put some things down on paper.

I am truly sorry for what has happened to us. Whatever respect you had for me when we were married is gone.

"Well, now, there's a No Shit Sherlock if ever I've heard one." I gave each cat a gentle noogie between the ears.

It's not gone because you lost it, but because I didn't give you reason to keep it.

Whatever hurt and sadness we are both feeling right now—

"Who sez *I'm* sad?"

—is only there because of the happiness we once had. It is the loss of that happy feeling that I miss.

After you left me I handled that situation so poorly. I'm sorry. Maybe if I had performed differently we wouldn't be where we are today. Before you and I separated we were in a crisis situation. I knew it but didn't admit or handle it too well.

If I had let you leave that night and go to your mother's for the weekend things would have been different. That would have made me face up to the problems involved and they would have been solved because I would have done anything to not lose you. I didn't want to face up to the problems so I lost you.

"Facing up to problems doesn't appear to be your forte."

I think that there should be some kind of mandatory cooling off period before anyone can file for divorce. A period of time where no contact is permitted.

"Contact. Now there's a word of many levels. For instance, Wife Beater. Hello? Can I get a Rule NiSi?"

If that had happened I would not have panicked and made a pest and damn fool out of myself. I would do anything to go back in time but that's not possible. I know that no matter how much I wish it to be possible and even if you wanted us to try a reconciliation it could not happen. Things have gone to far and it is now out of our hands.

I told you the other night that I love you and I do. There must be a soul, because I felt that love in a way that was more than just physically or emotionally.

I felt it coming from you also. I guess we both failed in "Marriage 101."

"OK, that would be Rosie two percent, Carl ninety-eight percent."

There are so many things that happen to me daily that remind me of us.

"Really? Like when *we* committed robbery? Or when *we* used credit cards fraudulently? Or when *we* beat people up?"

If there is a second life, I want to find you. I promise I will be a better person. I just wish we had taken more time to "smell the roses" and that's not your fault.

"Bing. Ass. O."

I close now my lady.

"Um, not yo' lady no mo."

Just know that I love you and miss you and our home.

"*My* home."

There will never by anyone like you in my life again. Forgive me for being such a damn blind fool.

Love, Carl

I lowered the letter to my lap, noting with relief and some pride that Carl's words meant absolutely nothing to me. Plus, I remembered well Dan Silkwood's pronouncement that this was the best con man he'd ever seen. With the divorce trial a little over a week away, I recognized Carl's letter for what it was: a last ditch effort to regain control of me.

The phone rang. It was a hang-upper.

I placed the receiver in its hook and hugged my cats who'd stirred at the ringing of the phone.

"Not to worry, kiddos. Just a damn blind fool."

Shu-ling and I fell into a routine quickly. I was delighted to turn the kitchen over to her as she loved to cook. She owned a humongous yellow mixing bowl, the likes of which my kitchen had never seen. In it, she would whip up a huge batch of egg rolls. I could not get enough of them.

"Oh, Shu-ling," I'd plead, "please make some more!"

Her face would scrunch into a pained expression, even while pleased by the compliment.

"Aw, no, no," she'd say, "too many chop chop!"

Especially entertaining was Shu-ling's mispronunciation of *L*'s to *R*'s. One day, I overheard Shu-ling trying to instill a sense of rhythm in her piano student. Clapping out the beat, she urged him to do likewise, saying, "C'mon now, crap, crap, crap!" Another time, after meeting Vivien's Frank, Shu-ling shared her impression with me later: "I tink he prayboy." I assured her praying was not his game.

CHAPTER 52

JUNE JUSTICE

On the evening before the divorce trial, Vivien spent the night so she could accompany me to the proceedings the next day. This would be her—and Louise's—third try at serving as witnesses. At least school was out, so taking another sick day was not required. All signs indicating no postponement was brewing, our mood was cautiously light. Vivien and I told Shu-ling tale after tale of Carl's antics the past few months.

"How about the time Adam's office caught on fire?" Vivien reminded me.

"Oh God, I know! They never could prove it was Carl, but there was absolutely no doubt who'd done it. Luckily, the fire was small and burned out before it did any damage. I guess it was one of Carl's 'scare tactics' since, you know, he's such a tough guy." (Years later, in a newspaper interview featuring Adam, he'd responded to an inquiry about the craziest occurrence of his career: "Well," he'd said, "there was some bozo who, during a divorce case, tried to burn down my office.")

I remembered something else. "Oh yeah, I thought it was classic when Carl called me, one day when he was still living in the house, and accused me of stealing the silver. You know, the silver I hid shortly before the..." My balled fist at my head completed the sentence. "Now...why would he have noticed it was gone in the first place? Think he was gonna sell it? Oh, or maybe he was throwing a formal dinner party for several of his jailbird buddies."

Vivien spoke. "I think one of Sinclair's—bless his feline soul—crowning achievements was when he batted a home run with that neck brace weight! Hell, I wasn't even there and I laugh out loud just imagining it!"

"Truly a sight to behold in person, I assure you," I giggled with glee. "Of course, in retrospect, I really don't think there was a damn thing wrong with his neck; he just needed a good excuse not to work."

"Lord, so how many jobs did he actually have? Since the time you met him, what, nearly four years ago?"

I looked at my two friends. "That would be, um, let me see..." I made as if to count my fingers, "...would you believe...*fifteen?*" To the gasps of disbelief, I added, "Yeah, people kept hiring him. The man could sell air-conditioners to an Eskimo." I paused. "Truly a shame, you know, because he had unbelievable talent—*potential*, as they say—but he was one certifiable lazy ass."

Our laughter was interrupted by the phone's ringing. I rolled my eyes. "Speaking of lazy asses..." I would've ignored the call but Vivien urged me to go ahead and answer, to see what Carl could *possibly* have to say at this final hour. Shu-ling, equally enthralled with all the drama, nodded eagerly. With a dubious look expressing this would be nothing more than the same ol' same ol', I picked up the receiver and listened to Carl's urgent entreaty:

"Hon, it's just a sin, you know. Do you not think that one, two, maybe five years from now, there might be a chance for us to start over? Because, if you don't—" A breathy pause. "—I don't think I can go on, hon." A muffled sob. "I can't do it." Another pause, with some rustling in the background. And with that, I heard a loud 'bam!' followed by a strangled intake of breath and a rustling sound. Then silence.

I hung up the phone, looking towards Vivien and Shu-ling, a bit of horror in my expression, but mostly excitement and hope.

"Omigod. Did the—'scuse me, Shu-ling—motherfucker do what I think he just did? Did he blow himself away?!"

We waited anxiously for the tape recorder to rewind. We listened intently to Carl's tearful spiel and then heard the *shot*.

Immediately, a look of disgust spread over Shu-ling's face, as though she'd just heard the weakest punch line ever.

"Not gun!" she cried. "That not gun! Rook!" She grabbed a can of hair spray and slammed it loudly onto the table. It made a sound not at all unlike the one we'd just heard.

"Wonder if he'll show up at the trial tomorrow?" Vivien asked, deadpan.

Not half an hour later, the phone rang again. "Can't wait to see who this is," I smirked. I heard a strange, high-pitched voice asking to speak to a Ms. Beaversluce. I held the phone away from my ear and looked at the two women, announcing, "Well, it's official. The man's gone crazy." Howls ensued.

Immediately Carl's voice squawked from the receiver.

"Who the hell are you talking to? Oh, yeah, I hear laughter... well, yeah, isn't this just a fucking party! Hey, you won't be laughing after that trial, you can bet your a—"

I hung up. The phone rang again immediately. I picked up, hung up and quickly forwarded my calls to Dial-A-Prayer. Moments later, the phone made its forwarding chirps. I picked the phone back up and punched in a few numbers.

"On second thought, the man has had all kinds of chances to get right with God, but it obviously hasn't worked." I punched in a couple more numbers and hung up the phone. "Looks to me like it's time for the Crisis Center. After all, he is suicidal."

And so, at long last, I was to get my day in court. The trial began with Adam's complimenting the judge on the color of his shirt and the judge reciprocating with a nod of approval at the rose in Adam's lapel. "Wore it just for you, your honor."

Nauseated by this ass-kissing exchange, I had to force it out of my mind since I was being called to the stand. As I ascended the couple steps, I suddenly felt weighted down by a wave of negativity and foreboding, punctuated by my wildly beating heart. I glanced at the table situated slightly below and to my right, where Carl, Lazarus-like, sat, his face set in a menacing glower.

"Could you please describe the night of December 19th," Adam asked me. Now was my chance to let the judge see how badly I'd been mistreated. To my dismay, the voice coming from within me sounded small and unsure. Carl's eyes, dark tombs, bored holes through me. Surely, Adam would prompt me with questions so I could expand on certain aspects, but none were forthcoming.

I was momentarily encouraged when Adam almost offhandedly offered the photos Vivien had taken of my bruises and cuts—was it really six months ago? Hope evaporated as I watched the judge merely glance at the pictures, unimpressed. I'd counted on Vivien's and Louise's testimonials as to Carl's incessant harassment to sway the judge's ruling in my favor. But then, to my stupefied amazement, I heard Adam say, "No, your honor, I'll call no witnesses."

The judge, his interest in the case minuscule at best, looked at the two attorneys. "It appears to me like justice would be better served if you two boys would go into the adjoining room and come up with a settlement."

Dumbfounded, I waited in the hall with Vivien and Louise while the attorneys discussed things.

Louise, thoroughly irritated with the proceedings, looked at me with a mix of anger and apprehension. "Well," she said, "I wasn't going to tell you this, but guess what your attorney—your defender, right?—said to me right before the trial began?"

"I don't think I want to hear this," I whispered.

"He said, and I quote, 'How about refreshing me on all this, would you?'"

I hung my head in defeat.

"I'm afraid Adam's selling you down the river," Vivien moaned.

About twenty minutes later, Adam called me into a small side room. "It looks like you'll only have to pay Carl three thousand dollars, his equity in the house. You'll have to take responsibility for the Cougar since your name's on the title and Carl has no income to pay for it."

"What?!!" I screamed. "You're telling me this like I should be relieved! Like this is fair! Those pictures of me with bruises, stitches, and the rib wrap? The judge hardly looked at them! What about the phone calls, the car chases, some sort of private eye on my tail, the robbery, the robberies—?"

"Now, I, a lot of that is circumstantial evidence, the pictures were barely telltale—you know, you really should've taken them the day of the, uh, the incident..."

I stared at my attorney in disbelief. "So, you're telling me what went down today was *justice*?"

Adam shrugged and sighed at me as a parent might when the child discovers there's no Santa Claus. "Now, now, Rose, you know, justice is a dark alley with a gun pointed at you from both ends."

I sat in stunned silence. To hear this gem of wisdom from the one person on whom I'd counted to fiercely represent me, to stand up for me...well, he may as well have gone ahead and shot me right then and there. So much for my day in court.

Later that day, after the trial, Carl called. "You've got a jerk for an attorney," he said gleefully.

Some months later, Lucy would cross-stitch a small plaque containing the quote from Shakespeare's *Henry VI*:

> The first thing we do,
> Let's kill all the lawyers.

CHAPTER 53

BEACH ESCAPE

Four days after the circus in court, I headed south with Mama, both of us in dire need of respite. Perdido Key, Florida, possibly the most beautiful spot on the entire Gulf Coast, proved ideal for decompressing. The two weeks would not pass, however, without annoying interruptions.

Shu-ling, at home with the cats, would call multiple times to report that Carl's calls had not stopped. In one, he'd screamed at her, threatening to call the Irondale police because no one was supposed to be in the house. In another, he'd said he was sending a truck to pick up his stuff.

"Trust me," I said to my frightened roommate, "the boy will not be calling the Irondale Police. They are not his fans. As for sending a moving van, Vivien spoke with Carl's attorney who swears Carl will be doing no such thing." Sensing Shu-ling was not at all appeased, I added, "I think he's exactly what that cop said a while back, 'just a bunch of hot air.'" I realized Shu-ling's lack of response was due to her confusion over 'hot air.' "I mean, he's a whole lotta talk and a whole lotta doing nothing."

Early in the second week, a special delivery envelope containing the divorce decree was delivered to the condo. Holding my breath, I began to read the judge's final word on the case, depressingly close to Adam's prediction. I wanted to scream. What an idiot I'd been to think that justice would be rendered. I was too deflated to do anything but sink onto the couch.

On June 8, I celebrated my thirty-third birthday. With worry and compassion, my mother looked at her haggard daughter.

"You've been through a terrible time," she said.

I regarded my dark, sunken eyes in the mirror. I was absolutely exhausted, having run on nothing but fumes for the past half year. My bikini barely clung to my five-foot-three frame, now a walloping eighty-eight-pounds. The bathing suit top was mostly filled with air. *Wow, who'da thunk my boobs coulda gotten any smaller? They're concave!* I smiled ruefully remembering Gilly's non-sugar-coated comment. Yep, Rosie-Rose, you *do* look like shee-ut!

But what I felt within my emaciated self was the return of an undercurrent, now a fresh, rippling stream which had finally emerged from its long hidden spring deep within. Its waters were unpolluted and life-giving. Like my body, my mind was still more fragile than not, but it, too, was benefiting from all the soothing beguilements the beach had to offer.

Sitting at surf's edge, I rocked in rhythm with the waves, all powerful, all peaceful, all symbolic of the cycle of life. I wondered if even the most morose soul could remain impervious to the healing properties of watching the ocean. Impossible.

On June 21, Mama and I made our way home, both improved in our own ways. Mama appeared to have gotten a slightly stronger grip on the mantra that life does indeed go on. My batteries had recharged enough to summon new determination to go forward. I knew with dead certainty I would *never* let this maniac—or any other, for that matter—put me into that sniveling, helpless, fetal position again.

As we pulled into Mama's driveway, we were pleased to see Gimpy hurrying from next door to welcome us home. "Well, if it isn't the widow and the divorcee! So good to have you back! It's been so boorrrrrring!"

I walked into my own home hugely relieved to find it still standing, and to see Shu-ling sitting on the couch with my cats. She looked ten times more relieved to see me. I barely got out a greeting before the phone began ringing, and Shu-ling's expression clearly stated, *'This is not what I bargained for.'*

"Trust me, this will end tomorrow. I'll have an unlisted number before the day's out."

I picked up the phone and held it away from my ear. Carl's voice was dripping with sympathy. "Gee, hon, I'm really sorry those lawyers burned you with the car. That's really too bad, but, well, I really don't have a solution for—"

CHAPTER 54

THE LONG...

True to my word, and because I realized trying to keep my own phone number would never be a viable option, I contacted the phone company the next day to request an unlisted number. Only Mama and Vivien would know it for a while. But while my phone suddenly became blessedly quiet, Mama, who simply refused to change her number, wasn't so lucky. She would be beleaguered with hang-uppers, curses, and veiled threats for months to come.

Next, I bit the bullet and called Ford Motor Credit to tell them they needed to repossess the Cougar or accept my payment terms of the seven-hundred-and-fifty-dollar balance. I gritted my teeth as I spoke to the collection agent.

"You may not believe me," I said, "but I will eventually make good on this horribly unfair expense. Right now I can do ten dollars a month. Take it or leave it."

One day, with Shu-ling accompanying me, I went to the mall to buy a new bedspread, another move towards erasing any memory of Carl. It had been eons since I'd actually gone shopping and I looked forward to the excursion. We were walking towards Penny's when suddenly I heard someone call my name. I froze, slowly turned, and then broke into a delighted grin. Standing at the entrance of Marsh Piano was the owner, Jeannette, the sweet lady who'd patiently indulged my three-year prelude of gazing longingly at the piano which would eventually be mine. Jeanette had sincerely shared in the excitement I had felt when signing the dotted line a couple years earlier. On this day, she looked glad to see me but also wore a puzzled expression.

"So, did you ever sell your piano?" For a second time, I froze in my tracks at such an odd question.

"Huh?" My clueless expression caused Jeanette to look even more puzzled.

"Your piano! Did you sell it?"

"What are you talking about?"

Jeanette's puzzlement turned to mild fright. "Well, your husband came by—let's see, I guess it was several months ago, and he said y'all were going to sell the piano." Seeing my blank look, Jeanette hurried on. "Yeah, your husband—oh, and he was so charming! So funny!—said y'all were selling it because y'all were going to move and it'd be too expensive to move the piano. He said you weren't teaching anymore, so there wasn't enough money coming in to keep up the payments. Besides that, he said you never played it anyway and it was just sitting around." Jeanette hesitated, watching my eyes fill with incredulity. "Yep, he wanted to sell it back to us that very day, but I told him that wouldn't be possible since the piano was in your name."

She paused a moment, recalling their exchange. "Seems like he quit being so charming after that. He left in a huff." Jeanette looked at me. "I thought it was all kinda odd."

"*Odd* doesn't begin to describe it, believe me."

"So...did y'all move? Did you sell the piano?"

Almost wearily I stared at Jeanette. "Nope. Not moving. Didn't sell. Divorced." I gave a greatly condensed version of my ordeal. "I think everything's going to be fine now," I concluded, hoping my voice didn't sound unconvincing. "I'll tell you one thing, though. I'm *never* selling that piano."

Jeanette look relieved. "Oh, that's good. He was a little scary, you know? He got irritated with me when I told him we couldn't buy it back."

"Scary is right," I agreed. As if to move on, I introduced Shu-ling, explaining that our being roommates was due in great part to the piano. We stood in silence for a moment, each considering the wild story that had just been told.

"Unbelievable," said Jeanette.

"Yep, unbelievable," I said.

"Rearry unberiebabuh," chimed in Shu-ling, shaking her head.

"See?" I said to Shu-ling as we returned home from the mall, "I have to keep reminding myself things could've been worse. I mean, he *didn't* sell the piano, he didn't find the silver, he didn't hurt the cats, he never found the gun..." I drifted off, declining to add that I wondered if it still could be worse. Even if the past few days had been a peaceful interlude, I remained wary, knowing such periods are often referred to as the quiet before the storm. As we pulled into the drive-way, I stopped the car so I could check the mail. I was puzzled to find an issue of *Sports Illustrated*. Only the day before I'd received *TV Guide*. Some crazy mix-up, most likely, not worth bothering with.

Still sorely riled by what I considered the extremely bad rap by the hands of my own attorney as well as the judge, I could hardly believe I was sitting in another attorney's office, this by my own volition. I sat before Richard Jagger, the city's premier—and therefore most expensive—*divorce* attorney, who'd been kind enough to allow me a gratis session, to see whether filing an appeal was worthwhile. He listened patiently to my brief-as-possible summary of the last three years. Then he carefully looked over the decree.

"You do realize, of course," he said, "the bottom line is always money. You have a steady income and he doesn't have a pot to pee in. There are court fees, attorney fees, a car needs to be paid for... Three thousand dollars is a very small amount to pay to get rid of the son of a bitch."

"But—" I stuttered. "Why in the hell should I have to pay *anything* for his pee pot?! Plus, *I'm* the one paying for the car! It's like I'm being punished for being a responsible person!"

Jagger sighed like someone who recognized a dead end when he saw one. "I'm not saying I agree, but I can promise you any judge will look at this and consider it a fair settlement."

"So," I said, "what you're trying to tell me is that I'm shit out of luck."

"Bingo." He regarded me with a mixture of pity and cynicism. "My advice to you is to let it go."

I looked at Jagger, whose assessment came as no surprise. I took small pride in managing to hold back tears of rage...not at him, but at the insanely unjust justice system. I thanked Jagger for his time and his honest appraisal, exited his office, and walked swiftly to my car. I flopped into the driver's seat, slammed the car door, and only then allowed the tears to burst forth for a good five minutes. Then I grabbed a Kleenex, wiped my nose, and squared my shoulders as I looked at myself in the rear-view mirror.

"Better buck up, Rosie-Rose. Do what the man said: Let it go."

I drove straight home and immediately fixed my favorite toddy. I headed to the deck where the cats were lazing around. The evening was surprisingly pleasant for late June in Birmingham, and the warm, soothing breeze seemed to have been ordered up especially to begin quietening the freight train that roared through my head. I had to admit Jagger was right about dropping it. If I were to appeal this case, it would be at the very least another year, another year of excuses for Carl to continue hassling me. I was bound and determined to get this man, this excuse for a man, out of my life.

I brought my knees to my chest, my feet at the edge of the seat, and I hugged myself. I closed my eyes and looked within, something I'd done so little of until recently. I felt like I was looking over a torn landscape, everything wrecked and lifeless, except for one tiny sprout of green amid the ruins. *Welcome back, gut!*

CHAPTER 55

...HOT...

Because 'letting go' could occur more easily with Carl completely out of the picture, I spent several days finalizing arrangements for the retrieval of his paltry pile of belongings. Once again feeling the need to call on my friends to withstand whatever shenanigans Carl might pull, I asked Vivien to be present for the transfer of goods. This would be the first time I had actually been in the same setting with Carl—other than court rooms—since the 'Mama, there's-a-robber!' day. I was none too certain Carl would behave.

Vivien and I had decided I best remain out of sight. I maintained my insistence in refusing to deal face-to-face with Carl: first, he'd forfeited all rights to communication that night of terror; second, there was no point. That I'd allowed so many interminable phone conversations was mainly to stop the phone from ringing, partly to keep Carl's frustration at bay, and slightly, I had to admit, to satisfy my own curiosity. What would this guy say next?! But talking over the phone—or, should I say, listening to his rants, raves, and futile persuasions—was one thing; being within an arm's reach of Carl was entirely another.

Not surprisingly, he showed up two hours before the appointed time. Vivien sentineled herself behind the garage door while I perched, unseen, at the top of the stairs. Awkwardly cradled in both hands was the gun, its cold, heavy metal completely foreign against my palms. I tried to calm my thumping heart upon hearing Carl's fists bang on the door. Oh, how I would have loved to see his expression as he watched the door slowly rise to reveal legs which were Vivien's, not mine. As soon as I heard Carl speak, I knew he was beside himself with frustration and fury.

"And just where the fuck is Rosie?"

Vivien, petite like me, was no physical match for Carl's hefty six feet. Yet her voice was calm and neutral as she simply said, "Rosie's not here, but here's your stuff."

"Noooo! I need to talk to her! Where is she?!" I expected to hear Carl explode past Vivien. Seeing as the Irondale Police had just pulled up out front as a precaution, Carl checked his aggression. "You scrawny little bitch! I don't know how in the hell you got to be so involved in this!"

Vivien ignored the irony of this statement and said simply, "The agreement is for you to pick up your things and leave."

Carl snarled and threw his bundled clothes to the ground. "I'll sue you for messing with my personal possessions. And you can tell Rosie I'll sue her for throwing away my gun!" He turned on his heel, stormed to his car, slammed the door and sped off.

Vivien closed and locked the garage door and headed to the stairwell where I still sat, the gun hanging loosely in my lowered hands, head raised skyward in utter relief and gratitude. Vivien sat beside me, her right arm enclosing my shoulders in comfort and friendship.

"Yeah," she mused, deadpan as ever, "I guess I shoulda apologized for being such a nosy bitch."

I nodded quickly. "So, you ol' scrawny, nosy bitch, exactly how *did* you wind up here?"

We walked back into the garage, ruefully observing the unretrieved items lining one side of the wall: a glass-topped dining room table and a few rumpled pieces of clothing.

"Wow, quite a collection he's amassed in his thirty-nine years," Vivien said.

"Of course you realize this means he has to come back..." I moaned.

"Hmmm, think that was by design?"

"Well, my design will be to get this crapola carted out of here... and delivered to his current jail of residence."

Vivien nodded at the gun still in my hand. "So, do you have any idea how to use that thing?"

"Not the foggiest. If Carl had pushed past you and come up these stairs, I just would've had to throw it at him."

That same evening, Shu-ling and I sat at the piano with the Bizet duet, greatly improved since our first go-round. The piece was taking nice shape and beginning to sound like music. So engrossed were we in our workplay that, when the phone rang, we both nearly fell off the bench.

I got up, expecting either Vivien or Mama, the only ones possessing my new number. I answered, but heard nothing at all. It was a hang-upper. I assured myself this was most likely a wicked coincidence. I turned to join Shu-ling but the phone immediately rang again. After fifteen rings, I picked up the phone. Nothing, then a dial tone.

"Dang it, dang it, dang it!" I yelled. "Somehow that son of a bitch has gotten my unlisted number!"

CHAPTER 56

...SUMMER

Furious that 'letting go' was a lot easier said than done, and knowing full well it was a no-no, I took it upon myself to get face-to-face with Carl's latest attorney—the others having tired of him. I marched into Walter Booker's office after several more days of hang-uppers as well as several foiled attempts to arrange the removal of Carl's stuff. After brief introductory pleasantries which I found absurd, I lit into a plethora of examples of Carl's continued harassment measures, particularly the obtaining of my unlisted phone number.

Booker, who looked slightly amused by my exasperation, offered to file a new Rule NiSi.

"Huh?" I was astounded. "You mean you'd file a Rule NiSi against your own client?"

"Seems to me that's what's needed to stop the harassing."

I studied him for a moment, making an effort to keep my lip from curling up. "Why in the hell are you even representing this monster?"

Booker chuckled softly. "Well, I wouldn't go so far as to call him a monster." He chuckled a second time. "But, for sure, the boy is confused."

Booker's offhand statement nearly sent me over the edge. Once again, the legal system was slapping me around, pulling the rug out from under me, and making a mockery of what was just and sane. Referring to Carl's dishonest, cruel, violent, twisted and totally irrational behavior as *confused* had to be the epitome of understatement.

I looked at Booker, who was still amused by his assessment of Carl. He was actually a nice looking man, well-dressed, with an educated, mild-mannered bearing. And yet, he chose—*chose*—to represent someone like Carl.

"Right," I said, thoroughly disgusted. "As if Carl's the only one who's confused."

Shortly upon returning from this distasteful encounter, I found in my mailbox a collection letter, albeit very polite, from *Sports Illustrated*, gently reminding me that payment was due. Up until now, I had received but ignored several more magazines, thinking it wasn't my damn problem. Still full of ire from the meeting with Booker, I plopped down at my desk, figuring it was high time to quell this tempest in a teapot. I composed the following letter:

July 23, 1981
Dear Sirs:

How absolutely charming to see Vince Ferragamo's lovely visage staring out at me from my mailbox the other day! What a pity that it was on a magazine to which I most definitely did not subscribe. Nothing against *Sports Illustrated*, of course; I simply never filled out a subscription order.

But I think I know who did.

You see, since I divorced my husband, it seems the poor man has nothing better to do than to hassle me, and this little trick of sending me magazines in my name is right up his alley. I've also received *TV Guide* (I watch TV approximately thirty minutes a week) and today was visited by UPS with a $45 C.O.D. package.

Now, I don't know what means you have handling such situations—I hardly think this is unique; there are a lot of sickos out there—but any punishment you might wish to administer upon this particular offender, up to and including a jail sentence of say, life, is just peachy keen with me.

His name is Carl C. Ballini, and, as far as I know is still staying with his parents, the Carl D. Ballinis, at 3125 45th Terrace S., St. Pete, Fla., 33720, phone 813-645-3892. Maybe you could write them and tell them their 39-year-old child needs a spanking.

In the meantime, please stop sending me your magazine—since you can be sure not to receive payment from me—despite the pretty pictures of Vince. I'd rather you'd just send me Vince. Better yet, send me Vince's wallet.

I do apologize for the mix-up here and hope Carl hasn't caused you too much trouble, but, to quote his own attorney, "The boy is confused."

Sincerely,

Rosie Browning

Shu-ling and I were in the kitchen making a new batch of egg rolls, me doing everything I could so she wouldn't have 'too many chop chop.' The phone rang. We looked at each other, wondering if this was going to be another hang-upper.

"Hello?" I asked, bending to the lower cabinet to get a chopping board.

"How ya doin', girl?"

I stood up and slapped the board on the counter. "Carl, how did you get this number?"

"Are you going to be nasty?"

"Are you going to tell me how you got this number?"

"No."

"When are you going to get your stuff?" I asked, almost off-handedly. I was livid that Carl had gotten my number, but had to expend zero effort in containing my anger.

"Well, the judge has allotted a certain period of time that I have to give you notice."

"No, he hasn't. It isn't in the decree."

"No, I never said that. What I said was the judge has allotted time. You will get notice. That's not why I called."

I unwrapped a head of cabbage and began chopping for all I was worth. "Why do you think I got an unlisted number? I don't want to talk to you. All I want to know from you is how you got this number."

"All I want to let you know is that I miss you dearly."

Rolling my eyes in disgust, I shoveled the tiny shreds of cabbage into Shu-ling's mammoth mixing bowl.

"Mmm-hmm. How did you get it?" I asked, now grabbing some cooked shrimp and the knife.

Carl laughed. "Don't blame me. Blame Ma Bell."

"You got it though Southern Bell?"

"Rosie, I'm not going to answer that. Do you really think I'm that stupid? Maybe you are that foolish. Anything can be purchased and I got it last Thursday. I miss you lady, I really do."

I swiped the shrimp morsels into the bowl. I watched Shu-ling spoon some mixture into a wrapper, moisten an edge and roll it up in a matter of seconds.

"Carl, do not call me again."

"OK, the only time I would call you is if I wanted to talk to you. Um, are you doing, doing anything with anybody, seeing anybody?"

"Hey, Carl, get your informer."

A small laugh from Carl. "Don't be so damn cold; that reflects back on you and everybody else concerned cause you're not that cold." A pause. "OK, hon?"

With a huge smile, I showed Shu-ling my first attempt at rolling, a huge glob of mixture escaping one end.

"Goodbye, Carl."

"Rosie, you could have hung up a long time ago if you didn't give a shit."

After a long sigh and a short laugh, I said, "Well, you are right about that."

I hung up. Five minutes later the phone rang again.

"Hey, don't hang up right away. Look, I have the opportunity to go to the Bahamas...with separate rooms...If I sent you a ticket..." A finely restrained snort from me. "And I know, you know, don't laugh."

"Carl, I'm not laughing." I laughed. "I just—I don't believe it."

"Hon, is there anybody else right now?"

"Goodbye Carl."

As I hung up the phone, I heard Carl whine, "Don't hang up! Fuuuuck!" I leaned my forehead on the receiver. *God, the balls of this man...*

Shu-ling was frying the egg rolls now. I smiled in anticipation.

The next day, while I was getting my second unlisted number, Mama was doing her own phone dealing. Up to this point, she'd agreed with me that staying in the background was the safest strategy in dealing with Carl. But now, with no relief in sight from Carl's continued calls, Mama called Penny, Carl's mom. Listing Carl's prolonged malfeasance, emphasizing the beat-up, she begged Penny to please try to influence Carl to back out of this, to leave both of us alone, to face the music, and to get on with his life.

When I inquired about Penny's reaction, Mama said, "Total, absolute indifference. Resignation, really. It was rather frightening, a bit. Depressing."

The very next day, Mama received a call from Carl, who blasted her for harassing his mother, adding he would sue her for slander.

The following day, my mailbox held not a tempest in a teapot but a storm. Copies of *U.S. News* and *Money*, along with a notice from *Time* magazine advising my account had been transferred to corporate collection. I returned to my desk to compose a generic memo—that would eventually be mailed to a total of seventeen publications:

It is with this xeroxed memo that I must advise you that I did not subscribe to your publication. If you will read the copy of the attached letter I recently sent to *Sports Illustrated*, I believe you will understand the absurd situation we are in: I am receiving and am being billed for goods I don't want and/or can't afford and you are doling out your product for free...hardly the way to clinch those windfall profits.

As each day seems to bring a different publication or package, thereby causing the sender unnecessary expense, it is my sincere hope that at least one of you will track down this "prime suspect" and collect the damages due. That the man has harassed me unduly is *the* understatement of the decade, but most frustrating is the fact that no one—not the phone company, the postal service, and, most assuredly, not the legal system—seems able to halt his antics. Perhaps you are the exception.

If I can be of any assistance, please let me know.

Apparently, one of the magazines proved exceptional. Like magic, the subscriptions ceased!

CHAPTER 57

PUTTING A LID ON IT

These persistent aggravations, though, generated fewer and fewer rises from me, and not because I'd gone numb or fetal. I was taking full ownership of that recently discovered weapon: indifference. The most powerful reaction I could exhibit to Carl's flailing, failing attempts to engage me was no reaction at all.

This is not to say I wouldn't have loved to throttle the son-of-a-bitch to within an inch of his life. But I had no intention of *ever* being the aggressor or stooping to Carl's level. I would maintain indifference *so long as* he kept the hell away from me. Should he be idiotic enough to ever darken my door...well, I did have a gun.

Best be learning how to use the silly thing, was my thinking.

To that end, I called upon good ole Gabe, who'd remained solicitous of my well-being ever since the 'pot party raid.' He was more than happy to instruct me on my virgin run at shooting a gun ('a freaking cannon,' as he called the Bulldog 44).

I entered the closet-like cubicle and clamped the huge ear protectors over my head. Planting my feet shoulder-width apart, extending arms straight in front, gripping the gun, I stared straight ahead at a large poster hanging at the far end of a sort of bowling lane. No fun game here, this was serious business, as the paper displayed the outline of a human figure, its only detail being a red heart. Inanimate as the outline was, I suddenly felt a stream of sweat pouring from my armpits to my waist at the thought of actually trying to kill a human being, no matter how depraved. I felt a withering humiliation, much as I'd experienced when retrieving Carl from jail, of even being in such surroundings. I wanted no part of guns.

And yet, I conceded, I did. Considering the terror of that cold December night, and the barrage of hassles since, I raised the gun, aimed at the little red heart, and fired. The recoil sent me stumbling backwards.

"Holy cow!" I said to Gabe. "I didn't know *fire* actually came out of guns when you shoot them!"

Reeling in the shuddering poster, Gabe nodded, laughing at my stunned reaction. He pointed to the outline, stationary now. "You got him," he said. The red heart was no longer there.

Exactly three months after the final divorce decree, I went as mandated to Carl's lawyer to hand over a check for three thousand dollars, Carl's 'fair share.' At first I had intended to write a long cover letter detailing my disgust with and lack of respect for the entire legal system, Carl's attorneys being a couple of the slimiest examples. Then I considered a brief, caustic comment, something like 'fair share, my ass.' Indifference stepped in, however, and convinced me to take the high road by saying absolutely nothing.

Well, almost nothing. As I handed over my check—money borrowed from Mama, to be repaid within three years—I couldn't resist re-posing one question. As Booker accepted the check, with a look that he had just gotten away with something, I asked, "So, tell me again why it is you represent this guy?"

Booker shrugged as if to place blame on a twisted legal system, and most certainly not on his own moral shortcomings. "Money, I guess."

That would be *my* money. I willed myself not to scream in his face, instead gazing at him in utter contempt. Booker, who'd long ago forgotten how to feel shame, reciprocated with his own unflinching gaze. I exhaled briefly, turned, and left.

As bitter a pill as this was for me to swallow, I knew it removed another excuse for Carl to prolong his delusion that any sort of bond remained between us. With every step further from the office, I felt less furious, less glum. I'd clamped the lid down a notch or two tighter. The stench of Carl's garbage was fading and would, I knew, eventually evaporate altogether.

My mood continued to lighten as I drove home. Shu-ling greeted me at the front door, holding a tray of freshly fried egg rolls. "Rife is good!" she exclaimed, repeating one of my mantras.

I grinned, grabbing an egg roll and hugging my roomie. "You got that right," I said with gusto. "Life *is* good!"

After a scrumptious dinner, a lively session at the piano, and a hot bath, I nestled into bed, jockeying for room amidst the feline component. I picked up my journal, no longer hidden from prying eyes and no longer neglected due to self-implosion and escape. Granted, Carl's distractions of the past several months had precluded longer, more introspective entries, but tonight, I promised, I would take time for one. I smiled as my hand seemed eager to greet the familiar shape of a pen, readying to resume a favorite ritual.

I began to write, noticing I did so in the same clear, confident handwriting that had suddenly reappeared the preceding New Year's Eve, when I had huddled on the bed at Vivien's, ribs wrapped, hairline stitched, and body bruised. Even in my pain back then, I'd taken solace in knowing I'd gotten back on the right track. Tonight, I wrote from a little further down that track, the one with the signpost reading, Life is Good. Ten pages later, I looked over my entry, noting phrases here and there that reflected my journey:

... so glad to report that I am now divorced but ... embarrassed ... allowed myself to get mixed up ... have been scarred ... am quite shaken ... just hold out financially ... going to be good again ... will take time ... hope to become more honest, consistent, thoughtful ... opportunity to start anew, to control my destiny, to better myself ... promise—I must— think my actions through beforehand ... not worried ... have had that rush of excitement ... the hint, or the promise, of anticipation ...

Subsequent journal entries of similar vein would become the norm. Assorted calamities, worthy of Erma Bombeck fodder, would of course crop up, but by and large, I was the one on the conductor's podium. My orchestration would include more notes of tennis, piano, dance, friends, and...even...dates. The latter would be played out in much lighter tones, my having no intention of embarking on another intimate relationship anytime soon. In short, every day with Carl further out of the picture was one for which I would express deep gratitude and growing optimism:

November 10, 1981 - ...I have this feeling inside of me, this low steady hum, that things are turning around for me....

November 19, 1981 - ...toilet overflowing, so you'd think the day was a shitty one. However, it is Nov 19 and it is not my fourth wedding anniversary!

December 19, 1981 - One year...

December 28, 1981 - ...Ball tomorrow...wearing my wedding dress..surely hope tomorrow night's occasion doesn't hold consequences nearly as calamitous as those held on 11/19/77

The sun has dipped behind the tall screen of lush Leyland cypresses, no longer rustled by the now-departed breeze. Against the late afternoon hush, the glider's creak sounds peaceful and reassuring, like low-tide waters.

I flip past the happy passages of late 1981 in search of remaining references to this unhappy period of my life. I'm pleased to note a diminishing supply.

Carl had made no definitive exit—flamboyant, acquiescent or otherwise—from my life. I do know for a fact he had made several entrances and exits from prison following our divorce, serving the various charges he could no longer elude. But as each day, month, and year passed, my preoccupation with all things Carl sort of petered out into nothingness.

As did Carl, I suppose. Oh, I can recall more than one occasion that prompted a flicker of lingering paranoia: an unfamiliar car passing my house at a suspiciously slow rate; the occasional hang-up-per/sit-and-breather phone call; an airport PA system page for a Mr. Carl Ballini, while I sat waiting for a flight. (Still employing his spies, perhaps?) That unsettling announcement had set my antennas all a-twitch but, like Carl's mean-spirited threats, absolutely nothing came of it. Because of repeat vacations to the Gray Bar Hotel, along with the advent of Caller ID, not to mention Carl's extreme lazy-ass quotient, these speculative harassments petered out as well.

Dimming light pervades the early autumn evening. I begin stacking up journals and calendars, gathering up loose papers and letters. As I stand, something flutters to the ground.

What's this? I pick up an overlooked letter. The return address reads The Sinclair Group; the postmark is a very faded March 30, 1992, some *twelve years* after the divorce decree. I smirk. *Riiight.* I vaguely remember this other, very belated apology letter. I scan the words quickly, scoffing once again at how the seemingly innocuous, even friendly tone could deceive at first glance. I settle back onto the glider and summon up one of my favorite—albeit slightly obnoxious—skills: reading between-the-lines...

Rosie,

I know I am the last person you expected to be hearing from, but I've thought about writing you for a long time.

I want to apologize for my behavior to you so very long ago. I know I did before but never in a rational, sober state. I violated a trust that night when I struck out at you.

'Struck out,' you say? Is that sort of like a 'spat'? Shouldn't you have said, 'beat the shit out of you'?

It was a trust that you probably had in me and one that I know I had in myself. I never thought that I could strike any woman, much less one that I loved so deeply. Those words you spoke "I was faking it" when you described the previous night burned into me. No excuse but that was the cause.

Oh, I see. I was the dishonest one. Maybe I'm wrong here, but I believe you just tried to say,'See what you made me do?'

I was loosing control for some time before that but was afraid to talk to you about it.

I'll fill you in a bit on my life.
Mmm...can't wait to hear this...

"The Cap'n" died in August 1984. A bad cancer (not lung) with a lot of pain.

What? No heart surgery?

Fortunately it went quickly. Penny died some time in Jan 1990.

I imagine that you've guessed that The Sinclair Group is named after that cat of yours.

You sly, slimy, balls-y sonofabitch. How dare you.

If you have cable, you might have seen my ad's on T.N.T., WTBS, ESPN or the Nashville Network.

Who gives a shit.

It's just Cleo and me now. I own a home on the beach and she loves the water.

And I repeat...

The problem with prose is that it can be flat. This letter is not meant to be that way. I have had relationships but have still not met anyone that filled my life and heart as you did. I've been off liquor now for 6 years and have realized how I allowed it to control my life. How many times did you tell me that? Many of the things I was accused of were false back then,

Oh, please... I see the 'changed man' is still playing The Big Secret card.

...but you would have to have been in the position of being falsely accused before you could understand. I know you have not been in that position and that is not the purpose of this letter.

That purpose being...? Let's see...my forgiveness? Friendship? A response of any kind, shape or form?

I hope you are well and happy and that life is treating you well.

So long as you're not in it, life is good.

Love, Carl

P.S. I really am so sorry that I fucked it up!

As I lower the letter to my lap, the phone rings, startling the blue blazes out of me and Sollie. I take a sideways glance at the LCD. *Oh, wouldn't that be rich...* It's Lucy.

"Hey, whatcha doin'?" Lucy chirps.

I summarize how I've passed the day tripping down Memory Lane. "And I just finished reading that *apology letter* he wrote me more than a decade after the divorce, remember?"

"Well, no, since I can't remember what I read in the paper this morning."

"Listen to this..." and I read the letter, including my critiques. When I finish, we sit in silence several moments.

"I don't suppose he included that check, did he?" Lucy's referring to a long-ago conversation when, on a whim, we'd attempted to calculate Rosie's Carl Expense. Starting with the joke of a 'fair share' divorce decree, we added ten sick days (taken for things like DUI's, jail, wrecks, robberies, attorneys), his godforsaken Cougar, and, the biggie, a triple-size thirty-year mortgage. Oh, and pain and suffering.

With a dramatic simper, I spread the envelope wide and jiggle it upside-down. "Nope! 'Fraid the boy fell about one-fifty-K shy of true atonement."

After another rueful silence, Lucy asks, "Do you ever wonder what he's doing? Where he's living?"

I ponder a moment. "No...but you know, sometimes—*very rarely*—I get the vaguest of urges to Google him, but then I just don't. I'll attribute one percent of that to fear, and I mean fear of starting the hassles back up. But the rest is absolute indifference...you know, my other best friend."

"What if he just showed up one day?"

"Well, first, I don't think I'd skitter off like some silly scared wabbit! But, what is he now, seventy-five? seventy-six? I doubt he's the monster he was." I pause. "But you know what they say: 'once a conman, always a conman.' I know I would never, ever allow myself to trust—or care about—the first syllable coming out of his mouth."

"Amen."

"Actually, if he showed up on my doorstep, I'd use the line from that e-card you told me about the other day. You know: 'Hey! Train Wreck! ...Not Your Station!'"

Laughing, we end our conversation with a simultaneous 'Loves ya and I loves ya!' and hang up. I give Sollie a rousing rub. "Lawd, lawd," I say, "I do believe we've spent enough time thinking about bad people!" Sollie, fully awake instantly, turns her attention to the slight movement in the nearby monkey grass. She catapults from the glider in hot pursuit of a chipmunk, foolish enough to leave its cover.

I shake my head again and shrug, having long ago accepted all this mess as water under the bridge. Plus, looking around my sanctuary of a yard, I have to admit, although the going had been slow initially, what with having to tend arid and unfertile soil—and I'm not referring solely to my yard—I had, in fact, eventually bloomed where I was planted.

And where I'm planted at the moment, I realize, is becoming far too chilly!

My arms encircle my journals as if in a gentle hug. For some reason, they feel lighter than when I brought them out here. I call Sollie who, amazingly, appears at once, tail raised in happy greeting.

"C'mon, you, let's get inside. We're done here."

EPILOGUE

Not only am I chilly, I'm hungry! But first, Queen Sollie demands her Fancy Feast. She weaves figure-eights around my ankles, seemingly in appreciation but, I suspect, more in entitlement. For myself, I opt for an easy favorite: popcorn! While the kernels pop and fill the house with that irresistible aroma, I race to the bedroom to don my comfiest lounge wear. Holding my bowl of dinner in one arm and Sollie in the other, I plop down in my recliner. Munching away, I realize, despite my earlier proclamation, I'm not quite done with my day's ruminations.

"Hey, let's think about some good people for a change...like, me!" I try to hug Sollie but laugh at her instant Heisman trophy strong-arm pose. "You mean, you don't want to hear what I've gained from today's Quest? Too bad! Here goes..."

I contemplate Carl's laggard letter of apology. Even aided by over a decade of retrospect, Carl's take on what went down in our relationship remained deluded. An expression of wry acknowledgment passes over my face. Ripping away my own screens of delusion—about relationships and, well, life in general—has been no easy task. Clarity has broken through at different stages and in different degrees. Sometimes it came through in sudden, apocalyptic brilliance—such as the certainty I had best leave the house that scary night. At other times, clarity has appeared in a slow, gentle dawning—such as the acknowledgment, nurturing and trusting of my own battered soul.

Crowning my insights is the imperative that I listen to my gut. That 'still, small voice within' has proved time and again to know what's best. If your gut tells you what you're seeing is a flag, it's a flag.

I can't answer for sure why I ignored my gut during those early courtship days, already fraught with lack of respect. But I have a couple viable conjectures:

Number One, I had always taken for granted I was operating under what I believed a very strong self-concept. But below the surface must have lurked all those childhood-rooted doubts and feelings of unworthiness which everyone must come to grips with. Despite my strong persona in most arenas, as pointed out to me much later by an astute counselor, I was woefully inept at standing up for myself *emotionally*. Until Carl, my belief in myself had never been tested. Each time he imposed his will on mine was, for me, like flunking a test even though I knew the answers. I just didn't know I knew them. I got *confused*.

Later, even when not so confused, I remained paralyzed from utter exhaustion and palpable fear. While Paul Simon might tout 'there must be fifty ways to leave your lover,' I counter with the adage that 'things are easier said than done'; 'hittin' the road, Jack' requires a boatload of gumption.

Number Two, being a Southern woman and, at that time, having no notion of the Cinderella complex, I was positive the fairytale was obtainable. I don't mean castles and princes; I'm talking big, lusty, extraordinary love. So spellbound was I by Carl's brilliant facade—so full of the *extra*—I failed to give proper respect to the *ordinary*.

Even when I'd realized early on in the marriage I'd gotten nothing close to the fairytale, I still hung around in that bad place for three mostly miserable years. Why?! See Number One.

The hopeless undertaking of trying to change someone is nowhere on my current to-do list. As Vivien said so long ago: "People can change, they just won't." Simply accepting people the way they are requires way less energy than trying to fix their faults. These days I apply my considerable fix-it skills solely to things material, leaving all things human well enough alone.

Here's something: Nothing—*nothing*—is more debilitating than fear. Not grief, not pain, not low self-esteem. Fear is the worst.

Granted, what Carl inflicted upon me was slight compared to what other women have suffered by their men. But. Make no mistake, when entrapped emotionally or physically by another human being, you are in a toxic, dangerous bond that has nothing to do with love.

How about those picky ways for which I was so often mocked? A smug grin plants itself on my face. *Still got 'em!* Especially my Number-One-Picky-Ways Mantra: Don't settle. Goodness, the energy I'd expended trying to discount Carl's glaring shortcomings while aggrandizing his mercurial gifts! I'd run myself ragged emotionally, financially and, ultimately physically to prove my choice worthy and viable. Never was there was a sadder case of 'That's my story and I'm sticking to it!'

My lips scrunch up. Has the resumption of picky ways served me well? Seeing as I have yet to allow another person into my life—*really* into my life—it's possible early dismissals of 'almost' relationships were ill-advised. Then again, some flaws—too needy, too religious, too married, too boring—are simply too prickly to embrace.

The aforementioned astute counselor shed some light on why I would even consider such flings of futility. Discussed, of course, was the all-important issue of trust: wounded by Carl as I was, I would find trust hard to come by again. As a result, I would only allow myself to enter a relationship that I *knew subconsciously at the outset* wouldn't work, thereby validating and sustaining my distrusting nature. With time's passing, I have put less and less stock in that (albeit) interesting theory. I attribute my failure to find fulfilling love to plain and simple bad luck. While no longer naive, and possessing greatly honed skills of character judgment (and flag recognition!), my primary inclination is, still, to trust.

I cock my head in reflection. Or, am I wrong about this? Could I possibly be kidding myself that my heart is still open to love when in fact it's closed and impenetrable? Maybe I've plum given up on love. My head sways gently from side to side, mocking the *maybes* and *maybe-nots*. I smile indulgently, opting to *listen to my gut* which is not buying this giving-up garbage.

With a wry smile, I consider my age: seventy. If the love of my life is out there, he best be making his appearance. Time's a-wastin'! And, in view of the decidedly shortened time line ahead, it might not be a bad idea to ease up on the picky/mantra bit. Perhaps make a few concessions. I frown. Perhaps not. I chuckle. See? I'm *still* confused! Now I laugh, remembering another of Vivien's quotes, probably my all-time favorite: "Hey, we're all fucked up. Some more than others."

Along with the acceptance that I might always be *a little* confused has evolved my slow realization that I am, in fact, happy. Who would've thunk? This, despite another slow dawning of the formerly unthinkable proposition that I might spend the rest of my life alone. I think of my silly self-assessment from earlier in the day: 'but for a hole, I'm whole.' Well, guess what? The hole is still there but it's a pinhead compared to what it used to be. Furthermore, it'll always be there, maybe even grow larger or smaller. Because—I feel giddy with a newfound insight—life is too full of wacko shifts for *anyone* to ever be perfectly happy, perfectly whole. One thing for sure, I am not alone. My life is rich with love—yes, love—of friends and family, activities, and good health.

Sollie has somehow sensed that now would be a good time to jump back into the chair and curl up next to me. I move the empty popcorn bowl to the side, place a hand on my purring cat, and look around the comfortable room. Maybe I'll build a fire on this first chilly night of the season! I smile at how much I now embrace— and most times prefer—my singledom, so free from constraint and complications.

My quest, begun early this morning, has brought me full circle to an even deeper state of awareness and contentment. My concern about the 'hole' in my life lessens even more as I acknowledge that not all holes are bad. Take, for instance, the hole in the middle of a bundt cake. Who could complain being at the bottom of that hole, surrounded by all that warmth, comfort, and heady aroma? I decide I'll think of the life I've baked up for myself as a delicious chocolate bundt cake which, even with its hole and lack of icing, is yummy all on its own.

An expression of coy anticipation dances across my face: Now, should the love of my life show up even at this late date...well, that would be icing on the cake.

AFTERWORD

While my tale has ended, you may perhaps be wondering how other characters' tales turned out. As for my Inner Circle—Vivien, Lucy, Louise—I am now closest to Lucy, even though all four of us manage occasional reunions to catch up and reminisce about all that has gone down the pike. Louise, having seemed content to devote herself solely to her teaching career, surprised everyone by finding—without looking for!—her soul mate. They married in mid-age and are nearly twenty years into the happily-ever-after thing. Vivien is at peace as well, now in her third marriage, this time to a man fourteen years her junior (an ex-student, if truth be told), who has treasured her since Day One. (Vivien's second marriage was, yes indeedy, to Frank, occurring some three years past my ordeal, and lasting about ten years until some strange woman showed up at Vivien's home to announce she and Frank were engaged. Ah, but that's a whole other story...) As for Lucy, her relationships have never gotten as far as marriage but, like me, she has come to appreciate the myriad positive aspects of the single life. Cindi, funny and wise as ever, married a hockey-player and followed him to Canada, where she is a sought-after piano teacher. Shu-Ling teaches piano as well in her private studio in Taiwan. Her letters to me always begin with, "Hey Rosie-Rose, You marry yet?"

And what, you might ask, about Carl?

I trust you now understand why I felt obliged to change the names of all characters and why I never once searched for any information regarding Carl's whereabouts/doings.

Not nearly so wary of waking a sleeping beast, a sleuthing, CSI-loving friend went to Google and beyond, rounding up Carl tidbits, not the least of which was a very sketchy people-finder account of his death, 'survived by a loving family.'

I smelled a rat. Call me paranoid, cynical, histrionic...whatever...knowing Carl's scheming nature, I would not put it past him to fake his own death, possibly to elude authorities or the IRS. Curiosity piqued, however, I joined in the search, conducted shortly before publication of this book, for an official obituary. Finding nothing conclusive to dispel my distrust on that aspect, I did put full stock into articles containing the following, sometimes chilling particulars:

In July 1982 (while Carl's hassling of me had barely slowed down), Carl was employed as Food and Beverage Director of a nightclub above a Tampa hotel. Hardly a chilling item, but it once again begs the question: How in the hell did this guy keep getting hired?

Upon the 1984 death of his father, Carl set about manipulating his mother to sign over the deed to her house and wound up kicking her out in the bargain. This came to light in a 1987 lawsuit, *filed by his mother*, citing cracked ribs, multiple bruises, harassing phone calls, and death threats. Sound familiar? No small wonder the woman seemed half-numb whenever I saw her. And no small wonder this mom was not at all proud of her son.

Remember his brother, who supposedly served time for involuntary manslaughter due to a bar fight? A 1957 article relates that, when he was seventeen, he was imprisoned for raping then slaying a fifteen-year-old classmate on Lover's Lane. Carl's brother was described as a quiet, bible-carrying, split personality.

This was one effed-up family.

To this day, Carl's Big Secret remains a mystery to me.

In December 1993, Carl, after having long been under suspicion and surveillance, was finally arrested in Tampa for maintaining 'quite an operation' of fraudulent credit card use. He'd scan obituaries for high-end professionals with good credit history, apply for cards, and proceed to bilk banks for a cool thirty to sixty thousand. When arrested, he 'offered no resistance' and led officials to his two-bedroom apartment where he 'lived alone.' This would be where Carl wrote to me, in that last apology letter of 1992, that he was leading a quiet, sober existence with his dog Cleo. Looks like my between-the-lines comments weren't nearly so cynical as one might have thought.

While I'd had quite enough reminder of how bad to the bone my ex-husband was, my sleuthing friend was not about to give up her search for solid proof of Carl's death. She revisited the grave-finder website and dialed the contact number. This is what she was told:

Carl did indeed die at the age of seventy-five on September 28, 2015 of throat cancer and heart disease. Two contacts (his brother and a woman) never visited, never returned messages from the hospital, and never claimed Carl's body. After being held in cold storage for about a month, his body was cremated. The ashes were held for nearly a year, no one ever coming forward. Finally, per the state medical examiner's protocol, Carl's ashes were unceremoniously dumped into the Gulf of Mexico.

So. Apparently there was no coming to Jesus, no sweet saint of a woman turning him around, and there sure as hell was no 'loving family.' Carl died alone and unloved. Sad, yes, that a man of such *potential* chose a life of bravado, deceit and violence, but you'll see no tears running down my cheeks. My thinking is the man received his just deserts.

ACKNOWLEDGEMENTS

I always enjoy reading an author's acknowledgements at the end of a book because I always go into daydream mode thinking of what I *might* say to all the folks who *might* help me on my book that *might* get written one day. Well, what do you know? *Might* is history! My book is a done deal and I don't know who's more grateful: me, or the following folks to whom I offer my most humble gratitude:

To Judy Renfroe who, long before the days of internet, gave me several books on writing, publishing and marketing, pens, pencils, erasers, etc., all packed into a huge cake box from a bakery named 'Sweet Expectations.' Perfect.

To Marcia Mouron, my most avid local cheerleader and reader of countless drafts. To Dianne Booth who, along with Marcia, read the very first all-over-the-place draft. (A bit more than y'all bargained for, huh?) To several others who read various drafts and offered thoughtful suggestions and constant encouragement: Judy Bryant (you really went overboard!), Pam Payne, Louise Schrimsher, Sally Harper, and Lilette Robinson. To Barbara Huffman, who shared many wise tips she'd garnered along her route to publication. To Nina Lockard, whose sleuthing talents made for a more interesting Afterword. And to others who kept me believing in myself, including Mary Butterworth, Laura Groce, Barbara Klyce, Michele Slick, Wrenne Taylor, and Diana Turnipseed.

A special shout-out to my recently discovered friends and Beta readers at Scribophile: Bonnie, Jen, Lynn, Annie and Marla. Your sage insights—provocative, humorous, always kind—proved as beneficial as those of any professional editor. You helped make my manuscript...maybe not perfect, but good enough! Thank you.